BEER HIKING

PACIFIC NORTHWEST

THE TASTIEST WAY TO DISCOVER
WASHINGTON, OREGON, AND BRITISH COLUMBIA

T0004119

Beer Hiking Pacific Northwest
The tastiest way to discover Washington, Oregon, and British Columbia
By: Brandon Fralic and Rachel Wood

ISBN: 978-3-907293-70-6
Published by Helvetiq (Lausanne, Switzerland)
Graphic Design: Anthony Pittet, Lucas Guidetti Perez, Daniel Malak
Cover Illustration: Felix Kindelán, Daniel Malak
Printed in China
First Edition March 2018
Second revised and expanded edition September 2022

www.helvetiq.com
www.facebook.com/helvetiq
instagram: @helvetiq

BEER HIKING
PACIFIC NORTHWEST
THE TASTIEST WAY TO DISCOVER
WASHINGTON, OREGON, AND BRITISH COLUMBIA

HEL
VETiQ

TABLE OF CONTENTS

1

INTRODUCTION

ABOUT THE AUTHORS

Brandon Fralic and Rachel Wood are pioneers of Beer Hiking in the Pacific Northwest. In 2013 they launched Beers at the Bottom (beersatthebottom.com) to highlight hiking trails and craft breweries in Western Washington. Since then they've sampled hundreds of hikes and brews at home and abroad, publishing stories along the way. Together, they've written for Washington Trails, REI Coop Journal, and OutdoorsNW among others.

Brandon Fralic is a freelance writer and photographer based in Bellingham, WA. A native of Washington state, he grew up hiking between the North Cascades and San Juan Islands. Brandon has written extensively about trails, travel, and beer for a variety of publications including Northwest Travel & Life, Outdoor Project, Modern Hiker, and more.

Rachel Wood received her Master's Degree in Creative Writing from Western Washington University. She has several years' experience working in the craft beer industry and has co-written pieces with Brandon on beer travel and hiking throughout the Pacific Northwest. Born and raised in Washington state, some of her fondest childhood memories are camping trips to the ocean.

HIKING AND BEER

The Pacific Northwest. Its very name evokes images of waves crashing, evergreens dripping, waterfalls cascading down, down, down. Lush rainforests and glaciated volcanic peaks; wildlife scurrying about. Here, hiking trails abound. And when it comes to beer? All hail the almighty hop.

For many Pacific Northwesterners, craft beer and hiking are the perfect pairing. We connect the two without thinking about it. How many breweries on the West Coast associate their brand with the great outdoors? How many use mountains and waterfalls for their logos, or market their aluminum cans for outdoor adventure? Of course, the roots connecting hiking and beer run much deeper; they are intricately intertwined. The very waters flowing from our mountain rivers and streams eventually make their way — often over hiking trails — right into our pint glasses.

Because breweries rely on clean water sources to create their products, environmentalism is as important for brewers as it is for hikers. Lately, we've seen a welcome shift on the part of breweries to go "green" — using solar energy and spent grains to power their operations, partnering with local farms and suppliers, and even creating farmhouse ales from ingredients grown on site. These conservation efforts directly relate to the land stewardship goals shared by hiking enthusiasts.

To say that craft beer and outdoor recreation are booming in the Pacific Northwest is no overstatement. Both Industries generate billions annually in economic impact. But impressive as they are, it's not about the numbers. We engage in beer hiking for fun — it's what we like to do. And we invite you to do the same. Because there's nothing more refreshing than a cold, frothy pint after a long day on the trail.

ABOUT THE BOOK

A Brief History of *Beer Hiking Pacific Northwest*

You are holding the Second Edition of *Beer Hiking Pacific Northwest*. It's safe to say that the world is a very different place than it was In 2018 when this title was first released. The changing landscape of craft beer (Hazy IPAs were "new" in 2018!) and the dramatic impact of Covid-19 on small businesses meant that a full overhaul of this book was necessary. In this updated edition, you will find: three new hikes, nine new brewery recommendations, plus updated trail, beer, and brewery details.

In some ways, we started writing this book years ago. On a rainy April afternoon in 2013, we were browsing the "Northwest" section of Bellingham, WA's longtime favorite Village Books. While browsing, we came to a conclusion: there's a hiking guide for just about everyone. Hiking with dogs, with kids, with bad knees — there are guides to help anyone who wants to explore the beauty of the Pacific Northwest. But something was missing.

Like many Pacific Northwesterners, we are trail and ale enthusiasts. When planning a trip we look for two things first: hiking trails and craft breweries. A day on the trail for us ends with a pint in a nearby taproom. But a hiking guide for beer lovers? It wasn't on the shelf.

We decided to change that and one day write the book ourselves.

In July of 2013 we took our first steps by launching the online beer hiking guide, Beers at the Bottom. The blog led to other opportunities to share our beer hiking adventures in a variety of magazines and web outlets. We kept an eye out for others who were creating in our niche, and fatefully found *Beer Hiking Switzerland* through a Google search. Discovering that book's international publisher, Helvetiq, was a serendipitous case of the right people connecting at the right time. We hope that this guide will kickstart (or add to) your own beer hiking adventures. Cheers!

Defining the Pacific Northwest

Definitions of The Pacific Northwest (PNW) vary wildly — sometimes including Alaska, Northern California, Idaho, and beyond — always encompassing the core US states of Washington and Oregon, and the Canadian province of British Columbia (BC). For the purpose of this book, we've adopted a narrow "Cascades to Coast" definition of the Pacific Northwest: roughly the Cascade and Canadian Coast Mountains, and coastal areas to their west.

Of course, there are always exceptions. No PNW beer hiking book would be complete without a visit to Central Oregon's high desert and the "Beer Town USA" of Bend. In Washington, a trip east over the Cascades brings us to Yakima, where the majority of the nation's hops are grown. Further north, Winthrop is an Old West-themed resort town at the eastern edge of the North Cascades, with a single brewery and endless hiking opportunities.

For the most part, though, we find the lands between the mountains and Pacific coastline best for beer hiking. Perhaps it's the sheer number of trails and ales: with countless hikes and hundreds of breweries to choose from, opportunites are endless. In Washington, over 400 breweries operate statewide, the majority of which are located west of the mountains. And where there are breweries, there are often trails. Thousands of miles of trails crisscross Washington state; nearly 700 miles of trails exist in Washington State Parks alone. This book provides a sampling — a tasting tour, if you will — and jumping off point for further explorations in the PNW and beyond.

In general, we paired hiking trails and breweries based on proximity. In Washington, for example, there is only one brewery (North Fork) for hundreds of miles of Mount Baker-area trails. In cities where there is a high concentration of breweries — like Seattle, Portland, and Vancouver — we did our best to choose a brewery near the suggested hike. Sometimes we suggest a brewery that we found unique or interesting, like Portland's Ex Novo. While there are breweries closer to Forest Park, Ex Novo was the world's first non-profit brewery. Rest assured that if a brewery is worth the drive, we've made an effort to include it.

Trail and Beer Ratings

All ratings in this book — both beer notes and hike difficulties — are subjective. Some hikers might find what we consider a "moderate" hike to be difficult or even easy. Just like some craft beer drinkers may think that the bitterness or sweetness of a specific beer differs from tasting notes we have described. Please do not consider our ratings as definitive, but as a reference to help you choose the right hike or beer for your taste.

Safety

Never drink and drive! The number of awe-inspiring wild places in the Pacific Northwest make it a hiker's playground. But we always need to remember that the wilderness is still wild. One of the best ways to stay safe is to be prepared. Make sure you hit the trail with the Ten Essentials (see page 16), but also take the time to learn about any dangers you might encounter on-trail. Familiarize yourself with how to handle wildlife encounters. Weather of the Pacific Northwest changes quickly — especially in the mountains — so it's also important to learn the safest ways to navigate through inclement weather. The Forest Service and organizations like Washington Trails Association have extensive resources to help you be as safe as you can on the trail. Know before you go!

While hiking, it's important to stay on the trail not only to protect the natural environment but also to avoid getting lost. Let a friend or family member know your hiking plans before setting out.

Conservation

In recent years, US National Parks have seen record numbers of visitors — hiking and outdoor recreation are on the rise, especially in places like the PNW. More people hiking means more boots on the ground, and that leads to more wear and tear on our natural places. To keep hiking trails and our wild places available for future generations there is one golden rule: Leave No Trace (LNT).

Leave No Trace means everything you packed in (including garbage and food scraps!) needs to be packed out with you. LNT practices also include staying on-trail to avoid damaging plants growing near the trail. Staying on the trails helps prevent erosion, keeping the natural environment intact and lessening the impact on the trails themselves. Learn more about Leave No Trace ethics at Lnt.org.

On the Beers

If there's one style that represents PNW craft beer, it's the India Pale Ale. Since this region is home to the lion's share of the world's hop fields, it just makes sense that the PNW would produce some hoppy brews. But when every brewery is known for its IPA, sometimes fantastic beers are overlooked. For this book, we did our best to highlight a wide variety of beers and touch on as many styles as we could. And yes, you will find a few IPAs in here as well — it wouldn't be a PNW guidebook without them.

We made every effort to ensure that all of the recommended beers can be enjoyed at the brewery year-round. But there are always exceptions. Some breweries are more experimental and put out new beers on constant rotation, meaning there isn't a set of core beers always on tap. The craft beer scene in the area is a dynamic one and new beers sometimes take the place of old favorites to keep up with the changing landscape.

The highlighted beers are also not the only thing worth trying at any given brewery — sometimes the best course of action is to grab a sample tray and really get to know the brewery's line-up. We chose these beers based on brewery recommendations, community reviews, and our own personal enjoyment. One thing is for sure though — we sampled hundreds of beers while researching this book, and can say without a doubt that there is some great beer out there!

(2)

HOW IT WORKS

CHOOSE THE BEER OR THE HIKE

NAME OF THE HIKE

STATE OR PROVINCE

NAME OF THE BEER

MAP *

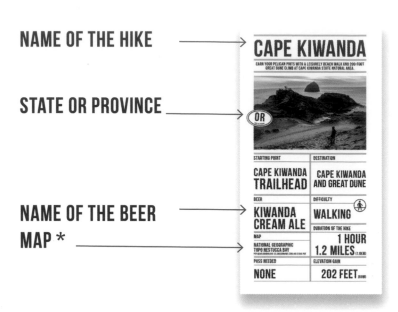

INFORMATION ABOUT THE BEER

INFORMATION ABOUT THE HIKE

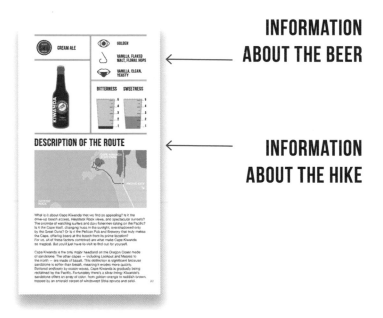

DIFFICULTY

Each hike is given a subjective difficulty rating. Ratings are based on a number of factors including hike length, elevation gain, and trail conditions. Easy trails are usually wide and well-maintained. The difficulty rating is also based on favorable weather conditions — poor weather and visibility can make a trail more difficult.

WALKING (EASY)

Easy trails are generally less than 3 miles round trip, with minimal elevation gain. These short excursions are great for beginner hikers, or those just looking to take a stroll.

HIKING (MODERATE)

Most of the hikes in this book are classified as hiking, or moderate trails. These hikes are roughly 5 miles round trip with 1,000 feet of elevation gain. Trail conditions vary from wide to narrow, but trails are generally well-maintained (unless otherwise noted).

MOUNTAIN HIKING (DIFFICULT)

Mountain hikes tend to be longer, in the 7+ mile-range. Any hike with more than 2,000 feet of elevation gain is considered difficult. Most of these hikes take place in the high country where trails can be narrow, steep, rooty, or rocky. These trails can be more dangerous, with exposed cliffs and the potential risk of falling. Some difficult trails require scrambling (using your hands) to reach the destination. Best for experienced hikers.

BEFORE DEPARTURE

TEN ESSENTIALS

Even if you're just heading out on a day hike, you should always be prepared. Here's a list of the Ten Essentials you should take with you on the trail.

- Navigation: Maps in this book are for reference only. The most reliable form of navigation is a topographic paper map and compass. Batteries die — don't rely solely on your phone!
- Hydration: Water is essential when you're hiking. Make sure you bring plenty along to keep yourself hydrated and ward off the potential for dehydration and heat stroke. Don't worry — no matter how much water you drink, you'll still be thirsty enough for a beer!
- Nutrition: Bring extra food along just in case you're on the trail for longer than you expect. Foods that are high in protein and can store for a while can be kept in your pack for emergencies.

- Rain Gear and Insulation: The weather can change quickly! Rain gear is especially important in the PNW. Bring an extra layer of clothing as temperatures fluctuate in the backcountry.
- Fire Starter: In case of emergency, a watertight container of waterproof matches is invaluable to a lost hiker for warmth and cooking.
- First Aid: From minor cuts and scrapes, to more major injuries, you need to be prepared.
- Tools: From a pocket knife to a multi-tool, these small tools take on big jobs in the backcountry. And never underestimate the power of duct tape!
- Illumination: Whether the hike took longer than you anticipated or you really wanted to catch that sunset from the top, you could get caught in the dark. Bring a flashlight or headlamp so you'll be able to see the trail.
- Sun Protection: Sunglasses, hats, and sunscreen keep you from getting sunburned and protect your eyes from the bright glare.
- Shelter: As simple as a space blanket or tarp — it could keep you dry in inclement weather or during an unexpected overnight on the trail.

HIKING SEASON

Seasons are always a factor when hiking in the Pacific Northwest. High country trails may not be accessible between late fall and spring due to snow levels. Always check with the land manager (listed for each hike) for current trail conditions before setting out. Local tourism offices can be a good resource as well.

WEATHER

Because conditions can change in an instant — especially in the mountains — it's best to always be prepared for wind, rain, snow, and anything else Mother Nature might throw your way. For accurate forecasts, check the following sites:

- United States: weather.gov
- Canada: weather.gc.ca

ADDITIONAL RESOURCES

For additional hiking and brewery information, we suggest the following sites:

Washington
- Hiking: wta.org
- Breweries: washingtonbeer.com

Oregon
- Hiking: oregonhikers.org
- Breweries: oregoncraftbeer.org

British Columbia
- Hiking: vancouvertrails.com
- Breweries: bcaletrail.ca

MAP

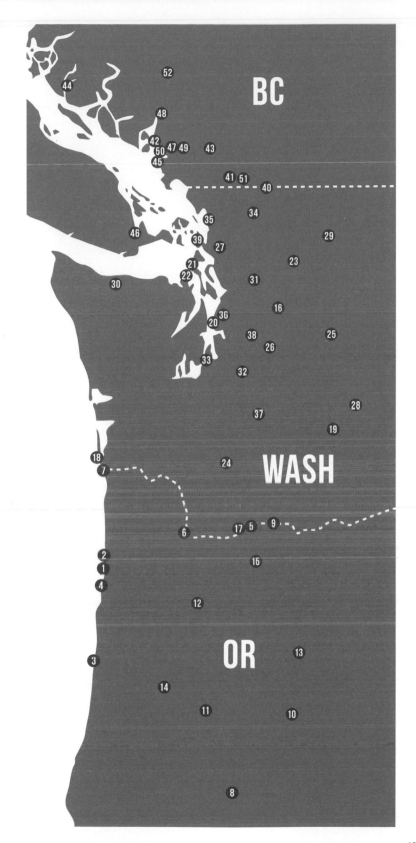

BC

WASH

OR

3

OREGON

CAPE KIWANDA

EARN YOUR PELICAN PINTS WITH A LEISURELY BEACH WALK AND 200-FOOT GREAT DUNE CLIMB AT CAPE KIWANDA STATE NATURAL AREA.

STARTING POINT	**DESTINATION**
# CAPE KIWANDA TRAILHEAD	# CAPE KIWANDA AND GREAT DUNE
BEER	**DIFFICULTY**
PELICAN KIWANDA CREAM ALE	# WALKING
MAP	**DURATION OF THE HIKE**
NATIONAL GEOGRAPHIC TOPO NESTUCCA BAY	# 1 HOUR 1.2 MILES (1.9KM)
PASS NEEDED	**ELEVATION GAIN**
# $10 DAY PASS	# 202 FEET (60M)

CREAM ALE

ALCOHOL 5.4% CONTENT

GOLDEN

VANILLA, FLAKED MALT, FLORAL HOPS

VANILLA, CLEAN, YEASTY

BITTERNESS

5
4
3
2
1

SWEETNESS

5
4
3
2
1

DESCRIPTION OF THE ROUTE

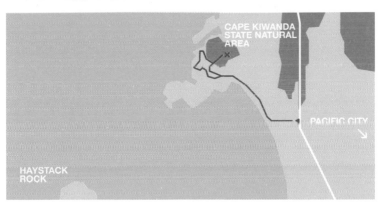

What is it about Cape Kiwanda that we find so appealing? Is it the drive-up beach access, Haystack Rock views, and spectacular sunsets? The promise of watching surfers and dory fishermen taking on the Pacific? Is it the Cape itself, changing hues in the sunlight, overshadowed only by the Great Dune? Or is it the Pelican Pub and Brewery that truly makes the Cape, offering beers at the beach from its prime location?
For us, all of these factors combined are what make Cape Kiwanda so magical. But you'll just have to visit to find out for yourself.

Cape Kiwanda is the only major headland on the Oregon Coast made of sandstone. The other capes — including Lookout and Meares to the north — are made of basalt. This distinction is significant because sandstone is softer than basalt, meaning it erodes more quickly. Battered endlessly by ocean waves, Cape Kiwanda is gradually being reclaimed by the Pacific. Fortunately there's a silver lining: Kiwanda's sandstone offers an array of color, from golden-orange to reddish-brown, topped by an emerald carpet of windswept Sitka spruce and salal.

Unlike most hikes in this book, Cape Kiwanda offers no defined trail. Wander as you will. We suggest a rough route, simply because beach trails change as swiftly as the winds and tides that govern them. Begin by walking down to the beach, then head north towards Cape Kiwanda. As soon as you reach the beach, Haystack Rock stands dead ahead. Not to be confused with the Haystack Rock at Cannon Beach; the basalt sea stack in Pacific City is actually 90 feet higher — but further offshore — than its famous Cannon Beach cousin.

Your leisurely beach walk ends abruptly once you reach the base of the Cape. Climb the beaten path to a fenceline, always staying within the posted boundaries. Cape Kiwanda is a potentially dangerous place, and a handful of fence-jumpers have met their death here over the years. Rangers sometimes patrol the area, alerting visitors to the risk. Kiwanda has earned the title of Oregon's deadliest cape.

Follow the fence out to the Cape's north side, where you can once again see Haystack Rock peeking over sculpted sandstone cliffs. Tumultuous waters slosh and swirl below in the Punchbowl. Further north, the cliffs rise even higher. Once you've had your fill, climb up the Great Dune for even bigger views.

Huff, puff, and kick your way up the sand dunes. Atop the Great Dune, look north towards Sand Lake and beyond to Cape Lookout, jutting nearly 2 miles (3.2 kilometers) straight into the ocean. Return the way you came, or pick a new descent route to slide down the dunes on your butt. Back at the parking lot, be sure to stop in at Pelican Pub for a Kiwanda Cream Ale.

Want to extend your hike? From Pelican Pub, walk the beach south approximately 1.5 miles (2.4 kilometers) to Bob Straub State Park. From here you can continue an additional 2 miles (3.2 kilometers) south along Nestucca Spit. This undeveloped, car-free coastline is full of birds, wildlife, and — according to one sign — even dragons!

TURN BY TURN DIRECTIONS

1. Walk west from the large parking area to the beach.
2. At 0.1 miles (0.16 km), turn right (north) and walk towards Cape Kiwanda.
3. At 0.3 miles (0.5 km), begin climbing the saddle between Cape Kiwanda and the Great Dune.
4. Follow the fenceline once you reach the top of the Cape. Then climb to the top of the Great Dune before returning the way you came.

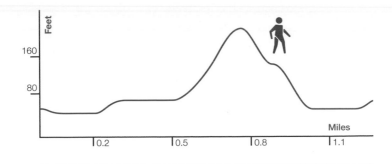

TRAILHEAD DRIVING DIRECTIONS

From Tillamook, take US-101 south for 11 miles. Turn right on Sandlake Road. Follow Sandlake Road 4.3 miles, then turn left to stay on Sandlake Road. After 6.5 miles, continue onto Ferry Road/McPhillips Drive Turn right on Hungry Harbor Road in 1.5 miles for parking at Cape Kiwanda near Pelican Brewery.

PELICAN PUB AND BREWERY

Pelican Pub is the Oregon Coast's original oceanfront brewery. Where else can you walk right off the beach onto a sand-sprinkled brewpub floor? Upon entering Pelican Brewery, one thing will clearly grab your attention (besides the sand) — this brewery has won a lot of awards! In fact, the first year Pelican entered the Great American Beer Festival, they walked away with three medals and the title of "Small Brewpub of the Year." They haven't slowed down since. Over 20 years since opening, Pelican is the fastest growing brewery in Oregon. Visitors from around the world now flock to the shores of Cape Kiwanda for unparalleled sunsets, paired with a pint of Pelican's famous Kiwanda Cream Ale.

TRAIL CONTACT INFORMATION
Oregon Parks and Recreation Department
725 Summer Street NE, Suite C
Salem, OR 97301
+1 503-842-3182
www.oregonstateparks.org

ACCOMMODATIONS
Surf & Sand Inn
35215 Brooten Rd.
Pacific City, OR 97135
+1 503-965-6366
www.surfandsandinn.com
Comfy, affordable motel approximately 1 mile from the brewery and Cape Kiwanda.

BREWERY/RESTAURANT
Pelican Pub and Brewery
33180 Cape Kiwanda Dr.
Pacific City, OR 97135
+1 503-965-7007
www.pelicanbrewing.com
Multi-award-winning, beachside brewery with full menu. Try Pelican's famous Tower of Rings!

TOURIST ATTRACTIONS INFO
Pacific City Chamber
Visitor Information Center
35170 Brooten Rd. Suite H
Pacific City, OR 97135
+1-888-KIWANDA
www.tillamookcoast.com

CAPE LOOKOUT

HIKE OUT THIS HUGE HEADLAND FOR THE CHANCE TO SPOT GRAY WHALES FROM A 400-FOOT HIGH BASALT CLIFF LOOKOUT.

STARTING POINT

CAPE LOOKOUT TRAILHEAD

DESTINATION

CAPE LOOKOUT

BEER

DE GARDE KRIEK

DIFFICULTY

HIKING

MAP

NATIONAL GEOGRAPHIC TOPO NESTUCCA BAY

DURATION OF THE HIKE

2-3 HOURS
4.8 MILES (7.7KM)

PASS NEEDED

OREGON STATE PARKS PASS

ELEVATION GAIN

900 FEET (274M)

SOUR CHERRY ALE

 RUBY HAZE

 FUNK, CHERRY SKINS, OAK

TART, CHERRY, CINNAMON

BITTERNESS | **SWEETNESS**

DESCRIPTION OF THE ROUTE

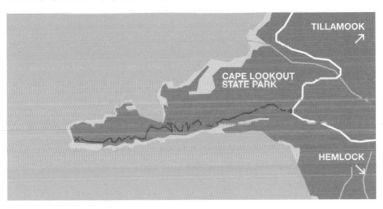

Of the Tillamook Coast's Three Capes — Kiwanda, Lookout, and Meares — Cape Lookout is easily the most remote and rewarding. No road leads to its viewpoint. In order to fully appreciate this state park's namesake lookout, visitors traverse over two miles along a rolling forested trail due west to the Pacific Ocean. Full of ups and downs, this trail is a fun year-round option for those looking to get away from the beach crowds. And with some luck, you may even spot a whale.

Cape Lookout is said to be one of the best areas for whale watching on the entire Oregon Coast. During fall, gray whales head south for warmer winter waters, following the coastline and detouring around Cape Lookout. Come spring, they head north again. Each trip spans approximately 6,000 miles in 2-3 months — an incredible journey between the waters of the Bering Sea and Baja California. Watch for spouts, and bring binoculars for the best viewing experience.

To reach this whale-watching wonderland, begin hiking along the Cape Trail. The first mile is easygoing, as it gently drops over 300 feet (91.5 meters) in elevation. Watch out for mud and standing water — this trail gets more than its fair share of precipitation. Half a mile in, come to a south-facing viewpoint — and the crash site of a B-17 bomber plane in the 1940s. A nearby plaque set in stone retells the event and memorializes its victims.

At 1.2 miles (1.9 kilometers), views open up north towards Netarts Bay Spit, Cape Meares, and the Three Arch Rocks National Wildlife Refuge. Is it just us, or do the Three Arch Rocks look like a pair of kissing turtles from here? Continue west for the roughest part of the trail. Halfway to the lookout, the trail turns into a rollercoaster — climbing and dropping several times — with rooty sections and lots of muddy puddles to navigate. Fortunately, the dense Sitka spruce and western hemlock forest provides adequate shelter from the elements.

Once you reach the end, a bench greets you atop Cape Lookout's sheer cliffs. Be careful out here — it's a long way down. Look south towards Cape Kiwanda and Haystack Rock. To the north, more views of Cape Meares and the kissing turtles. Watch for wildlife. Even if whales are not present, you may spot sea lions, seals, seagulls, or "comically elegant" brown pelicans. Back at the trailhead, it's possible to extend your hike along the North and South trails.

TURN BY TURN DIRECTIONS

1. Begin by walking west to the trailhead from the parking lot.
    Take the left trail for Cape Lookout.
2. At an immediate junction, continue straight on the Cape Lookout Trail.
3. Reach a viewpoint at 1.2 miles (1.9 km). The trail becomes rougher from here on out.
4. At 2.4 miles (3.8 km), reach the end of the trail.
    Return the way you came.

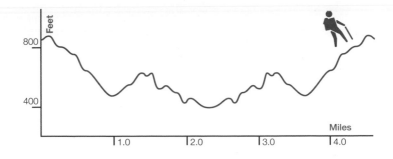

TRAILHEAD DRIVING DIRECTIONS

From Tillamook, take OR-131 West. Bear left on Whiskey Creek Road, then continue 8 miles (12.8 kilometers) to the trailhead parking lot.

DE GARDE BREWING

When de Garde Brewing's co-owner Trevor Rogers set out to find the location for his new brewing venture, the choice rested on something very tiny: microflora. Tillamook, OR offered what he was looking for — a delicate interplay of coastal air and farming country. Using harvested microbes and wild yeast strains, de Garde's unique line-up of Farmhouse Ales are unlike any other and completely wild. Barrel aged and traditionally crafted, de Garde's beers take time to ferment to perfection — anywhere from one year to four!

TRAIL CONTACT INFORMATION
Cape Lookout State Park
13000 Whiskey Creek Rd.
Tillamook, OR 97141
+1 503-842-4981
www.oregonstateparks.org/park_186.php

RESTAURANT
Upstairs Bar and Grill
4805 Netarts Hwy. W,
Tillamook, OR 97141
+1 503 815 1687
Seafood, pub grub, and a solid drink selection in Netarts.

TOURIST ATTRACTIONS INFO
Tillamook Chamber of Commerce
3705 US-101
Tillamook, OR 97141
+1 503-842-7525
www.gotillamook.com

BREWERY
de Garde Brewing
6000 Blimp Blvd.
Tillamook, OR 97141
+1 503-815-1635
www.degardebrewing.com
"A truly wild brewery in Tillamook, Oregon."

ACCOMMODATIONS
Netarts Surf Inn
4951 Netarts Hwy. W,
Tillamook, OR 97141
+1 503-354-2644
www.pacificviewlodging.com
Simple, newly renovated vacation rentals just two blocks from the beach.

CAPE PERPETUA

CLIMB TO A VISTA OVERLOOKING OREGON'S RUGGED COASTLINE, THEN DESCEND TO THE TIDEPOOLS AND CHURNING WATERS OF CAPE PERPETUA ON THE TRAIL OF RESTLESS WATERS.

STARTING POINT

CAPE PERPETUA VISITOR CENTER

DESTINATION

CAPTAIN COOK'S SPOUTING HORN

BEER

YACHATS CETACEA

MAP

LOOK UP
WWW.FS.USDA.GOV

PASS NEEDED

NORTHWEST
FOREST PASS

DIFFICULTY

HIKING

DURATION OF THE HIKE

3 HOURS
4.7 MILES (7.5KM)

ELEVATION GAIN

750 FEET (228M)

PEPPERCORN SAISON

LIGHT GOLD

HONEY, DUSTY, PEPPERCORN

CRACKED PEPPER, HAY

BITTERNESS	SWEETNESS
5	5
4	4
3	3
2	2
1	1

DESCRIPTION OF THE ROUTE

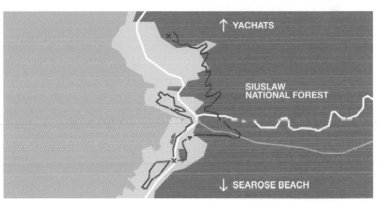

↑ YACHATS

SIUSLAW NATIONAL FOREST

↓ SEAROSE BEACH

Located just two miles south of the small coastal town of Yachats, Cape Perpetua rises 800 feet (244 meters) high from the battering waves of the Pacific Ocean. This hike combines three of Cape Perpetua Scenic Area's most picturesque trails in a tour de force of Oregon's rocky coast. Add in a stop at the Cape Perpetua Visitor Center and you can make a full day of your explorations.

From the Visitor Center, set out on the St. Perpetua Trail to climb up to the viewpoint near the top of the cape. A moderately strenuous hike, St. Perpetua switchbacks through a forest of Douglas fir, spruce, and hemlock. After about 1.2 miles (1.9 kilometers), you'll come to an open meadow — in the summer, wildflowers dot the scenery here. Keep climbing to reach the overlook. Look down at the coastal landmarks you'll be exploring next — like the swirling waters of the Devil's Churn — and try to pick out the spray of Captain Cook's Spouting Horn. Take the Whispering Spruce Trail to the Stone Shelter, remnants of the CCC buildings that were built here in the 1930s.

From the overlook on a clear day, you'll be able to see over 30 miles out to sea, and over 70 miles of coastline both north to Cape Foulweather and south to Cape Blanco. Take in the view and head back down to the Visitor Center to refill your water bottle. Now it's time to hit the beach!

From the Visitor Center, head out to the Cape Cove hikes: The Trail of Restless Waters and Captain Cook Trail. Visit this area around high tide if you can — from an hour before high tide to an hour after — when the crashing surf creates a magnificent spectacle. Cross under Highway 101 in the pedestrian tunnel and turn right onto the Cape Cove Trail. From here, you'll come to the Restless Waters Trail that leads to the Devil's Churn. A cut in the basalt shoreline, the waves crash in, rolling upon one another to compound in a swirling mass of seafoam. The sheer power of the Pacific is channeled into this narrow space, the waves coursing in like a herd of wild horses. Complete the Restless Waters loop and head south on the Cape Cove Trail to meet up with the Captain Cook Trail. This trail is perhaps the most well known of the trails in the area. The path is paved, making it accessible and easy for families with young children. In the summer months, the sharp tidepool-harboring basalt rocks swarm with visitors hoping to catch sight of the two superstars of Cape Perpetua: Cook's Spouting Horn and Thor's Well.

Both were formed from collapsed sea caves, creating a pressurized tunnel through which ocean waves are forced in impressive displays. Thor's Well has become a bit of a viral internet sensation — but in order to get that Insta-ready view into the mouth of the well, you'll need to prepare to get really wet. It's dangerous to get too close, as the waves in this area are unpredictable and "sneaker" waves frequent. Personally, we were more awed by the Spouting Horn and Cook's Chasm. A smaller version of the Devil's Churn, waters in the Chasm seem to boil in fury as the waves crash in, causing the Spouting Horn to shoot a puff of salt water high into the air. It's a symphony of water, seafoam dancing delicately on the rolling waves.

TURN BY TURN DIRECTIONS

1. Start on the St. Perpetua Trail next to the bathrooms at the Visitor Center.
2. At 0.2 miles (0.3 km), turn left at the junction.
3. At 0.3 miles (0.5 km), cross the street in the Cape Perpetua Campground and meet back up with the trail.
4. At 0.4 miles (0.6 km), cross Overlook Road and continue onto the trail.
5. At 1.3 miles (2 km), keep straight on the St. Perpetua Trail.
6. At just over 1.3 miles (2 km), stay left to take the Whispering Spruce Trail.
7. At 1.5 miles (2.2 km), return to the Whispering Spruce Trail start and head back down the St. Perpetua Trail to the Visitor Center.
8. At 2.8 miles (4.5 km), return to the Visitor Center and head to the left on the Cape Cove Trail.
9. At 2.9 miles (4.8 km), veer to the right to head under the highway.
10. At 3.1 miles (4.9 km), turn right on the Cape Cove Trail.
11. At 3.3 miles (5.3 km), stay left at the junction to take the Restless Waters Trail Loop.
12. At 3.9 miles (6.2 km), return to the start of the Restless Waters Trail and head left on the Cape Cove Trail.
13. At 4 miles (6.4 km), stay straight at the junction and head to the Captain Cook Trail and keep right.
14. At 4.3 miles (6.9 km), take the stairs down to the Spouting Horn and Thor's Well.
15. At 4.5 miles (7.2 km), come back to the junction with Cape Cove Trail. Return to the Visitor Center the way you came.

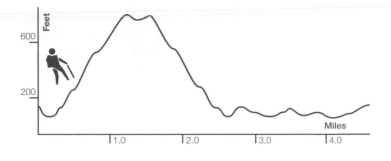

TRAILHEAD DRIVING DIRECTIONS

From Yachats, head south on Highway 101. In 3 miles (4.8 kilometers), turn left at the signs for the Cape Perpetua Visitor Center. The trailhead is located in front of the Visitor Center.

YACHATS BREWING

Yachats Brewing is the community hub for the picturesque beach town of Yachats, OR. Growing from a farmstore ripe with seasonal produce and natural food selections, the brewery started with just two original beers on tap. In May of 2016, the taphouse grew to feature a full service kitchen, over 16 different beers, and a selection of in-house kombuchas. Yachats Brewing is known for their Saisons, inspired by the rich coastal location they call home, infused with everything from Szechuan peppercorns to delicate rose petals and sage.

TRAIL CONTACT INFORMATION
Siuslaw National Forest
Cape Perpetua Visitor Center
2400 Highway 101
Yachats, OR 97498
+1 541-547-3289
www.fs.usda.gov/recarea/siuslaw/
recarea/?recid=42265

RESTAURANT
Yachats Brewing
348 US-101
Yachats, OR 97498
+1 541-547-3884
www.yachatsbrewing.com
Farmstore, brewery, and restaurant
specializing in natural food and Saisons.

ACCOMMODATIONS
Deane's Oceanfront Lodge
7365 US-101
Yachats, OR 97498
+1 541-547-3321
www.deaneslodge.com
Value-priced comfy, nautical-themed
rooms with ocean views and kitchenettes
available.

TOURIST ATTRACTIONS INFO
Yachats Visitor Center
241 US-101
Yachats, OR 97498
+1 541-547-3530
www.yachats.org

CASCADE HEAD

HOME TO A RARE ENDANGERED BUTTERFLY AND AN ABUNDANCE OF WILDLIFE, CASCADE HEAD'S GRASSY SLOPES ARE TRULY A PROTECTED TREASURE ALONG THE OREGON COAST.

STARTING POINT

KNIGHT PARK

DESTINATION

LOWER VIEWPOINT

BEER

RUSTY TRUCK MOONLIGHT RIDE BLACKBERRY ALE

DIFFICULTY

HIKING

MAP

LOOK UP
WWW.FS.USDA.GOV

DURATION OF THE HIKE

2 HOURS
3.2 MILES (5.1KM)

PASS NEEDED

NONE

ELEVATION GAIN

600 FEET (182M)

FRUIT BEER

 CLOUDY RUBY

 BLACKBERRY, YEASTY, SWEET MALT

 BLACKBERRY, WHEAT, MALTY

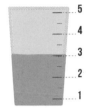

BITTERNESS   SWEETNESS

DESCRIPTION OF THE ROUTE

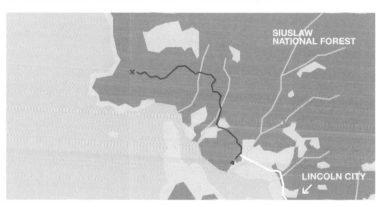

For 50 years, Cascade Head Preserve has created a protected grassland habitat for rare species of plants and animals. In fact, this unique coastal prairie headland is one of the few homes to the endangered Oregon silverspot butterfly. The area is managed by The Nature Conservancy, and hundreds of volunteers each year help to remove invasive species and maintain the trail system.

The Nature Conservancy Trail is a 3.4 mile (5.1 kilometer) traverse in full (for a 6.8 mile (10.9 kilometer) roundtrip hike), but we'll describe the lower section of this trail, which is accessible year round and furnishes exquisite views of the Three Rocks and the Salmon River Estuary. If time allows, hike the full trail to the upper trailhead, or add on a hike out to Hart's Cove. Cascade Head gets its name from the waterfall that literally cascades into the waters of Hart's Cove — a fantastic sight! Please note, however, that the road to Hart's Cove and Trail is only open between July 16 and December 31 each year.

The trail passes through sections of privately owned land. Between these private lands and the fragile grasslands, it's incredibly important to stay on the trail at all times. Begin at the parking area in Knight Park. From here, head out along the Nature Conservancy Cascade Head Trail. The trail follows along Three Rocks Road, veering onto boardwalks, then crossing the road to head down to the original trailhead, which was moved to help with parking issues for the private residences nearby.

From here, the trail is fairly rugged, with roots and stairs climbing steeply through old-growth forest dominated by Douglas fir and Sitka spruce. You'll notice frequent Siuslaw National Forest signs — alerting you to the borders of the Cascade Head Ranch neighborhood whose cooperation with the Forest Service and Nature Conservancy make this trail possible. This forest climb is the steepest part of the trail, but very short. At 1.2 miles (1.9 kilometers) you'll cross Teal Creek on a wooden bridge, and soon after come to the edge of conservancy land, marked by an informational board. Get ready for the true beauty to take over.

The headlands are windswept, especially in the winter when cold winds mix with ocean air to make the hike downright chilly, despite typically mild coastal temperatures. The single-track trail climbs steadily up the bluffs, cutting through the strikingly green prairie. The higher you climb, the more the Three Rocks come into view — seemingly marking the barrier between the Salmon River and the Pacific Ocean.

You'll find a turnaround point at what's known as the "Lower Viewpoint." However, there's no viewing platform, not even a sign. Instead, you can judge your endpoint in a few ways. You can keep track and hike out 1.6 miles (3 kilometers), or simply hike out to the farthest point out on the headlands before the trail turns back and starts to climb up a series of switchbacks. Take a big breath of sea air, admire the views, and head back the way you came once you've had your fill.

TURN BY TURN DIRECTIONS

1. From the parking area at Knight Park, head left to the Cascade Head Nature Conservancy Trail.
2. At 0.1 miles (0.16 km), cross North Three Rocks Road and continue on the trail following the green signs.
3. At 0.4 miles (0.6 km), cross Savage Road, following the green trail signs. Trail continues along the road.
4. At 0.5 miles (0.8 km), come to the original trailhead, continue on it and away from the road.
5. At 1.6 miles (2.5 km), arrive at the Lower Viewpoint.
6. Return the way you came.

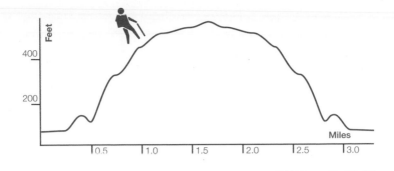

TRAILHEAD DRIVING DIRECTIONS

From Lincoln City, head north on Highway 101. Turn left on Three Rocks Road, turning left at the intersection with Savage Road to stay on Three Rocks Road. Knight Park is on the left.

RUSTY TRUCK BREWING CO.

When you walk into Rusty Truck Brewing Co. you'll instantly recognize its roots as a Roadhouse — the saloon feel to the interior, dollar bills tacked to the ceiling, and a stage ideal for a rockin' show. The brewery's namesake rusty-red truck still sits out front in its designated parking space (after a lengthy "debate" with the city). Now, Rusty is joined by a whole fleet of trucks, outfitted with taps and jockey-boxes to bring Rusty Truck's beach-worthy brews to thirsty beer lovers all over the Northwest. If you visit on the weekend, be sure to pack your dancing shoes!

TRAIL CONTACT INFORMATION
Hebo Ranger District
31525 Hwy. 22
Hebo, OR 97122
+1 503-392-5100
www.fs.usda.gov/recarea/siuslaw/
recarea/?recid=42717

Nature Conservancy
821 SE 14th Avenue
Portland, OR 97214
+1 503 802-8100
www.nature.org

ACCOMMODATIONS
Lincoln City Quality Inn
1091 SE 1st St.
Lincoln City, OR 97367
+1 541 996-4400
Great price, clean, spacious rooms,
and ocean views available.

BREWERY/RESTAURANT
Rusty Truck Brewing Co.
4649 SW Hwy. 101
Lincoln City, OR 97367
+1 541 994-7729
www.rustytruckbrewing.com
Come for the beer and stay for
everything this 101 Roadhouse has to
offer!

TOURIST ATTRACTIONS INFO
The Lincoln City Visitor
and Convention Bureau
City Hall, Fourth Floor
801 SW Hwy. 101
Lincoln City, OR 97367
+1 541-996-1274
www.oregoncoast.org

DRY CREEK FALLS

FOR COLUMBIA RIVER GORGE CASCADES WITHOUT THE CROWDS,
HIKE ALONG THE PACIFIC CREST TRAIL TO SECLUDED DRY CREEK FALLS —
A PICTURESQUE PLUNGE OVER MOSSY BASALT CLIFFS.

STARTING POINT

BRIDGE OF THE GODS TRAILHEAD

DESTINATION

DRY CREEK FALLS

BEER

THUNDER ISLAND YA YA EE IPA

DIFFICULTY

WALKING

DURATION OF THE HIKE

2 HOURS 4.6 MILES (7.4KM)

MAP

GREEN TRAILS COLUMBIA RIVER GORGE
WEST NO. 428S

PASS NEEDED

NORTHWEST FOREST PASS

ELEVATION GAIN

710 FEET (216M)

JUICY IPA

THUNDER ISLAND
Brewing Co.

GOLDEN

CITRUS,
TROPICAL FRUIT

DANK MANGO,
JUICY

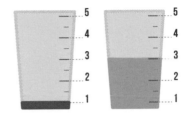

BITTERNESS   SWEETNESS

DESCRIPTION OF THE ROUTE

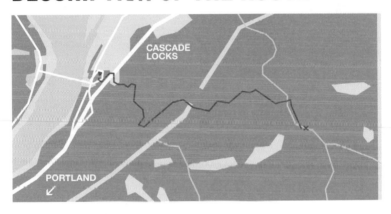

With the highest concentration of waterfalls in North America, the Columbia River Gorge is a waterfall hunter's paradise. Cascading down from steep basalt cliffs, many of these falls are accessible right off the highway, drawing crowds all year long. Seeking an escape? Dry Creek Falls is an easy hike away — if you know where to look.

Beginning at the Bridge of the Gods Trailhead and traversing along a section of the Pacific Crest Trail, the way to Dry Creek Falls is well maintained and easy to follow. Famous in the hiking world — where it's known simply as the PCT —the Pacific Crest Trail runs 2,650 miles (4,265 kilometers) between the Mexican and Canadian borders. The Dry Creek Falls Trail follows a mere 2 miles (3.2 kilometers) of the northernmost Oregon section.

From Toll House Park in Cascade Locks, cross the road that leads to the bridge and find a paved trail marked as the Pacific Crest Trail. This first section of the hike takes you through the edge of town before it delves deeper into the forested reaches of the Gorge. At 0.1 miles (150 meters), you'll come to Moody Street and walk up it to cross under the freeway, continuing to follow signs for the PCT. Continue up the road, until you reach a trail crossing at 0.2 miles (300 meters). Head to the left and hit the PCT proper.

The noise from I-84 dwindles as you make your way through a second-growth forest towering with bigleaf and vine maples. The trail climbs steadily but not steeply through the woods, and is rocky but well maintained. Oregon grape and multiple species of ferns — licorice, sword, lady and maidenhair — cover the forest floor in a carpet of lush green.

The sunlight glimmers through the verdant canopy above, making it seem as if you're walking through a tunnel of green. At 2.1 miles (3.3 kilometers), you'll come to Dry Creek and an old primitive road. Take your leave from the PCT and turn right to head up the road on a spur towards Dry Creek Falls. This section is a bit steeper, but the waterfall is just under 0.3 miles (480 meters) away. As you crest the hill, you'll start to see the lower cascades of Dry Creek come into view, small pools forming around larger rocks in the stream. At 2.3 miles (3.7 kilometers), you'll come to the falls.

Dry Creek Falls is a plunge stream, falling from a notch in the near-black basalt cliffs around it. Year-round, the stream of the falls rushes — which leaves its name a bit of a curiosity. At one point this stream had been diverted, creating a dry creek bed through this area. The stream has now been restored, and this Dry Creek is once again wet. The surrounding cliffs are covered in a plush tapestry of bright green moss, while ferns and small shrubs cluster at their base and around the pool created by Dry Creek Falls. Head back the way you came to Cascade Locks and beer awaiting!

TURN BY TURN DIRECTIONS

1. Cross the road to the Pacific Crest Trailhead.
2. At 0.1 miles (0.16 km), come to Moody Street and head to the right.
3. At 0.2 miles (0.3 km), turn left to continue on the Pacific Crest Trail.
4. At 2.1 miles (3.3 km), turn right onto the Dry Creek Falls spur.
5. At 2.3 miles (3.7 km), arrive at Dry Creek Falls.
6. Return the way you came.

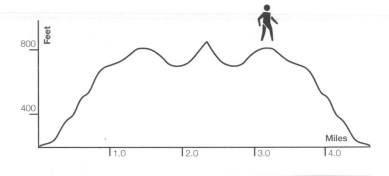

TRAILHEAD DRIVING DIRECTIONS

From Portland on I-84, take Exit 44 and proceed for 0.3 miles (480 meters). Then bear right onto the access road for the Bridge of the Gods to Stevenson. In 0.2 miles, reach the trailhead on your right, before the toll booth.

THUNDER ISLAND BREWING

Thunder Island Brewing's taproom has one of the best views of the Columbia River. Crafting fine ales in the shadow of the Bridge of the Gods since 2013, Thunder Island is a must for adventure and brew seekers alike. Welcoming weary PCT hikers finishing their Oregon journey, Thunder Island invites hikers to celebrate with a pint. The brewery has a "Trail Magic" program where visitors can pay-it-forward to a thru-hiker with a complimentary pint!

TRAIL CONTACT INFORMATION
Columbia River Gorge
National Scenic Area Office
902 Wasco Avenue
Suite 200
Hood River, OR 97031
+1 541 308 1700
www.fs.usda.gov/main/crgnsa/home

ACCOMMODATIONS
Best Western Plus Columbia River Inn
735 Wanapa Street,
Cascade Locks, OR 97014
+1 541-374-8777
www.bestwesternoregon.com/hotels/
best-western-plus-columbia-river-inn

BREWERY/RESTAURANT
Thunder Island Brewing
601 NW Wa Na Pa St.
Cascade Locks, OR 97014
+1 971-231-4599
www.thunderislandbrewing.com
Great eats, great beer, and a fantastic view!

TOURIST ATTRACTIONS INFO
Port of Cascade Locks
355 Wanapa St. at Marine Park
Cascade Locks, Oregon 97014
+1 541-374-8619
www.portofcascadelocks.org

FOREST PARK

STROLL THROUGH AN OLD-GROWTH FOREST AND PAST HISTORIC LANDMARKS
TO THE FAMED PITTOCK MANSION AND POSTCARD-READY VIEWS
OF DOWNTOWN PORTLAND.

OR STATE OF OREGON

STARTING POINT	DESTINATION
LOWER MACLEAY TRAILHEAD	**PITTOCK MANSION**
BEER	DIFFICULTY
EX NOVO ELIOT IPA	**HIKING**
MAP	DURATION OF THE HIKE
GREEN TRAILS MAP FOREST PARK #426S, TRAIL MAP AND VISITOR'S GUIDE TO FOREST PARK	**2-3 HOURS 5.2 MILES** (8.3KM)
PASS NEEDED	ELEVATION GAIN
NONE	**900 FEET** (274M)

INDIA PALE ALE

 AMBER

 CITRUS, PINE

GRAPEFRUIT AND MANGO

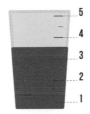

BITTERNESS   **SWEETNESS**

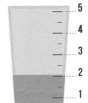

DESCRIPTION OF THE ROUTE

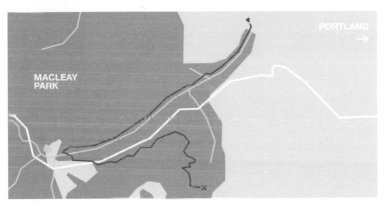

Northwest of downtown Portland, Forest Park is the biggest urban forest in the United States, with more than 80 miles of trails to explore on a respite from the city. Fern-lined and tree-covered, the trails meander past creeks and historic landmarks alike. If you have time for only one hike in this expansive park, the 5.2 mile (8.3 kilometers) Balch Creek to Pittock Mansion trail is an obvious choice.

A snapshot of the park's landscape, the trail begins by following Balch Creek on the Lower Macleay Trail as it snakes through a lush understory. The largest creek in the park, Balch Creek is lined with red huckleberry, salmonberry, and Oregon grape, its shaded shallows home to coastal cutthroat trout. This part of the trail is wide, gently climbing through a forest of western hemlock, red cedar and winding vine maple. Even during the day, you might be lucky enough to spot one of Forest Park's resident owls — five species including the barred owl make this forest their home.

At 0.8 miles (1.3 kilometers) you'll come to the first landmark along this trail — the Stone House. Sometimes ominously called the Witch's Castle, the structure is actually the decaying ruins of a former restroom built in 1929 (complete with running water). Storms and vandalism through the years have destroyed the structure's roof, but the Stone House is a great place to pause and take photos. Covered in moss with licorice ferns fanning out from its peaked sides, the place is slowly being reclaimed by nature.

After exploring the Stone House, continue west on the Wildwood Trail. The Wildwood Trail is 30.2 miles (48.6 kilometers) long, snaking through a large portion of Forest Park. This section of the Wildwood passes by trickling waterfalls, climbing upwards for 0.5 miles (0.8 kilometers) to a road crossing at NW Cornell Road. Cross the street and meet back up with the Wildwood Trail to begin your climb up to the mansion.

On this steepest section of the trail, you might find yourself waiting for large groups to pass on busy weekends. Yet the payout for the climb is well worth it. At a 4-way trail crossing, continue straight on the Wildwood Trail for the final push up to the top.

You'll come out on the far end of the Pittock Mansion parking lot — head left to find the mansion's grounds. Built by Henry and Georgiana Pittock in 1914, the mansion was restored and opened to the public in 1965. A fee is required to tour the mansion, but you can stroll the grounds and garden at your leisure. There is one sight not to be missed — the viewpoint of Downtown Portland around the back side. Take a seat at one of the many benches, snap a few photos, see how many of Portland's iconic bridges you can spy, and on clear days spot the snow-covered peak of Mount Hood. Return along the same route.

TURN BY TURN DIRECTIONS

1. From Macleay Park, head south on the Lower Macleay Trail where it begins under the Thurman Street Bridge.
2. At 0.8 miles (1.2 km), turn left onto the Wildwood Trail.
3. At 1.4 miles (2.2 km), cross NW Cornell Road and meet back up with the Wildwood Trail.
4. After crossing the road, continue straight on the Wildwood Trail toward Pittock Mansion.
5. At 2.5 miles (4 km), reach the Pittock Mansion Parking Lot.
6. Bear left and walk 0.1 miles (0.16 km) to reach Pittock Mansion.
7. Return via the same route to Macleay Park.

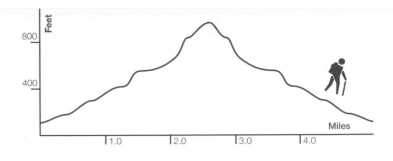

TRAILHEAD DRIVING DIRECTIONS

Take I-5 north to 405 north, and exit for Highway 30 west towards St. Helens, then take the first exit at Vaughn Street. Turn left at the first light onto 23rd, then right onto Thurman Avenue Turn right on NW 28th, then take an immediate left onto Upshur. In about three blocks, Upshur ends at Lower Macleay Park.

EX NOVO BREWING CO.

Opened in July of 2014, Ex Novo Brewing Co. is a benefit company in the Eliot neighborhood of Portland. With a mission to better the world, one brew at a time, Ex Novo donates 100% of its net profits to local and global charities. The restaurant's menu is eclectic, using local ingredients and changing with the season. With a small number of year-round beers, Ex Novo's tap list is ever-rotating through new, edgy small batch brews.

TRAIL CONTACT INFORMATION
Portland Parks and Recreation
+1 503-823-7529
www.portlandoregon.gov/parks

ACCOMODATIONS
Crowne Plaza Portland Convention Center
1441 NE 2nd Ave.
Portland, OR
+1 503-233-2401
www.cpportland.com
Upscale hotel close to public transportation and in walking distance from Ex Novo Brewery.

BREWERY/RESTAURANT
Ex Novo Brewing Co.
2326 North Flint Ave.
Portland, OR
+1 503-894-8251
www.exnovobrew.com
Community-minded brewery with a localvore-focused menu and rotating taplist. Growlers and bottled beers available to go.

TOURIST ATTRACTIONS INFO
Travel Portland
701 S.W. Sixth Ave.
Pioneer Courthouse Square
Portland, OR 97204
+1 877-678-5263
www.travelportland.com

WRECK OF THE PETER IREDALE AND COFFENBURY LAKE LOOP

STROLL ALONG THE SHORES OF MARSHY COFFENBURY LAKE, THEN HIKE OUT THROUGH SAND DUNES TO THE WRECK OF PETER IREDALE: ONE OF THE MOST ACCESSIBLE SHIPWRECKS IN THE GRAVEYARD OF THE PACIFIC.

STARTING POINT	DESTINATION
COFFENBURY LAKE	**WRECK OF THE PETER IREDALE**
BEER	DIFFICULTY
BUOY DUNKEL	**WALKING**
MAP	DURATION OF THE HIKE
LOOK UP WWW.OREGONSTATEPARKS.ORG	(LOOP) **2-3 HOURS** **4.2 MILES** (6.7KM)
PASS NEEDED	ELEVATION GAIN
OREGON STATE PARKS PASS	**MINIMAL**

DUNKEL

 BROWN

FLORAL HOP, CARAMEL

CARAMEL, CHOCO-LATE, CLEAN

BITTERNESS	SWEETNESS

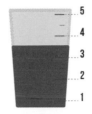 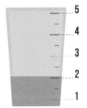

DESCRIPTION OF THE ROUTE

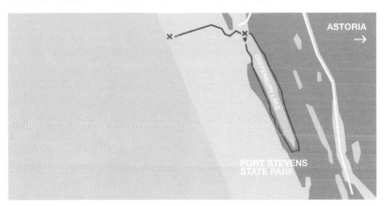

If there is anywhere in the Pacific Northwest to search for shipwrecks, it has to be Astoria, OR. Immortalized in the 80s classic *The Goonies*, Astoria's hilltop Victorian houses look down on the mouth of the Columbia River, evoking images of pirate ships and maps leading to long-lost treasures. But this tumultuous meeting of river and ocean has also earned the moniker, "Graveyard of the Pacific." The Columbia Bar, a formidable sandbar that's been the folly of many sailors, is the reason behind it. Over 2,000 ships have been lost in this area alone, and in 1846 an elite group of bar pilots was created to guide each ship through the narrow passage.

There may not be any buried treasures to discover, but you can hike out to remnants of one of these lost ships. Just off the coast of Fort Stevens State Park, the Wreck of the *Peter Iredale* is a popular Astoria destination. While you can literally drive up to the wreck, we suggest adding on a loop hike around the tranquil Coffenbury Lake so you can explore a bit more of the park.

Close to the park's camping area, Coffenbury Lake is a popular swimming beach and kayak destination during the summer months. The 2.4-mile (3.8 kilometers) loop trail around the circumference of the lake is an easy walk with chances for wildlife sightings. On the west side of the lake, the trail goes through the coastal forest which surrounds the lake. The Sitka spruce that dominates the coast is most prevalent, but there are cedar and red alder in the area as well. At the south end of the lake, you'll come to a marshy area, where the trail continues on a causeway through the marsh. Now on the east side of the lake, the trail keeps close to the shoreline. With open views of the lake, keep an eye out for waterfowl.

Once you make it back to the parking lot, head to the paved trail that goes past the bathroom. Follow this trail to the Sunset Trail, which will lead you to the remains of the *Peter Iredale*. A British four-masted sailing ship, the *Peter Iredale* was bound for the mouth of the Columbia River just before it ran aground when the crew became disoriented during a nighttime storm in October of 1906. Stuck in the silt and sand of Clatsop Spit, the crew evacuated safely. But during the wait for more favorable weather to tow the ship back to sea, the vessel listed, lodging itself into the sand. The hull was sold for scrap — today only the iron frame of the bow and a few ribs remain.

From different angles, the Wreck of the *Peter Iredale* takes on a cast of guises. From behind, the skeletal wreckage looks like a beached whale, the remnants of masts like nobby vertebrae. Looking up at the prow, you can imagine the vessel's original form; peering through the rusted wreckage you'll watch the crashing waves that sentenced the *Peter Iredale* to its sandy grave. The wreck is haunting at sunset. You may want to plan accordingly! Whisper the final toast Captain Lawrence pledged to his abandoned ship — "May God bless you, and may your bones bleach in the sands" — before heading back on the Sunset Trail to the parking lot at Coffenbury Lake.

TURN BY TURN DIRECTIONS

1. Start at the parking lot for Coffenbury Lake.
   Walk south through the picnic area to the footpath.
2. At 1.1 miles (1.7 km), turn left at the junction.
3. At 1.2 miles (1.9 km), turn left to continue on the lakeshore trail.
4. At 1.8 miles (2.8 km), continue straight through the swimming/picnic area.
5. At 2.4 miles (3.8 km), come to the parking lot where you started.
6. At 2.5 miles (4 km), continue on the paved pathway that goes past the bathrooms.
7. At 2.6 miles (4.1 km), turn left at the trail junction.
8. At 2.7 miles (4.3 km), turn right onto the Sunset Trail.
9. At 2.8 miles (4.5 km), stay left to continue on the Sunset Trail.
10. At 3.0 miles (4.8 km), continue straight to stay on the Sunset Trail.
11. At 3.2 miles (5.1 km), arrive at the parking area for the Peter Iredale.
    Take the trail down to the beach.
12. At 3.3 miles (5.3 km), arrive at the Wreck of the Peter Iredale.
    Take the Sunset Trail back to the Coffenbury Lake parking area.

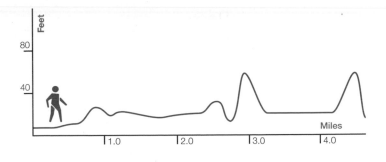

TRAILHEAD DRIVING DIRECTIONS

From Astoria on US 30/Marine Drive, exit onto Highway 101 S. Turn right onto E Harbor St, then left onto N Main Avenue A. Turn right onto SW 9th Street and then right onto NW Ridge Road Turn into Fort Stevens State Park by taking a left onto Peter Iredale Road. Continue to the Coffenbury Lake parking area on Crossover Road to the left.

BUOY BEER COMPANY

From its home on a pier in Astoria's harbor, Buoy Beer Company has a front-row seat to the bustle of the Columbia River. Sip on the brewery's Czech Pilsner or Dunkel like a true fisherman as you watch the Bar Pilots guide vessels past the Oregon side's red buoy. Buoy Beer Co. takes the seafaring history of Astoria to heart, brewing bold-flavored ales and lagers to offset the area's ofttimes stormy weather. As you walk into the cannery-turned-brewery, make sure to look through the glass window in the floor to the pier below— you might even catch sight of a seal!

TRAIL CONTACT INFORMATION
Fort Stevens State Park
100 Peter Iredale Rd.
Hammond, OR 97121
+1 503-861-3170
www.oregonstateparks.org

ACCOMMODATIONS
Windwater Bed and Breakfast Suite
172 Duane St.
Astoria, OR 97103
+1 503-338-8702
Book via Airbnb
Contemporary luxury loft-suite with breathtaking views of Astoria and the Columbia River — an ideal couple's retreat with a charming host.

BREWERY/RESTAURANT
Buoy Beer Company
1 8th St.
Astoria, OR 97103
+1 503-325-4540
www.buoybeer.com
Located in an old cannery building on the Astoria Waterfront.

TOURIST ATTRACTIONS INFO
Astoria Visitor Center
111 West Marine Dr.
Astoria, OR 97103
+1 503-325-6311
www.travelastoria.com

Maritime Museum
1792 Marine Dr.
Astoria, OR 97103
+1 503-325-2323
www.crmm.org

GARFIELD PEAK

TAKE THIS SHORT BUT STRENUOUS SUMMIT HIKE TO AN 8,000 FOOT PROMINENCE ALONG CRATER LAKE'S RIM FOR UNOBSTRUCTED VIEWS OF WIZARD ISLAND AND THE SURROUNDING CASCADE MOUNTAINS.

STARTING POINT	DESTINATION
GARFIELD PEAK TRAILHEAD	**GARFIELD PEAK**
BEER	DIFFICULTY
SKYLINE BREWING LIQUID VACATION	**HIKING**
MAP	DURATION OF THE HIKE
LOOK UP WWW.CRATERLAKEINSTITUTE.COM	**2-3 HOURS 3.4 MILES (5.4KM)**
PASS NEEDED	ELEVATION GAIN
NATIONAL PARKS PASS	**1,010 FEET (307M)**

DOUBLE INDIA PALE ALE

ALCOHOL **8.5%** CONTENT

 DEEP GOLD

 CITRUS, TROPICAL FRUIT

JUICY, PINEAPPLE, TANGERINE

BITTERNESS   **SWEETNESS**

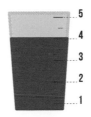

DESCRIPTION OF THE ROUTE

A sapphire gem in Oregon, Crater Lake is the deepest lake in the United States. Its impossibly blue depths formed in the caldera left behind after Mount Mazama's eruption some 8,000 years ago. A beloved place that has captured the hearts and imaginations of countless visitors, Crater Lake National Park was created in 1902 in order to protect this awe-inspiring landscape.

One of the more challenging hikes in the park, the Garfield Peak trail climbs to one of the highest prominences on the caldera's jagged rim. At 8,054 feet high (2,454 meters), Garfield Peak offers expansive views of the entirety of the water below, including the lake's two islands: Wizard Island and Phantom Ship. For this reason — and due to its easy access from Rim Village —Garfield Peak is one of the most popular trails at Crater Lake.

From the eastern end of Rim Village, head behind the Crater Lake Lodge to meet up with the paved Rim trail. The pavement soon falls away and the trail starts its ascent. The trail follows the contours of the rim for 0.5

miles (0.8 kilometers) through meadows and Mountain Hemlock, before turning north and providing the first views of the lake at a wooden bench.

From the bench, you'll be able to peer down the steep slope of the crater to the transparent crystalline-blue lake shore below. Look up and take in the craggy volcanic rock of Castle Crest. This formation predates the eruption that created the caldera below. From here, the trail is mostly exposed, making small switchbacks up Garfield's northwestern flank.

Along the trail, listen and watch for pika, Clark's nutcracker, and golden mantled ground squirrel who make their homes on the rocky slopes of the rim. Wildflowers bloom from the rocks: orange paintbrush and the small but hearty pearly everlasting. The only trees at this point on the trail are 5-needle whitebark pines, limbs twisting and gnarled providing no shade on the exposed trail. You'll eventually come to a stone-covered reservoir that supplies water to Rim Village. The flat top provides an excellent platform to take in the view and catch your breath before the final push up to the peak.

Reach the summit and find Crater Lake spread out before you. At this high vantage point, you're able to see the far reaches of the lake. Look northwest for views of cinder-cone Wizard Island, with The Watchman and Hillman Peak looming behind. To the east, you'll see Mt. Scott, the highest peak in the park. The Klamath Basin is visible to the south. From here, you'll also be able to see the rocky Phantom Ship, eternally moored along the lake's southern shore.

TURN BY TURN DIRECTIONS

1. From Rim Village, head to the back of the Crater Lake Lodge, turning to the right (east) on the paved Rim Trail.
2. At 300 feet (91 m), the paved path turns to a dirt trail.
3. At 0.3 miles (0.5 km), come to the wooden bench.
4. At 0.5 miles (0.8 km), reach the stone-covered reservoir.
5. At 1.7 miles (2.7 km), reach the summit of Garfield Peak.
6. Return via the same route.

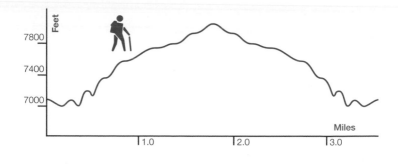

TRAILHEAD DRIVING DIRECTIONS

From Highway 138, turn onto Highway 209 (Volcanic Legacy Scenic Byway). Veer right to continue on the Rim Drive towards Rim Village. Turn left into the parking lot for the Rim Village Visitor Center and Crater Lake Lodge. Park near the back of the Lodge, near the trailhead if possible.

SKYLINE BREWING COMPANY

Brothers Ty and Ry Kliewer are full-time farmers in Klamath Falls, growing wheat, alfalfa and barley and raising cattle. And there's something else going on inside a renovated milking barn on the family's farm: one of Klamath Falls' favorite breweries. Welcome to Skyline Brewing Company, a true farm brewery. The brewery repurposes spent grain into cattle feed, while hops and yeast are used to make fertilizer. Though they don't have a dedicated tasting room, Skyline's beers can be found at a variety of bars and restaurants around Klamath Falls, including The Falls Taphouse — a highly rated, family-friendly, and spacious beer bar in downtown Klamath Falls.

USEFUL CONTACT INFORMATION
Crater Lake National Park
Rim Visitor Center
+1 541-594-3000
www.nps.gov/crla

BREWERY
Skyline Brewing Company
Klamath Falls, OR
+1 541-891-2528
www.skylinebrewingco.com

RESTAURANT/TAPHOUSE
The Falls Taphouse
2215 Shallock Ave.
Klamath Falls, OR 97601
www.facebook.com/thefallstaphouse
Family-friendly taphouse featuring food trucks, a spacious patio, and indoor seating.

TOURIST ATTRACTIONS INFO
Lake Cruise and Wizard Island Tour
+1 888-774-2728
www.craterlakelodges.com/activities/
volcano-boat-cruises
Take a guided boat tour of the lake out to explore Wizard Island Crater Lake.

ACCOMMODATIONS
Mazama Village Campground
Crater Lake National Park
+1 541-594-3000
www.craterlakelodges.com
Campground within the National Park.

HOOD RIVER WATERFRONT

THIS LEISURELY RIVERSIDE RAMBLE PASSES THROUGH PUBLIC PARKS AS IT FOLLOWS THE COLUMBIA, ALL WHILE OFFERING WALKERS FRONT-ROW VIEWS OF ONE OF THE BEST WINDSURFING DESTINATIONS IN THE WORLD.

STARTING POINT	DESTINATION
PORT MARINA PARK	**THE HOOK**

BEER	DIFFICULTY
PFRIEM IPA	**WALKING**

MAP	DURATION OF THE HIKE
LOOK UP PORTOFHOODRIVER.COM/WATERFRONT-RECREATION	**1.5 HOURS 3 MILES** (4.8KM)

PASS NEEDED	ELEVATION GAIN
NONE	**MINIMAL**

INDIA PALE ALE

BRIGHT GOLD

RESIN, CITRUS, PINE

GRAPEFRUIT, CANDIED ORANGE, PINE

BITTERNESS **SWEETNESS**

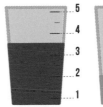 

DESCRIPTION OF THE ROUTE

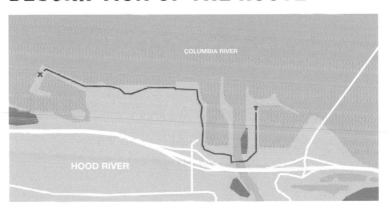

While there are plenty of worthy waterfall hiking trails in the nearby Columbia River Gorge, sometimes you just need to go for a walk in the park. And that's exactly what this urban trail provides: a short, easy path accessible from downtown Hood River — the perfect after-dinner sunset stroll.

Begin at Port Marina Park. Owned and managed by the Port of Hood River, this rectangular green space provides lawn and beach access to all. Once you've parked at the north end of the park, check out the beach before heading south on the paved trail. From here you can see the Hood River Bridge spanning the Columbia River to White Salmon, Washington, on the hillside. You'll pass a picnic shelter and the Marina Green — where you may witness an evening game of rugby — before coming to the History Museum.

If it's open, step inside the yellow-brick building for a dose of local history. Outside the museum, a large steam-powered paddlewheeler, or "sternwheeler" wheel is on display. It once belonged to the *Henderson*, a 160-foot sternwheeler built in 1901. The *Henderson* spent decades running up and down the Columbia River, between The Dalles and Portland, before its eventual demise in the 1950s. An interpretive sign describes its storied past.

After viewing the *Henderson* wheel, cross the nearby footbridge over Hood River at its confluence with the Columbia. Below, fisherman try their luck in the rushing waters, often wading out knee-deep to cast their lines. Continue along the trail as it skirts the Hampton Inn and Suites before turning north. At 0.8 miles (1.2 kilometers) you will reach the port's event site and public restrooms. Various events are held here throughout the year, from windsurfing and kiteboarding to a fall harvest festival.

During summer months, the Hood River Waterfront is alive with watersports. Many schools set up shop right here at the event site. An internationally recognized windsurfing destination, Hood River is known to many as the "windsurfing capital of the world." Strong winds rip through the Columbia River Gorge — a river canyon bisecting the Cascade Mountains — creating ideal conditions for wind-powered watersports. As you walk by, watch for surfers, boarders, paddlers, and more on the river.

Upon reaching Waterfront Park, you'll be greeted by nearly six acres of attractively landscaped community space. This family-friendly park provides a swimming beach, a kids, climbing wall and playground, restrooms and a covered picnic area. Due to its namesake beach access and walk-in boat launch, it's another hot spot during summer. Best of all, the brewery is right across the street.

Before you head in for a pint, continue your walk out to the Hook. Another windsurfing playground, the Hook creates a protected cove where beginners can learn the sport. Look for Mount Adams peeking through to the north as you walk along this aptly-named breakwater. From the Hook's west end you can see well beyond Wells Island — to Ruthton Point and beyond — deep into the gorge.

TURN BY TURN DIRECTIONS

1. Begin at the north end of Port Marina Park. Head south on the waterfront trail.
2. At 0.2 miles, turn right to stay on the Hood River Waterfront Trail.
3. At 0.3 miles, cross the footbridge over Hood River. Follow the trail to the right (north) after crossing the bridge.
4. At 0.4 miles, turn left at Nichols Parkway. Follow the trail along this road.
5. At 0.5 miles, turn right, following the path to the Hood River Event Site at 0.8 miles.
6. Enter Waterfront Park at 1 mile.
7. Continue half a mile out to the Hook. Return the way you came.

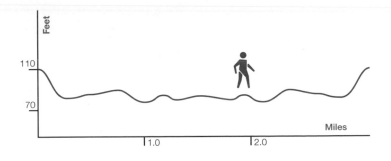

TRAILHEAD DRIVING DIRECTIONS

Drive I-84 east to Hood River from Portland, then take Exit 64. Turn left onto Button Bridge Road/Mt. Hood Highway, then immediately turn left onto East Port Marina Drive. Follow this road half a mile into Port Marina Park.

PFRIEM BREWERY

After a decade of brewing experience, Ken Pfriem achieved his dream and opened a brewery of his own in 2012. Since then, Pfriem Family Brewers have won dozens of awards, expanded their brewery, and opened a barrel-aging program. Pfriem's tasting room has a prime location on the Hood River waterfront, and offers craft beer lovers fine Columbia River views alongside a pint of Belgian-inspired brew.

TRAIL CONTACT INFORMATION
Port of Hood River
1000 E. Port Marina Dr.
Hood River, OR 97031
+1 541-386-1645
www.portofhoodriver.com/
waterfront-recreation

ACCOMMODATIONS
Hampton Inn and Suites Hood River
1 Nichols Parkway
Hood River, OR 97031
+1 541-436-1600
www.hamptoninn3.hilton.com
Conveniently located on the Hood River
Waterfront Trail.

BREWERY/RESTAURANT
pFriem Brewery
707 Portway Ave #101
Hood River, OR 97031
+1 541-321-0490
www.pfriembeer.com
Seasonal salads and classic pub grub
paired with fine pFriem beer.

TOURIST ATTRACTIONS INFO
Hood River County Chamber of
Commerce & Visitors Center
720. E. Port Marina Dr.
Hood River, OR 97031
+1 541-386-2000
www.hoodriver.org

NEWBERRY CALDERA LITTLE CRATER TRAIL

A MODERATELY DIFFICULT HIKE ALONG NEWBERRY CRATER, WITH VIEWS OF BEAUTIFUL PAULINA LAKE AND BIG OBSIDIAN LAVA FLOW.

STARTING POINT	DESTINATION
TRAILHEAD AT THE BOAT LAUNCH IN LITTLE CRATER CAMPGROUND	**LITTLE CRATER OVERLOOK**
BEER	DIFFICULTY
GOODLIFE SWEET AS PACIFIC ALE	**WALKING**
MAP	DURATION OF THE HIKE
USFS DESCHUTES NATIONAL FOREST, LOOK UP: WWW.AMERICANSOUTHWEST.NET	**(LOOP) 1-2 HOURS** **1.9 MILES** (3KM)
PASS NEEDED	ELEVATION GAIN
NORTHWEST FOREST PASS OR MONUMENT ENTRY FEE	**276 FEET** (84M)

PALE ALE

CLOUDY, PALE YELLOW

ORANGE, LEMON ZEST

TROPICAL, CITRUS, MANGO

BITTERNESS   **SWEETNESS**

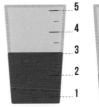

DESCRIPTION OF THE ROUTE

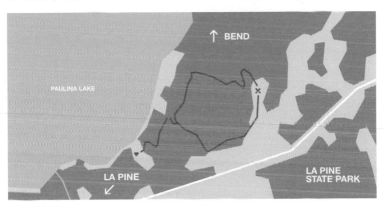

Newberry Caldera lives in the shadow of Oregon's more famous Crater Lake, but this volcano offers its own share of geological wonders. Still active, Newberry Volcano's caldera contains two lakes, multiple obsidian flows, and pyroclastic cones. The Little Crater Trail offers hikers the chance to get right into the heart of this volcano.

Starting along the edge of Paulina Lake, the larger of the two alpine lakes within the caldera, the Little Crater Trail climbs to the mouth of the Newberry cinder cone for views into the caldera, of East Lake, and of two obsidian flows. A relatively short hike, the Little Crater Trail can be combined with other side trips in the area to either Paulina Lake Hot Springs or the Big Obsidian Flow to extend your explorations.

Park at the day-use area next to the public boat launch. Head back up the road about 20 feet to find the Little Crater Trail. The trail is dusty and surrounded by tall thin pines as it makes its way up the side of the crater for 0.3 miles to the crater overlook. At the junction, turn right to head out on the east side of the crater, reaching the high point of the rim at 1.0 mile (1.6 kilometer). The trees obscure the depth of the crater, making its edges hard to define, resembling nothing more than a tree covered hillside. In the distance, you'll see the jagged top of Paulina Peak to the south, rising above the black glint of the Big Obsidian Flow. To the right, East Lake shimmers in the sunshine, and to the north the Interlake Obsidian flow looks like a permanent mudslide, frozen in time. You'll also find volcanic rock formations on the east rim that can be carefully climbed through.

At 1.3 miles (2 kilometers), you'll reach another junction. Go straight to head along the west side of the crater. Along this side you'll find a fissure in the rim, an important geological point of interest. Plants grow out of the cool crevasse, creating a deep grotto to peer down into. Descend the crater's west flank down grassy slopes, through bearberry and fallen lodgepole pines, twisted and sun-bleached. You'll catch beautiful views of Paulina Lake before making your way back into the pine forests. At 1.6 miles (2.5 kilometers) you'll arrive back at the beginning of the loop; turn right to return to the parking lot.

Want to extend your hike? Take the 1 mile (1.6 kilometers) out-and-back trail through the Big Obsidian Flow located across the street from Paulina Lake. An easy hike with interpretive signs, this educational walk takes you out through the glassy, jet-black obsidian fields— the lasting mark of the destructive shield volcano below. You can either drive to the Big Obsidian Flow parking lot, or alternately take the 0.6 mile (0.9 kilometers) Silica Trail that begins at the Little Crater trailhead.

Despite its high elevation (the Newberry Caldera is located in Oregon's High Desert), summer temperatures can be downright hot. Pack plenty of water and apply sunscreen generously.

TURN BY TURN DIRECTIONS

1. From the parking lot at the Paulina Lake boat launch, head back up the road 20 feet (6 m) to Little Crater Trail No. 53.
2. At 0.3 miles (0.5 km), come to the beginning of the Little Crater loop and head right.
3. At 1.3 miles (2 km), come to a junction and go straight.
4. At 1.6 miles (2.5 km), return to the beginning of the loop and turn right.
5. At 1.9 miles (3 km), arrive back at the parking lot.

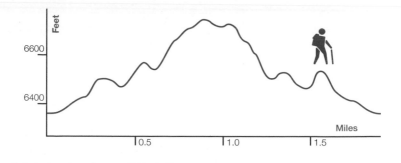

TRAILHEAD DRIVING DIRECTIONS

Head north on US-97 from La Pine. Turn right onto Paulina-East Lake Road. In 15 miles, turn left onto Little Crater Campground Road. Park at the day-use parking lot.

GOODLIFE BREWING

Named after the "Good Life" residents of Bend, OR, enjoy when it comes to craft beer and outdoor adventure, GoodLife Brewing creates well-balanced ales. The first Bend brewery to start canning, GoodLife ensures that its beers are ready for adventure, both inside and outside the taproom. Capturing this spirit, the brewery's full-time tropical and crisp Sweet As Pacific Ale is the perfect way to kick back post-hike.

TRAIL CONTACT INFORMATION
Deschutes National Forest
Crescent Ranger District
136471 Hwy. 97 North
Crescent, OR 97733
+1 541-433-3200
www.fs.usda.gov

ACCOMMODATIONS
Paulina Lake Lodge and Cabins
22440 Paulina Lake Rd.
La Pine, OR 97739
+1 541-536-2240
www.paulinalakelodge.com
Lakeside cabins with full kitchens and rustic furnishing.

BREWERY/RESTAURANT
GoodLife Brewing
70 SW Century Dr.
Bend, OR 97702
+1 541-728-0749
www.goodlifebrewing.com
Brewery/Restaurant with outdoor enthusiasts in mind.

TOURIST ATTRACTIONS INFO
Lava Lands Visitor Center
58201 S. Hwy. 97
Bend, OR 97707
+1 541-593-2421

Visit Bend- Bend Visitor Center
750 NW Lava Rd., Suite 160
Bend, OR 97703
+1 877-245- 8484
www.visitbend.com

NORTH FORK RIVER WALK

AN EASY HIKE STARTING FROM THE LONGEST COVERED BRIDGE IN OREGON, THE NORTH FORK TRAIL TAKES YOU ALONG THE WILLAMETTE RIVER AND OVERLOOKS RAPIDS, FISHING HOLES, AND REMNANTS OF A FORMER DAM.

STARTING POINT	DESTINATION
WESTFIR COVERED BRIDGE SCENIC BYWAY PORTAL	**ROAD 1910**
BEER	DIFFICULTY
3 LEGGED CRANE BRACEGRIDDLE	**WALKING**
MAP	DURATION OF THE HIKE
MIDDLE FORK RANGER DISTRICT (2013) WILLAMETTE NF MAP LOOK UP WWW.FS.USDA.GOV	**2-3 HOURS 6 MILES** (9.6KM)
PASS NEEDED	ELEVATION GAIN
NONE	**200 FEET** (61M)

ALCOHOL
5.4%
CONTENT

SPECIAL BITTER

 CLOUDY
GOLDEN BROWN

MALT, TOASTED,
TOFFEE

MALTY,
BROWN SUGAR,
HINT OF CITRUS

BITTERNESS **SWEETNESS**

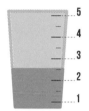

DESCRIPTION OF THE ROUTE

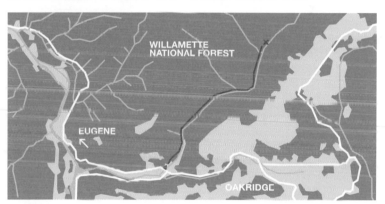

It's a bit of a mouthful — the North Fork of the Middle Fork of the Willamette River — but this section of river is an adventure lover's playground. With plenty of secluded swimming holes and fishing spots, the river's deep green waters draw many visitors to the small sister towns of Westfir and Oakridge.

You don't have to pull on hip waders or launch a whitewater raft to experience the beauty of these pristine waters; just head out on the North Fork River Walk Trail. It's a popular hiking and biking path, and there are plans to continue this section of the North Fork River Walk to connect with other sections of trails farther upstream.

Reach the trailhead by driving across the charming red Office Covered Bridge. Named for the nearby office of the former Western Lumber Mill, the Office Bridge is the longest covered bridge in Oregon. The town of Westfir was built as a company town for the lumber mill. Lumber operations in the area stopped in the 1970s to 1980s, but you can still experience a little bit of history along this trail — and at the old Office itself. Now the charming Westfir Lodge, the structure was built in 1925, has been lovingly restored, and makes a great base camp for adventures in the area.

Head out from the parking lot to the trail, passing by a small BMX park to your left. Between the BMX park and the miles of bike trails crisscrossing the foothills above, it's no surprise to learn that the Westfir-Oakridge area is a premier destination for mountain biking. After passing the BMX park, you'll cross under a railroad trestle before coming to the official trailhead at 0.1 miles (160 meters). Deciduous trees make their home along the riverbanks, making fall an ideal time to hike. The big leaf maples turn the trail into a tunnel of green or gold depending on the season. In the summer, the trail is shaded most of the way, keeping hikers cooled off (and leading them to swimming holes).

The trail is rolling, and a pleasant walk along the river. At 0.8 miles (1.2 kilometers), you'll come to the remains of the old historic dam, most likely remains from the timber company's mill pond. You can climb out to the remaining stone tower, or dip your feet in the cool water at its base. At 1.5 miles (2.4 kilometers), you'll find one of the popular swimming holes in the area. A large rock juts out into the river here, creating a perfect spot for sunbathing or taking up-close photos of the river.

Continue hiking along the river, coming to your turnaround point at approximately 3 miles (4.8 kilometers) where the trail comes to Forest Road 1910. Return back the way you came.

 ## TURN BY TURN DIRECTIONS

1. Head out on the trail to the right from Westfir Covered Bridge Scenic Byway Portal.
2. Come to the North River Walk Trailhead at 0.1 miles (0.16 km). Turn right to head out on the trail.
3. At 0.8 miles (1.2 km), reach the historic dam site on the river.
4. At 1.5 miles (2.4 km), reach the swimming hole.
5. At 3.0 miles (4.8 km), reach Forest Road 1910 and the turnaround point.
6. Return the way you came.

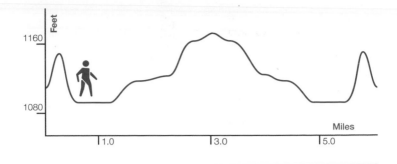

TRAILHEAD DRIVING DIRECTIONS

From OR-58, turn left toward Westfir. Cross the bridge and turn left onto Westfir-Oakridge Road. Turn left and cross the Office Covered Bridge. The parking lot for the trailhead is just on the other side of the bridge.

THE 3 LEGGED CRANE PUB

John Crane bought the Oakridge Public House — originally Brewer's Union Local 180 — and re-christened it the 3 Legged Crane Pub in January 2020. The heart of this beloved brewery lives on — one of the only true "Real Ale" breweries on the West Coast, the 3 Legged Crane brews in the British tradition of cask-conditioned and hand-pumped ales. A gathering place for the communities of Oakridge and Westfir, the pub is cozy and offers an always changing menu and live music. With a taplist of both cask and draft beers, there's a very real reason to wander through the wilds of Willamette National Forest and find yourself at the 3 Legged Crane.

TRAIL CONTACT INFORMATION
Middle Fork Ranger District
46375 Highway 58
Westfir, OR 97492
+1 541-782-2283
www.fs.usda.gov/detail/willamette/home/

ACCOMMODATIONS
Westfir Lodge
47365 1st St.
Westfir, OR 97492
+1 541-246-9007
www.westfirlodge.com
Bed & Breakfast in a restored historic lumber mill office, close to trails and full of rustic charm. Cozy accommodations and amazing food.

BREWERY/RESTAURANT
3 Legged Crane
48329 E 1st St.
Oakridge, OR 97463
+1 541-782-2024
www.3leggedcrane.com
Oregon's only Real Ale Public House and Brewery.

TOURIST ATTRACTIONS INFO
Travel Lane County
Eugene, Cascades, and Coast
754 Olive St.
Eugene OR 97401
+1 541-484-5307
www.eugenecascadescoast.org

WINTER FALLS LOOP
SILVER FALLS STATE PARK

CHECK OFF SEVEN OUT OF TEN WATERFALLS ON THIS ABBREVIATED
VERSION OF THE TRAIL OF TEN FALLS —A HIGHLIGHT REEL SHOWCASING
SOME OF THE FINEST CASCADES IN OREGON.

STARTING POINT	DESTINATION
STONE CIRCLE AT SOUTH FALLS LODGE	**WINTER FALLS LOOP**
BEER	DIFFICULTY
SANTIAM PIRATE STOUT	**HIKING**
	DURATION OF THE HIKE
MAP	**(LOOP) 3 HOURS**
OREGON STATE PARK SILVER FALLS	**4.7 MILES** (6.4KM)
PASS NEEDED	ELEVATION GAIN
OREGON STATE PARKS PASS	**650 FEET** (198M)

RUM BARREL-AGED STOUT

ALCOHOL 8% CONTENT

 BLACK

 COCONUT, JAVA, RUM

 TOASTED COCONUT, NUTTY, COFFEE

BITTERNESS **SWEETNESS**

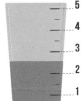

PIRATE

DESCRIPTION OF THE ROUTE

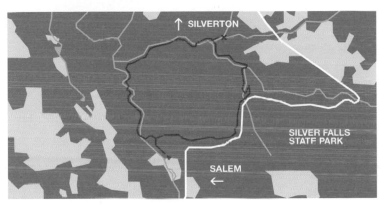

↑ SILVERTON

SILVER FALLS STATE PARK

SALEM
←

When it comes to waterfalls, Oregon offers some of the best in the Pacific Northwest. The Trail of Ten Falls is proof. Each of the waterfalls on this loop would be worthy of a visit on its own. They range in height from 27 to 178 feet, and several of them plunge over caverns deep enough to walk into. Combined, they create an unparalleled waterfall wonderland. If you've never visited this classic Cascadian destination, prepare to be wowed. There's nothing quite like walking behind these falls.

Begin your hike from the South Falls Lodge parking lot. The trail begins at the northwest end of the lot, between interpretive signs and near the restrooms. Read up on the history of Silver Falls State Park before proceeding. You'll learn about the construction of the Trail of Ten Falls thanks to hard work by the Civilian Conservation Corps and Works Projects Administration in the 1930s. These Depression Era laborers built the trail's bridges and rock walls, stairs, picnic shelters, and South Falls Lodge. Walk a short distance up the main trail to admire their work with a visit to the lodge.

Inside the lodge, you'll be greeted by a crackling fire, visitor information, and a seasonal cafe — a great place to relax and grab a bite to eat after your hike. For now, proceed past the lodge to a four-way junction called the Stone Circle. The loop begins here; you can hike in either direction. We recommend heading right (east) in order to save the best for last.

Head east on the Rim Trail through fir and hemlock forest to the Winter Falls parking lot. From here, you can continue on the Rim Trail to complete the full Trail of Ten Falls. It's worth the extra couple miles if you have time. For the shorter Winter Loop, turn left on the Canyon Trail and begin your descent, eventually dropping 500 feet (152 meters) to the canyon floor. On the way down, you'll pass Winter Falls — a nice warm-up waterfall to get you in the mood for more.

Soon you'll reach a short side trail to Middle North Falls. This is the first waterfall you can walk behind, and it's an exhilarating experience. Take the time to walk behind this wide, 106-foot (32 meters) tall sheet of water before continuing past Drake Falls to Double Falls. The tallest waterfall in Silver Falls State Park, Double Falls plunges 178 feet (54 meters) in a narrow stream, bouncing off rocks far below. Take a short side trail to access it.

Next up is Lower North Falls, a smallish 30-footer (9 meters). Ramble along Silver Creek for another mile on the Canyon Trail as it gently rolls up and down before reaching Lower South Falls. Similar to Middle North Falls in shape and size, Lower South Falls presents another opportunity to walk behind the water — and this time you don't have a choice! The trail passes through before beginning a stairway ascent out of the canyon to the grand finale.

At the end of your hike, South Falls steals the show. Dropping 177 feet (54 meters) over a cave sandwiched between basalt cliffs — glistening black above and moss-covered below — it's no wonder this is the most visited waterfall in Silver Falls State Park. Admire it from the bridge below, then continue on the Canyon Trail to walk into the falls' trickling cavern. Watch your head here — it's a bit of a limbo to get through. Then continue up the Canyon Trail to reach the Stone Circle and warm up at the lodge.

TURN BY TURN DIRECTIONS

1. From South Falls Lodge parking lot, take the main trail towards the lodge.
2. At 0.1 miles (0.16 km), turn right onto the Rim Trail.
3. At 0.7 miles (1.1 km), stay left on the Rim Trail.
4. At 1.3 miles (2 km), turn left for the Canyon Trail.
5. At 1.7 miles (2.7 km), stay left on the Canyon Trail.
6. At 1.9 miles (3 km), take the short trail to Middle North Falls, then continue on the Canyon Trail.
7. At 2.4 miles (3.8 km), take the short trail to Double Falls, then continue on the Canyon Trail.
8. At 3.5 miles (5.6 km), continue on the Canyon Trail at its junction with Maple Ridge Trail.
9. At 4.3 miles (6.9 km), reach the bridge at South Falls. Continue straight on the Canyon Trail to walk behind the falls.
10. At 4.4 miles, turn right, then stay right at a second junction to reach your starting point near South Falls Lodge.

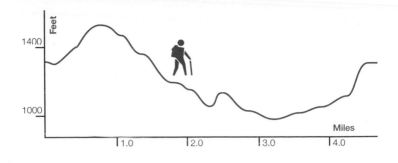

TRAILHEAD DRIVING DIRECTIONS

From Salem, drive east on Highway 22 to Exit 7, signed for OR Highway 214. Continue on 214 for approximately 4 miles (6.4 kilometers) to Silver Falls State Park. Turn left into the first entrance and continue to the end of the parking lot.

SANTIAM BREWING

You wouldn't expect much driving around the industrial park it's located in, but Santiam Brewing is warm, inviting and a ton of fun. Proudly flying the Republic of Cascadia flag, Santiam's taproom is an eclectic mix of decorations. And the beer list is just as creative. With a range of barrel-aged and cask ales on tap, Santiam has plenty to offer craft beer fans. Not many breweries can boast that people travel from far and wide for a taste of their rum barrel-aged coconut Stout. Santiam can. This hidden treasure is well worth the journey.

TRAIL CONTACT INFORMATION
Oregon State Parks
20024 Silver Falls Hwy. SE
Sublimity, OR 97385
+1 503-873-8681
www.oregonstateparks.org

ACCOMMODATIONS
Hampton Inn & Suites Salem
510 Hawthorne Ave. SE
Salem, OR 97301
+1 503-362-1300
www.hamptoninn3.hilton.com
Clean, comfy rooms, great service and, hot breakfast — just 2 miles from the brewery.

BREWERY/RESTAURANT
Santiam Brewing
2544 19th St. SE
Salem, OR 07302
+1 503-689 1260
www.santiambrewing.com
Kitchen offering American- and British-inspired pub fare.

TOURIST ATTRACTIONS INFO
Travel Salem Visitors Center
181 High St. NE
Salem, OR 97301
+1 503-581-4325
www.travelsalem.com

MISERY RIDGE LOOP

THIS STEEP, NARROW TRAIL MAY LIVE UP TO ITS NAME ON HOT SUMMER DAYS, BUT MISERY RIDGE PAYS OFF HANDSOMELY IN CROOKED RIVER, CASCADE MOUNTAIN, AND MONKEY FACE VIEWS YEAR-ROUND.

STARTING POINT	DESTINATION
SMITH ROCK TRAILHEAD	**SMITH ROCK SUMMIT**
BEER	DIFFICULTY
WILD RIDE NUT CRUSHER PEANUT BUTTER PORTER	**HIKING**
MAP	DURATION OF THE HIKE
OREGON STATE PARKS SMITH ROCK (AVAILABLE AT VISITORS CENTER)	(LOOP) **2-3 HOURS** **3.8 MILES** (6.1KM)
PASS NEEDED	ELEVATION GAIN
OREGON STATE PARKS PASS	**800 FEET** (244M)

PORTER

 MAHOGANY

 NUTTY

 SMOOTH, ROASTED CHOCOLATE

BITTERNESS	SWEETNESS
	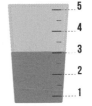

DESCRIPTION OF THE ROUTE

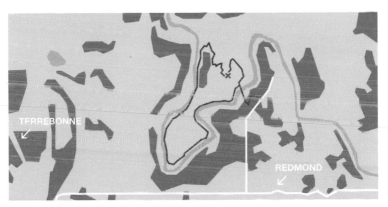

If you've only got time for one hiking destination in Central Oregon, look no further. Smith Rock State Park is home to 651 acres of golden-red volcanic rock formations set among a stunning desert backdrop. Soaring skyward from the high desert plateau — some 3,000 feet (914 meters) above sea level — this natural rock fortress features spires up to 550 feet (167 meters) tall. Misery Ridge Loop is the absolute best way to experience it all in a relatively short amount of time.

Like any self-respecting fortress, this rock castle's first line of defense is its formidable appearance. You'll notice it from the get-go. Parking lot views don't get much finer than those at Smith Rock. Grab a trail map from the visitors center — housed in a charming little yurt — before hitting the trail. A $5 day-use fee is required for parking.

Before climbing this tower, you must first descend to its doorstep. Follow the Canyon Trail, stopping for photos at an irresistible overlook above Crooked River. Surrounding Smith Rock on three sides, Crooked River snakes along, changing direction every so often and forming a moat to keep intruders at bay. Head down the Chute to reach a footbridge and water fountain at 2,600 feet (792 meters). Here, the climb begins.

Misery Ridge Trail starts off relentlessly, with a series of south-facing switchbacks exposed to the elements. Arrive early in the morning for the best hiking conditions. Summer temperatures can rise above 100 degrees here and there's little in the way of shade, so pack plenty of water. You won't find any above Crooked River.

Your first chance to see climbers in action is at Red Wall. Smith Rock is a world-famous climbing destination, attracting daring rock climbers since the 1960s. Stop for a moment and observe — it's a good excuse to catch your breath before more Misery. Views along the east ridge offer a welcome respite and a taste of what's to come. After ascending another steep series of dry, slip-inducing switchbacks, you'll top out at 3,280 feet (1,000 meters). Peer down on the trail, the river, the earthtone landscape below. You've conquered the castle, but this journey's not over yet. Continue along the ridge for Cascade volcano views, from Mount Bachelor and the Three Sisters to Mounts Washington and Jefferson, and even as far north as Hood. Black Butte rises in the foreground, appearing nearly as large as its Cascade cousins from such a distance.

When you notice a 350-foot (106 meters) pillar obstructing your view, you've found the famed Monkey Face. The park's crown jewel, Monkey Face is popular with rock climbers year-round. As you descend from the ridge, you'll notice a few gurney-and-crutches stations placed strategically along the trail. One can only imagine how many accidents happen here.

After descending a series of switchbacks and passing directly beneath Monkey Face, you're on the home stretch. Follow Mesa Verde Trail down to the river, and be sure to turn around for photos of the Monkey Face. It truly does resemble a monkey from this angle. Further along, a dip in Crooked River is a nice way to cool down, but watch for rattlesnakes lurking in the shadows. The River Trail follows Crooked River all the way back to the footbridge, where you'll make the final ascent back up to the parking lot. Fortunately, the brewery is just 9 miles (14 kilometers) away.

TURN BY TURN DIRECTIONS

1. Take the Rim Rock Trail north from behind the Visitors Center.
2. At 0.1 miles (0.16 km), turn left onto the paved Canyon Trail.
3. At 0.2 miles (0.3 km), turn right onto the Chute Trail.
4. At 0.4 miles (0.6 km), cross the footbridge and continue straight onto the Misery Ridge Trail.
5. At 1.2 miles (1.9 km), turn left onto the Mesa Verde Trail.
6. At 1.6 miles (2.5 km), continue straight onto the River Trail.
7. At 3.4 miles (5.4 km), turn right onto the footbridge and return the way you came.

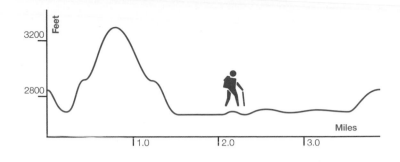

TRAILHEAD DRIVING DIRECTIONS

From Redmond, head north on US-97. Turn right onto Smith Rock Way. Turn left onto NE 1st Street/Lambert Road. Then, turn left onto NE Crooked River Drive and continue to the State Park entrance.

WILD RIDE BREWING

Just north of Bend, Oregon's beer capital, Wild Ride Brewing is carving out a flavorful niche of its own. Open since 2014, Wild Ride's vibe matches its edgy lineup of ales and lagers. Its slick and laid-back taproom has plenty of seating both inside and out. Visitors to the brewery can grab a pint and a bite to eat at one of the trucks in the food truck community on the patio.

TRAIL CONTACT INFORMATION
Smith Rock State Park Welcome Center
+1 541-548-7501
www.oregonstateparks.org

ACCOMODATIONS
The Lodge at Eagle Crest
1522 Cline Falls Rd.
Redmond, OR 97756
+1 877-859-5095
www.lhg.com
Unique full-service resort next to the Deschutes River.

BREWERY/RESTAURANT
Wild Ride
332 SW 5th St.
Redmond, OR 97756
+1 541-516-8544
www.wildridebrew.com
A variety of food trucks are located on the patio.

TOURIST ATTRACTIONS INFO
Redmond Chamber of Commerce
446 SW 7th St.
Redmond, OR 97756
+1 541-923-5191
www.visitredmondoregon.com

SPENCER BUTTE

HIKEABLE YEAR-ROUND, THIS 2,055-FOOT HIGH BUTTE OFFERS PANORAMIC
WILLAMETTE VALLEY VIEWS FROM JUST OUTSIDE DOWNTOWN EUGENE.

OR
STATE OF OREGON

STARTING POINT	DESTINATION
SPENCER BUTTE TRAILHEAD	**SPENCER BUTTE SUMMIT**

BEER	DIFFICULTY
FALLING SKY TORRENTIAL SOUR SERIES	**HIKING**

MAP	DURATION OF THE HIKE
LOOK UP WWW.EUGENE-OR.GOV	**1-2 HOURS** **2.2 MILES** (3.5KM)

PASS NEEDED	ELEVATION GAIN
NONE	**740 FEET** (225M)

BERLINER WEISSE

CLOUDY PALE GOLD

TART, SOURDOUGH

CANDY SOUR,
BREADY FINISH

BITTERNESS	SWEETNESS
5	5
4	4
3	3
2	2
1	1

DESCRIPTION OF THE ROUTE

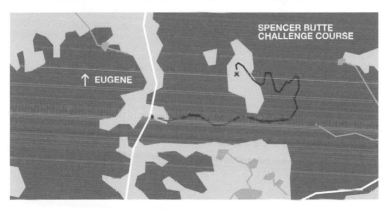

↑ EUGENE

SPENCER BUTTE
CHALLENGE COURSE

Oregon is a land of many buttes. These isolated mountains with steep sides and relatively flat tops rise high from surrounding lands, offering views in all directions to those who climb them. In Eugene, you can drive to the top of Skinner Butte, peer over the city, and spot Spencer Butte rising high just 6 miles away. Spencer's claim to fame? It's the tallest visible point when looking south from downtown Eugene. This visibility and accessibility are what make Spencer Butte such a popular gateway hike. For many University of Oregon students, first-time hikers, and would-be couch sitters, it provides an introduction to Oregon's diverse outdoor playground.

The trail begins with a gentle climb through dense Douglas fir forest on a wide, sometimes rocky dirt path. It is well maintained, but gets a bit mucky in the rainier months. Ferns aplenty will accompany you during the ascent, along with poison oak the higher you go. Remember the age-old adage, "Leaves of three, let it be" and you'll be just fine.

The native Calapuyian name for Spencer Butte was Champ-a te, which translates to "rattlesnake mountain". Signs in the park warn about rattlesnakes, as well as bear and cougar sightings. Of course, with the amount of foot traffic here, you're unlikely to encounter anything but the wily ground squirrels. Be aware of your surroundings, and always respect the wildlife.

Upon leaving the forest, the trail climbs over stone-cut steps to a bald summit with wide-open views. From here, look down on Eugene and Skinner Butte to the north. You may even be able to locate Falling Sky Brew Pub with binoculars — your post-hike destination. The Cascades rise to the east. Look for the Three Sisters directly east, and peer further south towards Mount Scott — visible only on the clearest of days. Turn your gaze west to the Coast Range, beyond which the Oregon coast and Pacific Ocean await. While we recommend returning via the same route, it's possible to turn this into a loop hike. A shorter, steeper trail runs down the butte's west side. "Trail is steep. Please use caution," reads the trailhead signage. It gains/loses the same amount of elevation as the main trail in roughly half the distance. From the summit it can be tough to locate if you don't know where to look. Fortunately, this trail is busy enough that you can always ask a local for directions.

TURN BY TURN DIRECTIONS

1. Hike east from the trailhead along the Main Trail to Spencer Butte.
2. At 0.6 miles (0.9 km), turn left at the junction.
3. At 1.1 miles (1.7 km), reach the summit of Spencer Butte.
4. Return the way you came.

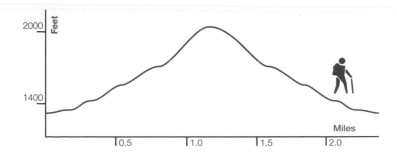

TRAILHEAD DRIVING DIRECTIONS

From downtown Eugene, drive south on Pearl Street. Continue on Amazon Parkway for 0.6 miles (1 kilometer), then turn right onto E 27th Avenue. After 0.1 mile (160 meters), turn left onto Willamette Street. Follow Willamette Street for 3.5 miles (5.6 kilometers) to the Spencer Butte Trailhead Parking Lot on the left.

FALLING SKY BREW PUB

With two locations in Eugene, OR, Falling Sky Brewing wants to "Let it Pour" when it comes to craft beer. When It opened in 2012, Falling Sky was unique to the Eugene beer scene for its emphasis on both beer and a curated craft food menu. Scratch-baked breads and house-cured meats make Falling Sky a foodie destination. Make sure to try something from their rotating Torrential Sours series (featuring a rotating fruit) or their Spruce Series, with each beer featuring spruce tips.

TRAIL CONTACT INFORMATION
For trail maintenance issues or volunteer opportunities, call +1 541-682-4800.
www.spencerbutte.com

ACCOMMODATIONS
Valley River Inn
1000 Valley River Way
Eugene, OR 97401
+1 541-743-1000
www.valleyriverinn.com
Comfy riverside hotel with nice views, a rock-and-roll history, and pet-friendly rooms.

BREWERY/RESTAURANT
Falling Sky Brew Pub
1334 Oak Alley
Eugene, OR 97401
+1 541-505-7096
www.fallingskybrewing.com
Pub grub, soup, salad, and sandwiches — plus great vegetarian options to pair with your beer.

TOURIST ATTRACTIONS INFO
Eugene, Cascades, and Coast
754 Olive St.
Eugene, OR 97401
+1 541-484-5307
www.eugenecascadescoast.org
Convenient visitors center In downtown Eugene, just half a mile from Falling Sky Brew Pub.

TOM DICK AND HARRY MOUNTAIN

IN-YOUR-FACE MOUNT HOOD VIEWS PAIR PERFECTLY WITH A
BREWERY SO CLOSE YOU CAN SEE IT FROM THE SUMMIT,
MAKING TOM DICK AND HARRY MOUNTAIN AN IRRESISTIBLE BEER HIKE.

STARTING POINT	DESTINATION
MIRROR LAKE TRAILHEAD	**TOM DICK AND HARRY MOUNTAIN**
BEER	DIFFICULTY
MT. HOOD HOGSBACK OATMEAL STOUT	**HIKING**
MAP	DURATION OF THE HIKE
GREEN TRAILS 461 GOVERNMENT CAMP	**3-4 HOURS 7.1 MILES** (11.4KM)
PASS NEEDED	ELEVATION GAIN
NORTHWEST FOREST PASS	**1,400 FEET** (427M)

OATMEAL STOUT

 DARK BROWN

 SMOKE, CHOCOLATE

CHARRED WALNUTS, COFFEE, DARK CHOCOLATE

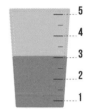

BITTERNESS   **SWEETNESS**

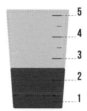

DESCRIPTION OF THE ROUTE

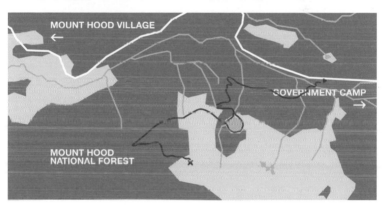

Tackle this trail on a sunny summer Saturday to fully appreciate its name. Every Tom, Dick, and Harry in Portland will be here hiking the day away. Located within 60 miles (96 kilometers) of the city — and just outside Government Camp — Tom Dick and Harry Mountain contains all the ingredients for a hit hike: ease of access, an easy-moderate trail to a pretty subalpine lake, the early bailout option, and breathtaking summit views. Visit during weekday mornings or late afternoons to beat the crowds.

Begin at the new parking lot off Highway 26, which was completed in 2018. Follow the paved path behind the restrooms, descending several switchbacks to the bridge over Camp Creek. No longer paved, the wide new trail rambles along for a mile before abruptly turning left and beginning to climb steadily. Rhododendrons line the trail, blooming pink in early summer. Overhead, dense pine forest provides shelter from the elements. Talus slopes offer a break from the tree cover, with views down into the valley and across to Mount Hood. You'll find yourself at the shores of Mirror Lake before you know it.

Go left at the junction to circle Mirror Lake. Short side trails lead to lake access and a view of your destination, Tom Dick and Harry Mountain. The mountain is actually named for its three distinct summit peaks, towering some 800 feet (243 meters) above the lake. Continue over boardwalks around Mirror Lake's south side to reach Mount Hood viewpoints aplenty. Here, the mountain's reflection can be seen in Mirror Lake's aptly-named waters.

Head left at the second junction. Most hikers call it quits here, so the crowds thin considerably as you make the final push up the mountain. Reach a large rock pile one mile from Mirror Lake. This curious cairn marks a bend in the trail — stay left to continue upwards. Enjoy an easygoing half mile beneath lodgepole pine, through seasonal wildflowers, beargrass, and more trailside rhododendron. Breaking from the woods, a short rocky section leads to Tom Dick and Harry's west summit. This sub-5,000 foot peak offers panoramic views, but your eyes (and camera) will be immediately drawn northeast to Mount Hood, rising high above all else. Mirror Lake twinkles below, cradled in its glacial cirque. Further north, Mounts Adams, St. Helens, and even Rainier are visible in Washington on clear days. Directly south, Mount Jefferson rounds out the volcano views. How many can you see?

Survey the surrounding Salmon-Huckleberry Wilderness and Mt. Hood National Forest. Peer down on Mt. Hood Brewing — a stone's throw away in Government Camp. If the mountain could speak, it might recommend stopping in for a pint. We certainly do!

TURN BY TURN DIRECTIONS

1. Begin at the signed Mirror Lake Trailhead.
2. At 1.8 miles (2.9 km), turn left at the junction to walk around Mirror Lake.
3. At 2.2 miles (3.5 km), turn left at the junction for Tom Dick and Harry Mountain.
4. At 3.1 miles (5.0 km), turn left at the large rock pile.
5. At 3.7 miles (5.9 km), reach the west summit.
6. Return to Mirror Lake, staying left at the junction at 5.2 miles (8.3 km).
7. At 5.3 miles (8.5 km), turn left to return to the trailhead.

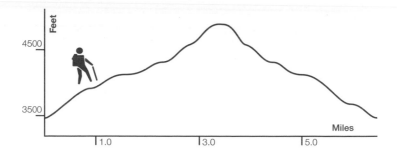

TRAILHEAD DRIVING DIRECTIONS

From Portland, travel 27.5 miles (44 kilometers) east of Sandy on US Highway 26 and turn right into the Skibowl West/Mirror Lake Trailhead parking area.

MT. HOOD BREWING CO.

The "Microbrewery with an Altitude," Mt. Hood Brewing Co. started in 1991, giving beer-loving visitors to Government Camp a reason to come down off the slopes. The brewpub is immediately welcoming, warm and rustic like a ski lodge, with retro-styled travel posters for each beer on tap. The beer is classically northwest in style. Take a seat at the bar and keep your pint frosty on the embedded ice rail while planning your next Mount Hood adventure.

TRAIL CONTACT INFORMATION
Mt. Hood National Forest
Zigzag Ranger Station
70220 E. Hwy. 26
Zigzag, OR 97049
+1 503-622-3191
www.fs.usda.gov/detail/mthood

ACCOMMODATIONS
Best Western Mt. Hood Inn
87450 Government Camp Loop
Government Camp, OR 97028
+1 503-272-3205
www.bestwestern.com
Located right next door to the brewery.

BREWERY/RESTAURANT
Mt. Hood Brewing Co.
87304 Government Camp Loop
Government Camp, OR 97028
+1 503-272-3172
www.mthoodbrewing.com
The Microbrewery with an Altitude!

TOURIST ATTRACTIONS INFO
Mt. Hood Cultural Center & Museum
8900 E Hwy. 26, Business Loop
Government Camp, OR 97028
+1 503-272-3301
www.mthoodmuseum.org
Museum, bookstore, art gallery, visitor information services, and more.

4

WASHINGTON

BARCLAY LAKE

AN EASY OUT-AND-BACK HIKE TO A WOODED LAKE,
SITUATED IN THE SHADOW OF BARING MOUNTAIN'S SHEER TWIN PEAKS.

STARTING POINT

BARCLAY LAKE TRAILHEAD

DESTINATION

BARCLAY LAKE

BEER

HAYWIRE BREWING DAIRYLAND

DIFFICULTY

WALKING

MAP

GREEN TRAILS 143 MONTE CRISTO

DURATION OF THE HIKE

2 HOURS 5 MILES (8KM)

PASS NEEDED

NORTHWEST FOREST PASS

ELEVATION GAIN

225 FEET (69.5M)

STOUT

BLACK

CHOCOLATE, ROAST

**CREAMY
BITTERSWEET
COCOA, ROASTY**

BITTERNESS	SWEETNESS

DESCRIPTION OF THE ROUTE

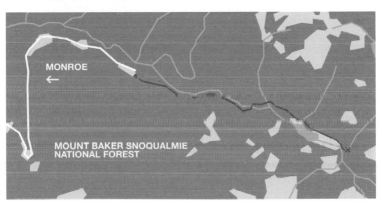

Minimal elevation gain, a serene mountain lake, and looming formidable peaks make Barclay Lake a popular hike. Beginning backpackers of every age have made camp on its shores, getting a front row seat for Barclay's stunning golden display at sunset. If you choose to forego camping out, this hike still makes an ideal way to stretch your legs in the wilderness.

From the gravel parking lot, head out onto the tree-covered trail. A positive aspect of its heavy usage, the trail is well maintained. The first section is well-packed gravel framed by wooden rails, but watch for muddy patches (especially from late fall to early spring).

The second-growth hemlock forest is moss-covered and quiet, with only the occasional chatter of squirrels or chirping of birds breaking the silence. Salmonberry and maidenhair ferns spring from the mossy forest floor, while mushrooms flourish in the damp environment. From the 0.9 mile (1.4 kilometer) mark, the trail stays close to Barclay Creek. At 1.2 miles (1.9 kilometers), the trail crosses a (sometimes slick!)

log bridge over the creek, reaching the north end of the lake after 1.7 miles (2.7 kilometers). If you'd like a little more adventure, you can bushwhack through towering lady ferns and blackberry bramble along the northwest end of the lake. Here, a rock pile offers views of the whole length of the lake — and unobstructed views of Baring Mountain.

Looking like a stand-in for Tolkien's Misty Mountain, Baring Mountain rises to the south, massive and imposing. The third-sheerest peak in Washington State, Baring looks like a jagged wall springing up from the lake's far edge. To the north, Merchant and Gun Peaks help form a valley in which Barclay Lake rests. Surrounded on all sides, the lake valley experiences a large amount of rain — nearly 200 inches per year! It's little surprise then that Baring Mountain is almost always partially clouded over, raindrops threatening at a moment's notice.

Continue along the trail to the left side of the lake. Campsites dot the shores, and you'll most likely encounter families teaching children how to stake a tent, or witness scout troops working towards another merit badge. The lake is also a popular fishing spot, so it won't take long for a fish to leap from Barclay's silvery waters with a splash. Take a seat on a log and enjoy a snack or picnic lunch before heading back the way you came.

 ## TURN BY TURN DIRECTIONS

1. From the trailhead, take the Barclay Lake Trail at the end of the parking lot.
2. At 1.2 miles (1.9 km), cross Barclay Creek via the bridge.
3. At 1.7 miles (2.7 km), arrive at the north end of Barclay Lake.
   Continue on the left side of the lake.
4. At 2.5 miles (4 km), arrive at the end of the lake.
   Return the way you came.

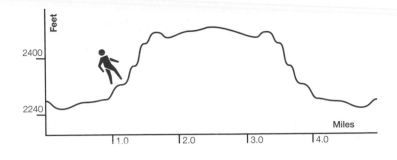

TRAILHEAD DRIVING DIRECTIONS

From Monroe, head east on US-2. Near milepost 41, turn left onto 635th PL NF. Stay on 635th until it turns into FR-6024. Continue 3.9 miles (6.2 kilometers) on the gravel road to the trailhead.

HAYWIRE BREWING CO.

Walking into Haywire Brewing's rustic taproom, you can feel the history of the building. Operating out of the hay barn of an old dairy farm, the Snohomish-based brewery is part of the Woodland Meadow Farms business collective. The milking parlor next door is now a wedding-venue and the open space out back hosts an annual Christmas tree farm. Haywire's beers reflect their farm-grown feel with offerings like the award-winning "U-Pick Pale" featuring strawberries, and the Pig Sty Rye IPA. Family-run, and community minded, Haywire is the place to drink in Snohomish Valley's past and present.

TRAIL CONTACT INFORMATION
Skykomish Ranger Station
74920 NE Stevens Pass Hwy.
PO Box 305
Skykomish, WA 90288
+1 360-677-2414

RESTAURANT
River House Cafe
444 Avenue A
Index, WA 98256
+1 425-883-9039
Cafe and BBQ with burgers and casual atmosphere.

ACCOMMODATIONS
Backpacking spots available at Barclay Lake.

BREWERY/FOOD
Haywire Brewing Co.
12125 Treosti Rd.
Snohomish, WA 98290
+1 360-568-2739
www.haywirebrewingco.com

TOURIST ATTRACTIONS INFO
Sky Valley Chamber of Commerce
320 Main St.
Sultan, WA 98294
+1 360-793-0983
www.skyvalleychamber.com

BEACON ROCK

VIEWS ATOP THIS 848-FOOT "BEATEN ROCK" ARE EXPANSIVE,
THOUGH THE JOURNEY MAY VERY WELL OVERSHADOW
THE DESTINATION ON THIS THRILLING ROCK-AND-RAIL RAMBLE.

WA
STATE OF WASHINGTON

STARTING POINT	DESTINATION
BEACON ROCK TRAILHEAD	**BEACON ROCK SUMMIT**

BEER	DIFFICULTY
WALKING MAN HOMO ERECTUS IPA	**WALKING**

DURATION OF THE HIKE

MAP	
GREEN TRAILS 429 BONNEVILLE DAM	**1 HOUR** **1.8 MILES** (2.9KM)

PASS NEEDED	ELEVATION GAIN
DISCOVER PASS	**578 FEET** (176M)

IMPERIAL INDIA PALE ALE

ORANGE GOLD

ORANGE ZEST, RESIN

TROPICAL, MANGO, HOPPY

BITTERNESS   SWEETNESS

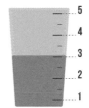

5
4
3
2
1

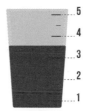

DESCRIPTION OF THE ROUTE

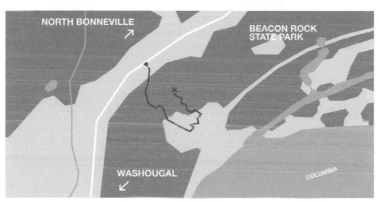

Long revered for its prominence above the Columbia River, Beacon Rock has known many names over the years. Natives once referred to it as "the navel of the world." American explorers Lewis and Clark initially called the rock "Beaten" in their journals, before changing it to Beacon during their return journey in 1806. It was known as Castle Rock for a stretch of years in the early 1900s. Beacon's various titles have suited it well. This core of an ancient volcano has stood the test of time, beaten by the Columbia River and ice-age flooding, castle-like in its formidable appearance. Today, the monolith is known once again as Beacon Rock.

A man by the name of Henry Biddle purchased Beacon Rock in 1915 for $1, promising to preserve it. And preserve it he did. Biddle spent three years building a trail to the top of the rock with no fewer than 52 switchbacks, constructing the stairs, ramps, and rails that are still in place today. The rock was later donated to Washington State Parks by Biddle's heirs for all to enjoy.

From the trailhead, it's less than one mile to the top with nearly 600 feet (182 meters) of elevation gain. Begin with a pleasant walk through the forest before reaching the first handrail. The trail's construction is unique — built directly into the side of the monolith, zig-zagging its way up at a moderate grade. It's been said that Henry Biddle was attracted to the very challenge of building such a trail. 100 years later, the trail remains — a testament to his success. Beacon Rock Trail is a wonder to behold, simply because nothing else quite like it exists in the Columbia River Gorge. It's a remarkably well-engineered trail in a gorge-ously scenic setting.

The Mighty Columbia rolls on hundreds of feet below, swirling around Pierce and Ives Islands. Lewis and Clark observed tidal influences from the Pacific Ocean here — over 120 miles (193 kilometers) from the mouth of the Columbia. To the west, you may be able to see as far downstream as the Crown Point Vista House, a prominent landmark on the Oregon side of the river. Across the river, Elowah Falls appears tiny from this distance, dropping over 200 feet. Upstream to the east, Bonneville Dam can be identified from the top of Beacon Rock.

An interpretive sign celebrates your arrival: "Congratulations on reaching the top of Beacon Rock!" The summit itself is quite rocky, leaving little standing room on busy days. Take your time marveling at river views on the way up or down, as they are somewhat obscured by trees atop this beacon. A gentle reminder that sometimes the journey truly is more rewarding than the destination.

TURN BY TURN DIRECTIONS

1. From the parking area, walk a short distance west to the Beacon Rock trailhead.
2. Follow the trail to the top — there are no junctions.
3. At 0.9 miles (1.4 km), reach the top of Beacon Rock.
4. Return the way you came.

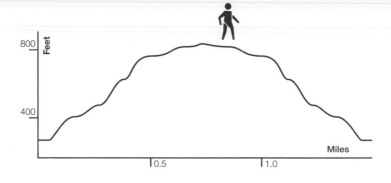

TRAILHEAD DRIVING DIRECTIONS

From Vancouver, drive east on State Highway 14 for 34 miles (54 kilometers). Beacon Rock is located on the south side of the highway.

WALKING MAN BREWING

One of the first breweries in the Columbia River Gorge, Walking Man Brewing opened in 2000. Since then, its beers have brought national awards home to the cozy taproom located in the historic downtown area of Stevenson, WA. In the summer, you can enjoy a pint out in the brewery's sun-drenched garden. In the cooler months, warm up inside with a pint and a slice, or snuggle up under the heated patio gazebo. Just head down the old saloon-esque building's stairs and stroll up to the bar for a big-flavored beer. For hikers, Walking Man is a home away from home.

TRAIL CONTACT INFORMATION
Beacon Rock State Park
34041 SR 14
Skamania, WA 98648
+1 509-427-8265
www.parks.state.wa.us/474/beacon-rock

ACCOMMODATIONS
Columbia Gorge Riverside Lodge
200 SW Cascade Ave.
Stevenson, WA 98648
+1 509-427-5650
www.cgriversidelodge.com
Riverside lodging steps away
from Walking Man Brewing.

BREWERY/RESTAURANT
Walking Man Brewing
240 1st St.
Stevenson, WA 98648
+1 509-427-5520
www.walkingmanbeer.com
Pub grub paired with stand-up brews.

TOURIST ATTRACTIONS INFO
Skamania County Chamber of Commerce
Visitor Information Center
167 NW Second Ave.
Stevenson, WA 98648
+1 800-989-9178
www.skamania.org

NORTH HEAD TRAIL
CAPE DISAPPOINTMENT STATE PARK

A ROLLING HIKE THROUGH COASTAL SITKA SPRUCE FOREST,
NORTH HEAD TRAIL LEADS TO WINDSWEPT CLIFFS AND AN ACTIVE
LIGHTHOUSE HIGH ABOVE THE PACIFIC OCEAN.

STARTING POINT	DESTINATION
MCKENZIE HEAD TRAIL PARKING AREA	**NORTH HEAD LIGHTHOUSE**
BEER	DIFFICULTY
NORTH JETTY THE MILKMAN KNOCKS TWICE	**WALKING**
MAP	DURATION OF THE HIKE
WASHINGTON STATE PARKS: WWW.PARKS.STATE.WA.US	**2 HOURS** **3.2 MILES** (5.1KM)
PASS NEEDED	ELEVATION GAIN
DISCOVER PASS	**500 FEET** (152M)

MILK STOUT

BLACK

COFFEE, CHOCOLATE, CHAR

ESPRESSO, CREAMY, ROAST

BITTERNESS   **SWEETNESS**

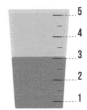

DESCRIPTION OF THE ROUTE

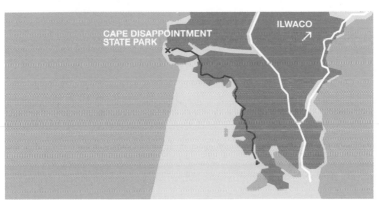

The phrase may be tired, but it's tried and true: Cape Disappointment does not disappoint. This state park in the southwest corner of Washington is a treasure trove of history and geological diversity. From the state's oldest lighthouse at the mouth of the Columbia River to wave-battered cliffs high above the Pacific Ocean, there's plenty to see, learn, and do in this 1,882-acre park. And unless you're a surfer, the best way to explore it is on foot.

Miles of hiking trails weave through old-growth forest and around freshwater lakes out to the crashing surf. We suggest hiking out to North Head Lighthouse for big ocean views. Park at the base of McKenzie Head and then cross the road and head north for North Head. The first quarter mile (0.4 kilometers) is a flat and easy warm-up, leading to the base of a hill. Here, the rollercoaster begins. Get your heart rate up with a 160-foot (48 meters) climb before dropping back to sea level on the other side. Then it's right back up again as you make your way to the North Head parking lot at 200 feet (60 meters).

Along the way, North Head Trail is constructed of bridges, boardwalks, and good old-fashioned dirt. In wet conditions, many sections of the trail become muddy. Watch for roots — and newts! Rough-skinned newts are common here during winter and spring. Frogs can be found as well, and the birds are too numerous to list. Once you reach the coast, watch for seals, sea otters, and even gray whales if visiting during winter.

At the parking lot, follow the Lighthouse Keepers Loop Trail out to North Head Lighthouse. This trail circles the lighthouse keeper's quarters, dropping 60 feet (18 meters) to the dramatic site of North Head Lighthouse. Built in 1898, this weathered beacon towers over the Pacific and continues to aid in navigation to this day. Visitors can pay a nominal fee to tour the lighthouse.

After completing the Lighthouse Keepers Loop, head back the way you came. You can extend your hike by climbing to McKenzie Head — a half-mile (0.8 kilometers) one-way trek to Battery 247, a relic from World War II. From here, peer down on North Jetty — the breakwater inspiration behind North Jetty Brewing's name. While the ocean views are nice from McKenzie Head, don't expect to catch a glimpse of the Cape Disappointment lighthouse from here. Southeast-facing views are (somewhat disappointingly) overgrown.

For the iconic waves-crashing-in-the-foreground viewpoint of Cape Disappointment Lighthouse, consider driving to Waikiki Beach. A popular surfing destination, the beach offers excellent wave-watching opportunities. Finally, you can drive to the Lewis & Clark Interpretive Center for a history lesson — and a show. Hike out to Cape Disappointment Lighthouse to witness the Columbia River crashing into the Pacific Ocean — an area known as "The Graveyard of the Pacific" due to over 2,000 shipwrecks that have occurred here. Built in 1856, this is the oldest active lighthouse in the state of Washington.

TURN BY TURN DIRECTIONS

1. Begin by crossing Fort Canby Road and picking up the North Head Trail.
2. Reach the North Head Lighthouse parking lot at 1.3 miles (2 km). Turn left to follow the path west.
3. Immediately come to a signed junction at the beginning of the Lighthouse Keepers Loop Trail.
4. Continue to North Head Lighthouse at 1.6 miles (2.5 km).
5. Complete the Lighthouse Keepers Loop by continuing along the trail.
6. At 1.9 miles (3 km), reach the North Head Lighthouse parking lot again and return the way you came.

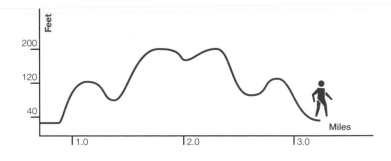

TRAILHEAD DRIVING DIRECTIONS

From Long Beach, take Highway 101 south to Ilwaco. Turn right on Spruce Street, then immediately left on 2nd Avenue Southwest. Continue onto WA-100 south/Robert Gray Drive for 2 miles (3.2 kilometers). Turn right onto Fort Canby, and follow this road 0.6 miles (0.9 kilometers) to the McKenzie Head Trail parking area on the left.

NORTH JETTY BREWING

Established on the Long Beach Peninsula in 2014, North Jetty Brewing is certainly bringing the fun to Washington's longest beach! You can't miss the bright red taproom just off Highway 101. Inside, the walls are decked out in seafaring decor, and an inviting fireplace nook welcomes windswept beach-goers in for a pint. One wall is dedicated to the founders of the family-owned-and-operated brewery. Proudly displayed, the names of these founding businesses and individuals are a reminder that North Jetty is a community gathering place for locals and tourists alike.

TRAIL CONTACT INFORMATION
Cape Disappointment State Park
244 Robert Gray Dr.
Ilwaco, WA 98624
+1 360-642-3078
www.parks.state.wa.us/486/
cape-disappointment

RESTAURANT
42nd Street Cafe & Bistro
4201 Pacific Way
Seaview, WA 98644
+1 360-642-2323
www.42ndstcafe.com
Roadside cafe across the street
from the brewery.

The Depot Restaurant
1208 38th Pl.
Seaview, WA 98644
+1 360-642-7880
www.depotrestaurantdining.com
Casual fine dining in a former train depot.

BREWERY
North Jetty Brewing
4200 Pacific Way
Seaview, WA 98644
+1 360-642-4234
www.northjettybrewing.com
Inviting taproom featuring rotating
selection of North Jetty Beers.

TOURIST ATTRACTIONS INFO
Long Beach Peninsula Visitors Bureau
3914 Pacific Way
Seaview, WA 98644
+1 360-642-2400
www.funbeach.com

ACCOMMODATIONS
Sou'wester Lodge
3728 J Pl.
Seaview, WA 98644
+1 360-642-2542
Retro trailers, lodge, and cabins.

COWICHE CANYON

TAKE AN EASY HIKE THROUGH A DESERT CANYON, CROSSING STREAMS AND PASSING HOP FIELDS — WITH AN OPTIONAL SIDE TRIP THROUGH THE VINEYARDS OF A NEARBY WINERY.

STARTING POINT	DESTINATION
COWICHE CANYON EAST TRAILHEAD	**COWICHE CANYON WEST TRAILHEAD**

BEER	DIFFICULTY
BALE BREAKER TOP CUTTER IPA	**WALKING** 

MAP	DURATION OF THE HIKE
WASHINGTON STATE DNR YAKIMA	**2-3 HOURS 5.2 MILES** (9KM)

PASS NEEDED	ELEVATION GAIN
NONE	**MINIMAL**

INDIA PALE ALE

PALE GOLD

ORANGE ZEST, PINE, GRAPEFRUIT

TANGERINE, DANK MANGO, RESIN

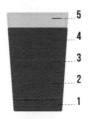

BITTERNESS	SWEETNESS
5	5
4	4
3	3
2	2
1	1

DESCRIPTION OF THE ROUTE

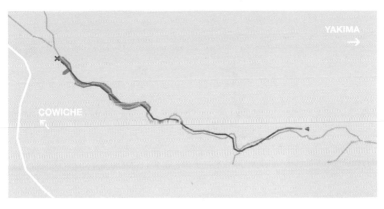

Cowiche Canyon (it's pronounced Cow-itchy) is a popular after-work and weekend hike just outside of downtown Yakima. Towering andesite and basalt walls guard a bustling ecosystem of plants and animals that make the banks of the swift Cowiche Creek their home. Families, trail runners, mountain bikers and even equestrians visit this vibrant landscape to journey on this placid trail.

Protected and maintained by the Cowiche Canyon Conservancy (CCC), the canyon and surrounding shrub-steppe are an incredibly unique area to explore. The CCC was founded in 1985, and over the past 30 years has accumulated 5,000 acres of protected lands and over 30 miles (48 kilometers) of trails. Cowiche Canyon Trail is perhaps the most iconic of these trails, allowing hikers glimpses of the many faces of this area.

The canyon is nearly three miles long, with a parking lot and trailhead on either end. The east trailhead off of Cowiche Canyon Road is closer to downtown, but requires driving down a short gravel road to get to the parking lot. From here, the trail is just ahead. Conservancy volunteers keep this trail, a wide gravel path, in top condition for the enjoyment of all.

To the left, you'll have views of the Cowiche Canyon Organic Hop Farm. The hops grown here are used each year by Seattle's Fremont Brewing to create its famed Fresh Hop series. If your visit happens in early fall, you might be lucky enough to see the harvest taking place.

You'll soon come to bridge 11, the first of 9 bridges you'll use to cross Cowiche Creek as it winds through the canyon floor (the trail has been rerouted, bypassing bridges 9 and 10). Mountain ash and aspen trees grow along the trail, turning a stunning blaze of gold and red in the fall. In the summer, yellow balsamroot and indigo lupine bloom along the slopes. It's easy to get caught up in the beauty of this area, but please be aware that rattlesnakes are frequently seen here. To avoid this possible danger, hike this trail during late fall, winter, or early spring.

At 0.8 miles (1.2 kilometers), you'll come to an intersection with the Winery Trail to the right. A fun side trip that will add 1.6 miles (2.5 kilometers) to your mileage, the Winery Trail climbs steeply out of the canyon to the vineyards of Wilridge Winery. Continue straight to stay on the Cowiche Canyon Trail.

The farther you walk into the heart of the canyon, the steeper the stacked basalt and layered andesite cliffs will rise. At 1.6 miles (2.5 kilometers), you'll enter into a narrow section of canyon, allowing for closer examination of the rocks. Be careful through this section, and a later section of narrow canyon just after crossing bridge 5 — rocks have fallen from overhead in these areas. At 2.2 miles (3.5 kilometers), you'll encounter the junction with the Lone Pine Trail to the left that leads to a trail network above.

Continue straight and come to the end of Cowiche Canyon at 2.6 miles (4.1 kilometers). Take a moment to read some of the trailhead signs about the canyon if you like, and then retrace your steps back through the canyon to the parking lot.

TURN BY TURN DIRECTIONS

1. At just over 0.7 miles (1.1 km), continue straight after encountering the East Uplands Trail to the left.
2. At 0.8 miles (1.2 km), continue straight at the junction with the Winery Trail to the right.
3. At 2.2 miles (3.5 km), continue straight at the junction with the Lone Pine Trail to the left.
4. At 2.6 miles (4.1 km), come to the end of the trail.
5. Return the way you came.

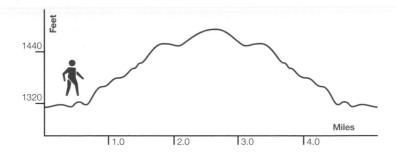

TRAILHEAD DRIVING DIRECTIONS

Heading west on US-12 from Yakima, turn left on Ackley Road.
Then turn left onto W Powerhouse Road. Then take a right onto Cowiche
Canyon Road. Follow Cowiche Canyon Road to the trailhead parking
at the end of the road.

BALE BREAKER BREWING COMPANY

If any brewery knows about hops, it's Bale Breaker Brewing Company
— growing hops has been the family business for three generations.
The brewery's "Baling Room" taproom is even located in a hop field
(Field 41 to be exact). It's little surprise then that Bale Breaker specializes
in hoppy brews — Pale Ales and IPAs abound on the taplist. Often taking
the top spot on the Best IPAs of Washington lists, the brewery's Top
Cutter IPA is not to be missed by hopheads.

TRAIL CONTACT INFORMATION
Cowiche Canyon Conservancy
302 N 3rd St.
Yakima, WA 98901
+1 509-248-5065
www.cowichecanyon.org

RESTAURANT
Cowiche Canyon Kitchen & Icehouse
202 East Yakima Ave.
Yakima, WA 98901
+1 509-457-2007
www.cowichecanyon.com
Award-winning restaurant with a great
happy hour.

TOURIST ATTRACTIONS INFO
Yakima Valley Tourism
10 North 8th St.
Yakima, WA 98901
+1 800-221-0751
www.visityakima.com

BREWERY
Bale Breaker Brewing Company
1801 Birchfield Rd.
Yakima, WA 98901
+1 509-424-4000
www.balebreaker.com
Brewery that showcases the power of
Yakima Valley hops.

ACCOMMODATIONS
Comfort Suites
3702 Fruitvale Blvd.
Yakima, WA 98902
+1 855-849-1513
www.yakimacomfortsuites.com
Complimentary breakfast and close to
the trailhead.

DISCOVERY PARK

TAKE A HIKE AT DISCOVERY PARK FOR PICTURESQUE VIEWS OF
THE OLYMPIC MOUNTAIN RANGE, THE WEST POINT LIGHTHOUSE,
AND SNOW-CAPPED MOUNT RAINIER.

STARTING POINT # NORTH PARKING LOT	**DESTINATION** # WEST POINT LIGHTHOUSE
BEER # FREMONT INTERURBAN IPA	**DIFFICULTY** # WALKING
MAP MAPS AVAILABLE AT PARKING LOT KIOSK	**DURATION OF THE HIKE** (LOOP) **2 HOURS** **3 MILES** (4.8KM)
PASS NEEDED # NONE	**ELEVATION GAIN** # 300 FEET (91.5M)

INDIA PALE ALE

ALCOHOL 6.2% CONTENT

YELLOW GOLD

GRAPEFRUIT, PINE, GRASS

LEMON ZEST, GRAPEFRUIT, RESIN

BITTERNESS   SWEETNESS

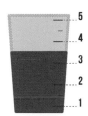

DESCRIPTION OF THE ROUTE

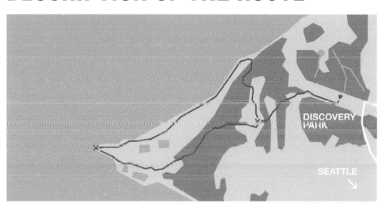

DISCOVERY PARK

SEATTLE

Covering 534 acres, Discovery Park is the biggest park on the Puget Sound. Meadows, woods, marshes, sea cliffs, and beaches can all be found within the park's boundaries, making it a favorite urban oasis for many Seattle residents. The views from the park don't get much more iconically Seattle either — ferry boats in the Sound with a backdrop of the Olympic Mountains, Mount Rainier looming massive and glaciated above the West Seattle skyline.

Discovery Park's best-known trail is the 2.8-mile (4.5 kilometer) Loop Trail (a National Recreation Trail) but there's even more to see beyond the Loop. Discovery Park is crisscrossed with trails, an ideal "choose your own adventure" place for getting in a hike. We'll give you our favorite route through the park, one that includes part of the Loop Trail, but also a walk along the beach and a visit to the West Point Lighthouse.

Start from the North Parking Lot, heading west from the southwest end of the lot. Grab a copy of a park map at the nearby infoboard for reference. The trail is paved for this first section and you'll begin to climb, following Kansas Ave. as it curves upward. Then pick up the Loop Trail and head through the forest before descending to the beach.

At 0.7 miles (1.1 kilometers), you'll start heading down to the North Beach Trail. This section loses elevation through a number of staircases and switchbacks through a thick alder forest. Once you hit North Beach Trail, you'll start to glimpse the Sound over the blackberry brambles. This is one of the most picturesque stretches in the park, with a view out to Shilshole Bay and the Olympic Mountains in the distance. It's here that the misty blue-gray image of Puget Sound so often equated with Seattle can truly be experienced. Looking further down the trail, the West Point Lighthouse comes into view and you might be lucky enough to catch sight of a harbor seal bobbing along the shore.

As you approach the West Point Lighthouse, you'll also pass by a marshy area — complete with a pond favored by waterfowl in the park. Follow the trail to the right onto the beach. There's not an official trail to the lighthouse from this side, but you can either skirt the fence line or walk on the beach along the bulkhead. You've reached the most western point in Seattle (where it gets its name) reaching out into Elliott Bay. The lighthouse is still active, and makes for an ideal model in a sunset picture — one that can only be overshadowed by Rainier. "Seattle's Mountain" rises from the West Seattle skyline to the south and at sunset is bathed in a neon shade of alpenglow. Round the point and cross the road to take the staircase-heavy Hidden Valley Trail back up to the Loop Trail before closing your loop and returning to the North Parking Lot.

TURN BY TURN DIRECTIONS

1. From the southwest corner of the North Parking Lot, walk west on the paved path.
2. At 0.2 miles (0.3 km), turn left at the junction.
3. At 0.3 miles (0.5 km), turn right onto the Loop Trail.
4. At 0.4 miles (0.6 km), continue straight at the trail junction with Texas Way.
5. At 0.5 miles (0.8 km), turn right, following signs to the North Beach Trail.
6. At 0.6 miles (0.9 km), continue straight on the trail.
7. Follow the trail downhill as it turns to the left.
8. At 1.5 miles (2.4 km), veer to the right on the North Beach Trail.
9. At 1.6 miles (2.5 km), you'll come to the end of the North Beach Trail. Skirt the fence line or walk along the beach around the point.
10. After rounding the point at 1.7 miles (2.7 km), get on the South Beach Trail.
11. Stay straight on the South Beach Trail for the next 0.2 miles (0.3 km).
12. At 1.9 miles (3 km), cross Utah Street and continue uphill.
13. At 2.0 miles (3.2 km), turn left at the Y-intersection.
14. At 2.1 miles (3.3 km), veer left onto the Hidden Valley Trail.
15. At 2.2 miles (3.5 km), continue straight on the Hidden Valley Trail.
16. At 2.5 miles (4 km), connect back to the Loop Trail and follow it back to the connection to the North Parking Lot.

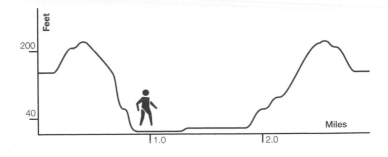

TRAILHEAD DRIVING DIRECTIONS

Take the Mercer Street Exit from I-5 and head west. Follow W Mercer Street onto Mercer Place; then take a right onto Elliott Avenue W. Elliott Avenue will turn into 15th Avenue W. Take the Nickerson Street Exit and keep right at the fork, continuing onto Emerson Street. Turn right onto Gillman Avenue W, which will turn into W Government Way, then Discovery Park Boulevard. Turn left onto Texas Way and follow it to the North Parking Lot.

FREMONT BREWING COMPANY

With a focus on community and sustainability, the brewery lives by a simple adage, "Because Beer Matters". Fremont is beloved by Seattle craft beer fans who crave everything from its classic Interurban IPA, to anticipated seasonals like Cowiche Canyon Fresh Hop and Bourbon Barrel Aged Abominable. Established in 2009, Fremont Brewing Company is a Seattle brewing institution. Because Beer Matters!

TRAIL CONTACT INFORMATION
Seattle Parks and Recreation
100 Dexter Ave. N
Seattle, WA 98109
+1 206-684 4075
www.seattle.gov/parks

RESTAURANT
Paseo Caribbean Food
4225 Fremont Ave. N
Seattle, WA 98103
+1 206-545-7440
www.paseorestaurants.com
A beloved Seattle sandwich shop serving Caribbean flair; be prepared for a line!

BREWERY
Fremont Brewing Company
1050 N 34th St.
Seattle, WA 98103
+1 206-420-2407
www.fremontbrewing.com
Known for its Fresh Hop and Barrel Aged beers — Hop-head and dark beer lovers can't go wrong.

TOURIST ATTRACTIONS INFO
Visit Seattle Market Information Center
Southwest Corner of Pike
and 1st in Pike Place Market
85 Pike St.
Seattle, WA 98101
+1 206-461-5840
www.visitseattle.org

EBEY'S LANDING

AMBLE ALONG SEASIDE PRAIRIE LANDS AND ROCKY BLUFFS BEFORE
RETURNING ON THE SHORE FOR OPEN OCEAN VIEWS AND BEACHCOMBING.

STARTING POINT

PRAIRIE
OVERLOOK

DESTINATION

EBEY'S
LANDING

BEER

FLYERS
PACEMAKER PORTER

DIFFICULTY

HIKING

DURATION OF THE HIKE

(LOOP) 2-3 HOURS
5 MILES (8KM)

MAP

USGS COUPEVILLE, NPS:
LOOK UP WWW.NPS.GOV

PASS NEEDED

NONE

ELEVATION GAIN

300 FEET (91.5M)

PORTER

ALCOHOL 5.5% CONTENT

DARKEST BROWN

ROASTY, ESPRESSO

CHOCOLATY, COFFEE, CHAR

BITTERNESS	SWEETNESS
5 4 3 2 1	5 4 3 2 1

DESCRIPTION OF THE ROUTE

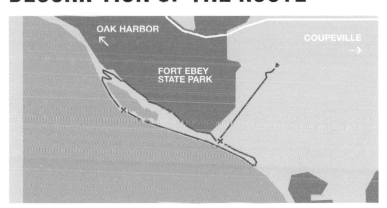

Ebey's Landing is a unique slice of Washington State history and landscape — prairie lands that stretch towards the Salish Sea, dropping dramatically down 300-foot (91 meter) tall bluffs. Named after the first European settler on Whidbey Island, Colonel Isaac Neff Ebey, this area is part of the United States' first national historical reserve, established in 1978. Ebey's Landing National Historical Reserve is a unique partnership between the town of Coupeville, Washington State Parks, Island County, and the National Park Service offering visitors a look into the agricultural, historical and cultural significance of the Pacific Northwest.

The hike begins at the Prairie Overlook, across from the Sunnyside Cemetery. Take the connector gravel path from the parking lot across the street to begin on Ebey's Prairie Trail. This trail takes you through the heart of Ebey's Prairie farmlands — wheat fields transition from green to golden through the seasons, swaying in the salt-kissed breeze. In 0.3 miles (0.5 kilometers) you'll come to the Jacob and Sarah Ebey house, now a visitor center. Stop in to learn about the history of the Ebey family, or continue on. At 0.8 miles (1.2 kilometers), the Ebey's Prairie Trail comes to a junction with the Bluff Trail. Turn right and you'll start the moderately steep climb of 260 feet to the top of the bluffs.

Upon reaching the crest of the bluffs, the narrow dirt trail follows the edge of the cliff, offering gorgeous views all around. Waves crash onto the shore below, and glaucous-winged gulls ride the airstream above. The trail moves from meadows to coastal forests that offer brief shade on the otherwise exposed trail.

At 1.9 miles (3 kilometers), you'll come to a fork in the trail. Head to the left to descend down the bluffs and meet up with the Beach Trail for the return journey. Two large switchbacks help the trail meet up with the shoreline, but can be steep. At 2.3 miles (3.7 kilometers), climb through the driftwood and meet the Beach Trail. Turn left to head back towards the other end of the beach. Here, you'll pass around the shores of Perego's Lagoon — this estuary is vital to many shore birds in the area.

It's best to plan this leg of the hike during low tide. This allows your return to be on an expanse of easily traversed wet sand. If not, you will spend your time outrunning waves or straining ankles on the rocky beach above the tideline. This is a hike ideal for beachcombers — look for sand dollars and midnight-purple mussel shells. At 3.9 miles (6.2 kilometers) the trail turns up the beach to the left, meeting back up with the Bluff Trail. At this point you'll find the Ebey's Landing State Park lot, an alternate starting location and parking lot. Turn left to continue on the Bluff Trail once more. The trail slowly climbs back up to follow along the prairielands. At 4.3 miles (6.9 kilometers), meet back up with the Ebey's Prairie Trail. Turn right and return back to the trailhead.

TURN BY TURN DIRECTIONS

1. From the parking lot, head on the gravel path to the south.
2. Cross the street to the Ebey's Prairie Trailhead.
3. At 0.8 miles (1.2 km), meet with the Bluff Trail and turn right.
4. At 1.9 miles (3 km), turn left at the fork.
5. At 2.3 miles (3.7 km), meet up with the Beach Trail, then turn left.
6. At 3.9 miles (6.2 km), turn left at the parking lot to meet up with the Bluff Trail again.
7. At 4.3 miles (6.9 km), turn right onto the Ebey's Prairie Trail.
8. Return to the parking lot.

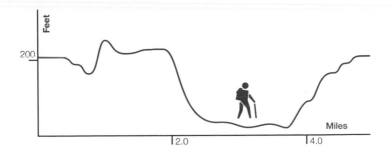

TRAILHEAD DRIVING DIRECTIONS

From Oak Harbor, head west on WA-20 towards Coupeville. Turn right onto S Sherman Road. Turn Right onto Cemetery Road. Park in the Prairie Overlook Parking lot on the left side of the road.

FLYERS RESTAURANT AND BREWERY

Inspired by and in tribute to Oak Harbor's naval and army aviation history, Flyers Restaurant and Brewery opened its doors in 2005. Owner and founder Jason Tritt built the award-winning brewery around his grandfather's aviation legacy — a legacy that now lives on in the photos and memorabilia around the community-loved taproom.

TRAIL CONTACT INFORMATION
Ebey's Landing National Historical Reserve
+1 360-678-6084
www.nps.gov/ebla

ACCOMMODATIONS/CAMPING
Fort Casey State Park
1280 Engle Rd.
Coupeville, WA 98239
+1 888-226-7688
www.parks.state.wa.us/505/Fort-Casey
Campground at a former coast artillery post with lighthouse on site. 21 tent sites and 14 full service sites are available.

BREWERY/RESTAURANT
Flyers Restaurant and Brewery
32295 State Route 20
Oak Harbor, WA 98277
+1 360-675-5858
www.eatatflyers.com
Aviation-themed brewery and restaurant known for its burgers and weekly live music.

TOURIST ATTRACTIONS INFO
Whidbey and Camano Island Tourism
905 Northwest Alexander
Coupeville, WA 98239
+1 360-678-5434
www.whidbeycamanoislands.com

FORT WORDEN

TAKE A HIKE THROUGH HISTORY, EXPLORE THE REMAINS OF FORT WORDEN
ARMY BASE, AND CLIMB ABANDONED GUN BATTERIES TO LOOK DOWN
ON THE WINDSWEPT PUGET SOUND BELOW.

STARTING POINT	DESTINATION
THE COMMONS AT FORT WORDEN	**ARTILLERY HILL COMPLEX**

BEER	DIFFICULTY
PROPOLIS SPRUCE	**WALKING**

MAP	DURATION OF THE HIKE
LOOK UP WWW.PARKS.STATE.WA.US	(LOOP) **1-2 HOURS** **2 MILES** (3.2KM)

PASS NEEDED	ELEVATION GAIN
DISCOVER PASS	**200 FEET** (60.9M)

FARMHOUSE ALE

 GOLD

 SPRUCE TIPS, WILDFLOWERS

CONIFER, CITRUS, HONEYCOMB

BITTERNESS	SWEETNESS
	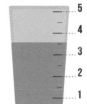

DESCRIPTION OF THE ROUTE

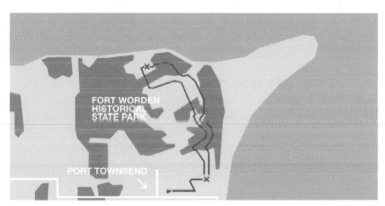

FORT WORDEN HISTORICAL STATE PARK

PORT TOWNSEND

Finished in 1904, Fort Worden was once a critical point in the "Triangle of Fire" — a collection of three forts constructed to protect the entrance to the Puget Sound. The fort remained an active military base until 1953, before it finally transitioned and opened as a state park in 1973. A curious mixture of concrete and natural beauty, Fort Worden is now a place for learning and outdoor recreation.

When Fort Worden became a state park, it welcomed two new additions to its grounds. The first was a campground near the beach and Point Wilson Lighthouse, and the second was Centrum. An arts organization, Centrum organizes musical performances, art festivals, and workshops throughout the year. Attendees often stay in the old barracks, or in the Victorian houses of Officers Row. Co-author Rachel roomed in the barracks during a creative writing seminar in the summer of 2012.

Winding through the former military complex, a network of trails allows hikers to explore this unique landscape. Our recommended route will allow you to experience the dramatic contrast of Artillery Hill against the lush sea bluffs of the coast. Begin in the Main Campus at the Commons Building where you can pick up a paper map to help navigate the maze-like trails. Once you leave the Commons, head west on the road towards Alexander's Loop. This road is named for Alexander's Castle, built by Reverend John B. Alexander in 1883. This red brick tower is one of the oldest buildings in the park.

After passing through cabins and the upper campground, you'll come to the staircase leading to the steep Madrona Trail. Winding through the waxy leafed forest of madrone trees, you'll meet up with Battery Way East, passing the entrance to the Memory Vault at 0.5 miles (0.8 kilometers). The Memory Vault is a hauntingly beautiful multimedia art installation that incorporates poetry and letters about the military history of the area. It's worth a few minutes of quiet contemplation. Continue on, veering right at the next intersection to head out on the Gun Line Road.

The concrete hulls of the former gun sites sit like abandoned shells on the hillside. If you dare, explore the cavernous rooms — just make sure you have a flashlight! Or, climb up the stairs and ladders to the top of a gun battery and look out at the waters of Admiralty Inlet and across to Whidbey Island. Continue on Gun Line Road through the tunnel, and then turn right onto the Tolles Trail at 0.9 miles (1.4 kilometers). Head down the steps to the final battery on this route, Tolles, with commanding views from its location on the bluffs. When you come to the battery, turn right to connect onto the Bluff Trail. The views here are spectacular, open and wide down onto the cliffs and the beach below. At 1.2 miles (1.9 kilometers), you'll come to an overlook with a breathtaking view above Point Wilson Lighthouse. Continue on the Bluff Trail, then continue straight on the JFK Trail, finally taking a right back onto Battery Way at 1.7 miles (2.7 kilometers) to head back to the Commons.

TURN BY TURN DIRECTIONS

1. From the Commons, head west for 0.1 miles (0.16 km) and turn left at the intersection onto Battery Way.
2. At just under 0.2 miles (0.3 km), turn right at the Y-intersection.
3. At 0.2 miles (0.3 km), take the first left you come to onto Alexander's Loop.
4. At 0.4 miles (0.6 km), take the stairs up to the Madrona Trail.
5. At just under 0.5 miles (0.8 km), connect with the Battery Way East Trail.
6. At the next intersection, reached at just over 0.5 miles (0.8 km), continue straight.
7. At 0.6 miles (0.9 km), veer right onto lower Gun Line Road.
8. At 0.9 miles (1.4 km), turn right onto the Tolles Trail.
9. At 1.0 miles (1.6 km), come to Tolles Battery and turn right to connect with the Bluff Trail.
10. At 1.4 miles (2.2 km), turn left onto the JFK Trail.
11. At just over 1.7 miles (2.7 km), turn right onto the road.
12. At 1.8 miles (2.8 km), turn left onto Battery Way.
13. From here, continue back to the Commons.

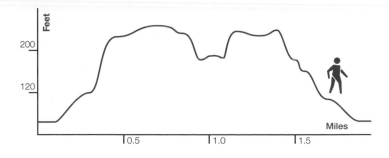

TRAILHEAD DRIVING DIRECTIONS

From the Port Townsend Ferry Terminal, take a left onto Water Street. Take a sharp right onto Washington Street, then the first left onto Walker Street. Walker Street will turn into Cherry Street. Follow Cherry Street all the way into Fort Worden State Park. Turn right onto Eisenhower Avenue and park in the gravel lot to the right.

PROPOLIS BREWING

Crafting a series of Farmhouse and barrel-aged beers, Propolis Brewing is a snapshot of the Port Townsend artist community in beer form. Taking inspiration from Belgian and French brewing traditions, along with influences of Old World ales no longer brewed wildly, Propolis' beers are hard to classify. The brewery first started selling its beers at local farmers markets before opening its taproom in early 2016. Part rustic farmhouse, part apothecary workshop, the taproom pays homage to the variety of wild herbs used in their brews. As their recipes change with the seasons, no two visits to Propolis will be alike.

TRAIL CONTACT INFORMATION
Fort Worden State Park
200 Battery Way
Port Townsend, WA 98368
+1 360-344-4400
www.parks.state.wa.us/511/fort-worden

RESTAURANT
The In Between
823 Water St.
Port Townsend, WA 98368
+1 360-379-2425
theinbetweenpt.com

TOURIST ATTRACTIONS INFO
Enjoy Port Townsend
2409 Jefferson St., Suite B
Port Townsend, WA 98368
+1 360-385-2722
www.enjoypt.com

BREWERY
Propolis Brewing
2457 Jefferson St.
Port Townsend, WA 98368
+1 360-344-2129
www.propolisbrewing.com
Brewery focusing on herbed farmhouse and wild ales.

ACCOMMODATIONS
Fort Worden Historical Lodgings
200 Battery Way
Port Townsend, WA 98368
+1 360-344-4400
www.fortworden.org/stay-here
Historic lodging including cabins, Victorian cottages, and campsites.

GREEN MOUNTAIN

CLIMB AMONG EMERALD FOREST AND FERN MEADOWS TO A HISTORIC
FIRE LOOKOUT WITH 360-DEGREE CASCADE MOUNTAIN VIEWS,
FOLLOWED BY BEER AT AN APPROPRIATE PACE.

STARTING POINT

FOREST
ROAD 2680

DESTINATION

GREEN MOUNTAIN
LOOKOUT

BEER

RIVER TIME
LIFE CHANGER SCOTTISH ALE

DIFFICULTY

MOUNTAIN HIKING

MAP

GREEN TRAILS CASCADE
PASS NO. 80

DURATION OF THE HIKE

6 HOURS
8.4 MILES (12.8KM)

PASS NEEDED

NONE

ELEVATION GAIN

3,300 FEET (1,005M)

SCOTTISH ALE

COPPER-BROWN

TOASTED CARAMEL

TOFFEE, BALANCED SWEETNESS

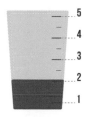

BITTERNESS	SWEETNESS

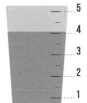

DESCRIPTION OF THE ROUTE

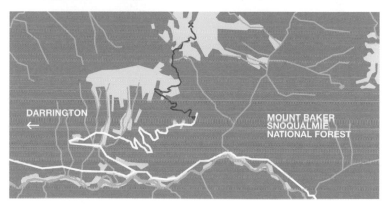

DARRINGTON
←

MOUNT BAKER
SNOQUALMIE
NATIONAL FOREST

Green Mountain is a place to be thankful for. The mountaintop lookout has survived over 80 years of vicious winter storms and threats of removal. Within the last decade, flooding and a landslide cut off access to the trailhead for several years. Fortunately, various organizations and volunteers have repaired the Suiattle River Road and preserved Green Mountain Lookout for hikers willing to make the drive to this challenging and immensely rewarding trek.

Speaking of the drive, the road to Green Mountain is long. Depending on your speed, plan on spending between 60 and 90 minutes driving from Darrington. It's easy to take the Suiattle River Road for granted when you're bumping along it, peering down on its namesake river and repeatedly asking the driver, "Are we there yet?" But for those who've never attempted Green Mountain, let us assure you: the drive is worth it.

Upon your long-anticipated arrival, it's finally time to hit the trail. It begins in the forest as any "green" trail should, winding through stands of

Douglas firs. Enjoy the shade while you can, as it becomes scarcer once you break out of the trees at around 1.5 miles (2.4 kilometers). Here, the landscape changes dramatically. Climb through colorful meadows, blooming with wildflowers during summer and bursting with berries in the fall.

The trail enters Glacier Peak Wilderness before dropping 100 feet to a pair of small ponds. Look up to Green Mountain Lookout from here, some 1,300 feet (396 meters) and one trail mile above. If you're tempted to turn around at this point, don't. You'll miss the best part.

Listen for pika, ptarmigan, and marmots as you climb. Marmots are notoriously fearless out here — you're most likely to encounter them on the final ascent, as they sun themselves and whistle from high rock perches. Always keep your distance and respect the wildlife. It's their home, after all. The lookout itself, standing at 6,500 feet above sea level, was originally constructed in 1933 by the Civilian Conservation Corps as a fire lookout. Today it is surrounded on three sides by a catwalk, allowing hikers to walk around back for views of Mount Baker to the north. Glacier Peak is the star of the show, but look in any direction and you'll find more peaks and valleys than we can name here.

Autumn is arguably the best time to hike Green Mountain. Colors are vibrant, and cooler temperatures keep the biting flies away. If you tackle this trail during summer, be sure to bring plenty of bug spray, water, and sunscreen.

TURN BY TURN DIRECTIONS

1. From the parking lot, head southwest on the Green Mountain Trail.
2. At 2.5 miles (4 km), drop 100 feet (30 m) to small ponds.
3. At 4.2 miles (6.7 km), reach the summit lookout.
4. Return via same trail to parking lot.

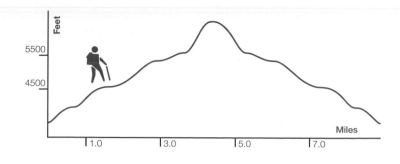

TRAILHEAD DRIVING DIRECTIONS

From Darrington, travel north on State Route 530 for 7.5 miles
(12 kilometers), turning right immediately after the Sauk River bridge onto
Forest Road 26 (Suiattle River Road). Follow FR 26 first on pavement,
then on gravel for 19 miles (30 kilometers), turning left onto FR 2680.
Continue 6 miles (9.5 kilometers) to the trailhead, near the road's end.

RIVER TIME BREWING

Founded in September 2013, River Time Brewing was originally located
next to the Sauk River. Today, River Time serves up fine craft beer with
a generous helping of friendly conversation from inside Darrington's Old
City Hall. A true place of history, this building was once the bustling
center of town — fire station, police station, library, dance hall — you
name it and it probably happened here. Now, you can kick back and
enjoy a beer at an appropriate pace.

TRAIL CONTACT INFORMATION
Darrington Ranger District Office
1405 Emens Ave. North
Darrington, WA 98241
+1 360-436-1155

Washington Trails Association
www.wta.org/go-hiking/hikes/green-mountain

TOURIST ATTRACTIONS INFO
Destination Darrington
www.destinationdarrington.com

BREWERY/RESTAURANT
River Time Brewing
660 Emens Ave. N
Darrington, WA 98241
+1 267-483-7411
www.rivertimebrewing.com
Relaxed, family-friendly tasting room
offering sandwiches, flatbread pizza,
and nachos.

HARRY'S RIDGE

EXPLORE THE SITE OF WHAT IS CONSIDERED THE MOST DEADLY AND
DESTRUCTIVE VOLCANIC ERUPTION IN THE HISTORY
OF THE UNITED STATES, WHILE TAKING IN THE BEAUTY OF
MOUNT ST. HELENS AND ITS RECOVERING LANDSCAPE.

STARTING POINT	DESTINATION
JOHNSTON RIDGE OBSERVATORY	**HARRY'S RIDGE**
BEER	DIFFICULTY
ASHTOWN STANDARD & BETTER	**MOUNTAIN** HIKING 
MAP	DURATION OF THE HIKE
GREEN TRAILS NO. 332 SPIRIT LAKE	**3-4 HOURS 8 MILES** (12.8KM)
PASS NEEDED	ELEVATION GAIN
NORTHWEST FOREST PASS + $8 FOR EACH ADDITIONAL PERSON.	**1,000 FEET** (305M)

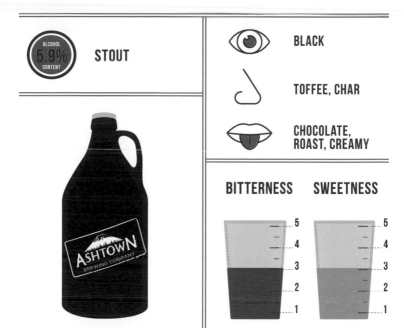

STOUT

ALCOHOL 5.9% CONTENT

BLACK

TOFFEE, CHAR

CHOCOLATE, ROAST, CREAMY

BITTERNESS

SWEETNESS

DESCRIPTION OF THE ROUTE

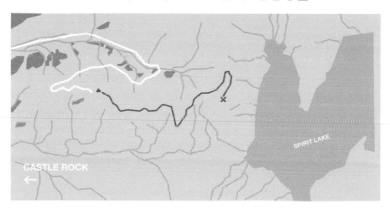

SPIRIT LAKE

CASTLE ROCK

On May 18, 1980, Mount St. Helens erupted, cataclysmically destroying 150 square miles of forest, unleashing devastating lahars through the Toutle River valley, and turning day into night as ash filled the air in Washington State. For years after, the area surrounding the mountain lay barren, described by many as a moonscape on earth.

Over 35 years later, life has returned to the area, creating a unique and dynamic landscape to explore. One of the best hikes to take in all of St. Helens' dramatic and deadly beauty is the Harry's Ridge Trail. The trail goes along a rolling ridgeline, dipping behind hummocks and providing fine views of Spirit Lake, Mt. Adams, and, of course, St. Helens looming large.

Start at the parking lot for Johnston Ridge Observatory and head inside to get your hiking pass for the National Volcanic Monument. From here, continue out along the paved "Eruption Trail" to connect with the Boundary Trail to Harry's Ridge. If you have extra time, the visitor center at the observatory offers a fascinating and comprehensive look at not only the 1980 eruption, but the history of the area as well.

The instant you hit the trail, St. Helens takes the stage as the star of this hike. You'll be able to easily make out the Lava Dome in the center of the crater, proof that the volcano has not yet returned to a dormant state. The Eruption Trail offers interpretive signs that tell the story of the volcano's eruption and its aftermath — but this portion of the trail is often crowded with visitors to the monument.

Once the pavement runs out and the trail begins fully, the crowds will thin and you'll gain some peace and quiet. Take a moment to look for grazing elk in the grassy meadows below — new residents in the area, these elk thrive on the open grassland, and are responsible for reintroducing 18 different plant species to the area. The trail rolls over the hilly landscape, short new-growth trees offering little in the way of shade. Off to the left, you'll be able to spy views of rocky Coldwater Peak rising above the hummocks left behind by the mudslide that cleared the terrain down to bedrock. At 1.6 miles (2.5 kilometers), you'll reach one of the more difficult parts of the trail. Here the trail cuts narrowly out along the slope of the ridge. Keep to the inside of the trail and watch your footing. After this perilous catwalk, you'll be awarded with your first view of Spirit Lake and Mount Adams at 1.9 miles (3 kilometers).

At 3.4 miles (5.4 kilometers), you'll reach a junction on the Boundary Trail with the trail leading up to Harry's Ridge. Turn to the right and climb steeply to the high point just 0.5 miles (0.8 kilometers) away. Watch your step along this length of the trail — you might spy a small, bright green Pacific Treefrog!

At the top of Harry's Ridge, the view is fantastic, the landscape a mixture of remnants from the blast and the regrowth of the area. The ridge was named after Harry Truman, the elderly owner of Mount St. Helens Lodge on Spirit Lake. Harry was a beloved folk hero in the months leading up to the eruption, and is presumed to have perished the day of the eruption after refusing to leave behind his lodge and 16 cats.

The bleached-grey log rafts still cover the banks of the brilliantly blue Spirit Lake, Mount Adams peaking over the edge of its shores. On clear days, you might even spy Mount Hood between Adams and St. Helens, creating a trio of volcanos in one view. From here, you'll also be able to make out, on the far side of the Lava Dome, the Crater Glacier — the youngest glacier in all of North America. Retrace your steps to make it back to Johnston Observatory.

TURN BY TURN DIRECTIONS

1. From Johnston Observatory, follow the paved Boundary Trail approximately 0.3 miles (0.5 km) to the end of the pavement.
2. Begin your hike here, continuing on to the Boundary Trail towards Harry's Ridge.
3. At 3.4 miles (5.4 km), come to the junction with the Harry's Ridge Viewpoint Trail. Head right onto the Harry's Ridge Trail.
4. Come to the high point of Harry's Ridge at 4.0 miles (6.4 km).
5. Return the way you came.

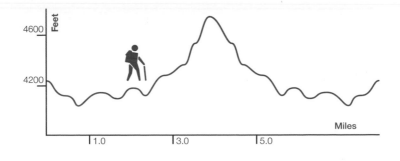

TRAILHEAD DRIVING DIRECTIONS

Take WA-504 east towards Toutle. When the road splits, head right towards Coldwater Peak and Johnston Ridge Observatory. Arrive at parking area 52.2 miles (84 kilometers) after turning onto 504.

ASHTOWN BREWING COMPANY

Longview's own Craft Brewery, Ashtown Brewing Company was started by cousins Erik and Jarrett Skreen in 2013. From the brewery's name to posters hanging on the taproom walls, Mount St. Helens looms large at Ashtown. In September of 2021, Ashtown opened a new and expanded space. Now complete with a kitchen and event area, Ashtown Brewing Company is ready to celebrate the resilient legacy of Longview.

TRAIL CONTACT INFORMATION
Johnston Ridge Observatory
24000 Spirit Lake Hwy.
P.O. Box 320
Toutle, WA 98649
+1 360-274-2140
www.fs.usda.gov

TOURIST ATTRACTIONS INFO
Mount St. Helens Visitor Center
3029 Spirit Lake Hwy.
Castle Rock, WA 98611
+1 360-274-0962
www.parks.state.wa.us/245/Mount-St-Helens

BREWERY/RESTAURANT
Ashtown Brewing Company
1145 11th Ave.
Longview, Washington 98632
+1 360-218-7519
www.ashtownbrewing.com

ACCOMMODATIONS
Eco Park Resort
14000 Spirit Lake Hwy.
Toutle, WA 98649
+1 360-274-7007
www.ecoparkresort.com
The closest accommodations to Mount St. Helens, complete with rustic charm.

ICICLE RIDGE

SWITCHBACK YOUR WAY UP THROUGH PINE FOREST AND SUMMER WILDFLOWERS TO A HIGH POINT OVERLOOKING THE BAVARIAN-THEMED TOWN OF LEAVENWORTH AND THE ICY-WATERS OF ICICLE CREEK BELOW.

STARTING POINT	DESTINATION
ICICLE RIDGE TRAILHEAD	**ICICLE RIDGE** EAST VIEWPOINT

BEER	DIFFICULTY
ICICLE BREWING DARK PERSUASION	**HIKING**

MAP	DURATION OF THE HIKE
GREEN TRAILS LEAVENWORTH 178	**2-3 HOURS** **5.2 MILES** (8.3KM)

PASS NEEDED	ELEVATION GAIN
NONE, BUT SIGN IN AT THE TRAILHEAD REGISTRATION	**1,910 FEET** (582M)

PORTER

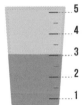

DARK BROWN

GERMAN CHOCOLATE CAKE

TOASTED COCONUT, CHOCOLATE, NUTTY

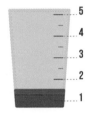

BITTERNESS	SWEETNESS
5	5
4	4
3	3
2	2
1	1

DESCRIPTION OF THE ROUTE

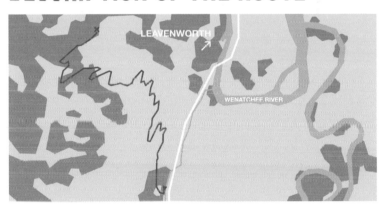

Stepping out onto the streets of Leavenworth, you'll feel like you're exploring a Bavarian mountain town. Gingerbread trim, murals straight from the pages of Heidi on the sides of buildings, and storekeepers dressed in lederhosen and dirndls — the entire town is committed to creating an alpine vacation spot just a mountain pass away from Seattle. While many visit to see Christmas lights or for the annual Oktoberfest celebration, Leavenworth is also a gateway to some of the most beautiful hiking in the state.

The Icicle Ridge Trail is a short drive from the bustle of downtown and offers hikers a truly bird's eye view of the town and surrounding peaks. Usually snow-free by spring, Icicle Ridge offers early-season hiking and some of the first wildflowers of the area. In the fall, the slopes come alive with shades of red and gold. No matter what time of year you hit the trail, it's sure to get your heart pounding.

A moderate 5.2 miles (8.3 kilometers) roundtrip, the trail switches up the slopes to a 2,900-foot (884 meter) high point above. Though the switchbacks help combat the grade of the climb, this trail still has a steady gain of 1,900 feet (580 meters) in less than 3 miles (4.8 kilometers). Pack plenty of water and tasty snacks to help motivate you during your trek. An Icicle beer should be enough motivation for the return trip into town.

The lower section of the trail criss-crosses beneath towering bigleaf maple trees — bright green in the spring and summer, turning a startling yellow with the first cool breath of fall. As you climb higher, the maples dwindle, and stands of ponderosa pine take their place. You will most likely share the trail with runners or other hikers, but assuredly you'll encounter other new friends along the way: chipmunks, squirrels, and even a few lizards if you look carefully.

At 2.4 miles (3.8 kilometers), you'll come to the top of the ridge, where a set of logs have been carved into a table and chair set — perfect for a shaded lunch. The trail meets the ridge in the low part of a saddle — so if you think the views from here are good, you're in for a treat. Head to the right and continue out to the ultimate viewpoint. The top of Icicle Ridge is full of wildflowers in the spring and summer, purple lupine carpeting the heights. Snags left from forest fires of the past rise from the brush. Watch for poison ivy, as it has been sighted in the area.

The views are incredible as you climb out of the saddle, and you'll reach an unobstructed viewpoint at 2.6 miles (4.1 kilometers). Look down on Leavenworth, Icicle Creek and the Wenatchee River. There are peaks in nearly every direction: Tumwater to the east, Edward Peak and Cashmere Mountain to the south, and Grindstone Mountain to the west. Soak in the alpine glory before heading back the way you came.

TURN BY TURN DIRECTIONS

1. Park on the left side of the gravel turnout, and head out on the Icicle Ridge Trail.
2. At 2.4 miles (3.8 km), reach the top of the ridge and turn right toward the viewpoint.
3. At 2.6 miles (4.1 km), come to a viewpoint at the end of the ridge.
4. Return the way you came.

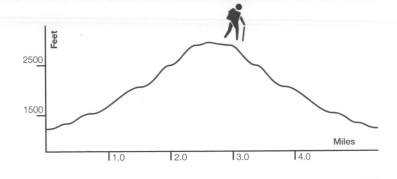

TRAILHEAD DRIVING DIRECTIONS

From downtown Leavenworth, turn left on Icicle Road at the end of town. Continue 1.4 miles (2.2 kilometers) to the Icicle Ridge trailhead sign. Turn right and then make a quick left. The trailhead parking lot is ahead.

ICICLE BREWING COMPANY

Owners Oliver and Pam Brulotte opened Icicle Brewing in 2011. From humble beginnings popping kettle corn on weekends, they now offer a tap list of award-winning beers. Icicle Brewing has become a Leavenworth establishment, with a craft beer take on the town's Bavarian theme. The best seat in the house is of course the ski chairlift hanging next to the bar, where you can sit back and truly appreciate the brewery's irresistible tagline — "From the top of the mountain, to the bottom of your glass...."

TRAIL CONTACT INFORMATION
Wenatchee River Ranger District
600 Sherbourne
Leavenworth, WA 98826
+1 509-548-2550
www.fs.usda.gov/recarea/okawen/
recarea/?recid=57123

RESTAURANT
München Haus
709 Front St.
Leavenworth, WA 98826
+1 509-548-1158
www.munchenhaus.com
Bratwurst, Icicle Brewing pints, and German music in a heated outdoor garden.

TOURIST ATTRACTIONS INFO
Leavenworth Visitor Center
940 US-2
Leavenworth, WA 98826
+1 509-548-5807
www.leavenworth.org

BREWERY
Icicle Brewing Company
935 Front St.
Leavenworth, WA 98826
+1 509-548-2739
www.iciclebrewing.com
A friendly, festive, and delicious brewery in the heart of the Bavarian wonderland of Leavenworth.

ACCOMMODATIONS
Obertal Inn
922 Commercial St.
Leavenworth, WA 98826
+1 509-548-5204
www.obertal.com
Comfortable accommodations in the heart of downtown Leavenworth, just steps away from nearby breweries.

IRA SPRING TRAIL

HIKE ALONG AN EXPOSED TALUS RIDGE WITH VIEWS OF THE SNOQUALMIE PASS CORRIDOR BEFORE DESCENDING TO PLACID MASON LAKE.

STARTING POINT	DESTINATION
IRA SPRING TRAILHEAD	**MASON LAKE**
BEER	DIFFICULTY 
DRU BRU SCHWARZ	**MOUNTAIN** HIKING
MAP	DURATION OF THE HIKE
GREEN TRAILS SNOQUALMIE PASS GATEWAY NO. 207S	**3 HOURS 7 MILES** (11.2KM)
PASS NEEDED	ELEVATION GAIN
NORTHWEST FOREST PASS	**2,420 FEET** (737M)

SCHWARZBIER

ALCOHOL
4.8%
CONTENT

FILTERED
DARK BROWN

ESPRESSO,
CHOCOLATE

SMOOTH, CHAR,
BITTER DARK
CHOCOLATE

BITTERNESS   SWEETNESS

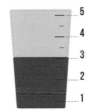

DESCRIPTION OF THE ROUTE

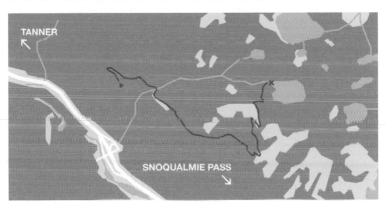

TANNER

SNOQUALMIE PASS

An easy day trip escape from the grind of busy downtown Seattle, the Ira Spring Trail is almost as beloved by the hiking community as its namesake. Named in honor of Ira Spring, photographer, trail advocate, and guidebook author, the trail climbs steadily to the ridge connecting Mount Defiance and Bandera Mountain before dropping to Mason Lake. In the summer, the south-facing talus-covered ridge is dotted with a colorful display of wildflowers. During fall, these same slopes explode with bright red as the huckleberries change with the season.

From the trailhead, the first 0.1 mile (0.16 kilometers) of the gravel trail climbs through new growth of alder, vine maple, and thimbleberry. The not-so-distant rumble of I-90 traffic is omnipresent, only drowned out occasionally by the trickle of streams and Mason Creek, reached at 0.8 miles (1.2 kilometers). Constructed with funds provided by the Spring Trust for Trails, a sturdy bridge allows for a safe crossing over the fluctuating flow of Mason Creek. At midspan, you can enjoy a picturesque tree-framed view of pointed McClellan Butte.

The trail climbs at a steady, moderate grade upwards for the first 1.6 miles (2.5 kilometers). Then, the true ascent begins. Sure to make your heart pound, this steep portion of trail climbs up through the now dense forest of fir and hemlock. At 2.7 miles (4.3 kilometers), you'll come out of the forest onto the open slopes. Isolated noble fir trees, identified by their upright cones, break up the rocky slopes. Look and listen carefully for the pika who live in the talus slopes on the side of the ridge.

At 2.8 miles (4.5 kilometers), you'll come to the junction with the Bandera Mountain Trail. From here, turn around for open views of Mount Rainier, looming glaciated above Mount Kent and McClellan Butte. You can peer down on the Middle Fork of the Snoqualmie River as it zig-zags below. Head to the left and continue up the final stretch.

When you reach the top of the ridge at 3.1 miles (4.9 kilometers), look carefully for a small copper-colored plaque on one of the large boulders near the edge of the trail. This is Ira Spring's Overlook — gazing out on the landscape Ira Spring himself dedicated the majority of his life to protect. Through his photographs and words, Spring opened up the trails of the Pacific Northwest to all, advocating for conservation of and education about wild spaces. The overlook is a place of solitude and remembrance.

Here, the trail descends rapidly 300 feet (91 kilometers) to the shores of Mason Lake. In a half cirque, this member of the Alpine Lakes Wilderness is clear, deep and placid. Lounge on a sunny lakeside boulder to rest up or enjoy lunch. To the south, Bandera Mountain looms large and tree-covered. At 3.5 miles (5.6 kilometers), turn around before the trail veers from the lakeshore to meet up with the Mount Defiance Ridge Trail. Continue back the way you came to the trailhead parking lot.

TURN BY TURN DIRECTIONS

1. From the trailhead, take the Ira Spring Trail at the end of the parking lot.
2. At 1.6 miles (2.5 km), stay left and begin the steep climb.
3. At 2.8 miles (4.5 km), stay left at the junction with the Bandera Mountain Trail.
4. At 3.4 miles (5.4 km), come to Mason Lake.
5. At 3.5 miles (5.6 km), turn around as the trail veers from the lakeshore.
6. Continue back the way you came, arriving back at the trailhead at 7.0 miles (11.2 km).

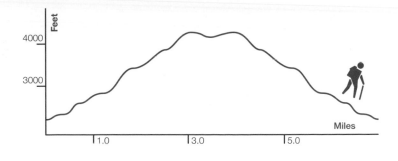

TRAILHEAD DRIVING DIRECTIONS

On I-90 east from Seattle take Exit 45 and turn left. Continue onto FR-9030. Stay left at the fork for Mason Lake Road, FR-9031. The parking lot is 3.8 miles (6.1 kilometers) from the highway.

DRU BRU

Located in the heart of the Summit at Snoqualmie, Dru Bru focuses on German styles using authentic ingredients. But by throwing in the high impact flavor of Yakima Valley hops, the brewery puts a decidedly hoppy spin on these classic styles. Crisp and sessionable, its award-winning recipes are a refreshing pick-me-up after a day on the trail or slopes. The tap room is a great place to relax apres-hike and watch a few ski videos on the big screen. Dru Bru has now expanded with a production facility and taproom in Cle Elum, just east of Snoqualmie Pass.

TRAIL CONTACT INFORMATION
Snoqualmie Ranger District-
North Bend Station
902 SE North Bend Way
North Bend, WA 98045
+1 425-888 1421

RESTAURANT
The Commonwealth
10 Pass Life Way #1
Snoqualmie Pass, WA 98068
+1 425-434-0808
Burgers, sandwiches, and comfort food in a relaxed setting.

TOURIST ATTRACTIONS INFO
Snoqualmie Valley Chamber of Commerce
38767 SE River St.
Snoqualmie, WA 98065
+1 425-888-6362
www.snovalley.org

BREWERY
Dru Bru + Squatch Box
10 Pass Life Way #3
Snoqualmie Pass, WA 98068
+1 425-434-0700
www.drubru.com
Brewing German-style beer at the top of Snoqualmie Pass.

ACCOMMODATIONS
The Roaring River B&B
46715 SE 129th St.
North Bend, WA 98045
+1 425-888-4834
www.theroaringriver.com
Comfortable Bed and Breakfast on a hilltop overlooking Middle Fork Snoqualmie River.

LITTLE MOUNTAIN

FEATURING TWO SKAGIT VALLEY OVERLOOKS AND OVER NINE MILES
OF MULTI-USE TRAILS, THIS LOW-ELEVATION MOUNTAIN OFFERS
THE PERFECT CURE FOR CABIN FEVER ANY TIME OF YEAR.

STARTING POINT	DESTINATION
LITTLE MOUNTAIN **PARK** EAST TRAILHEAD	LITTLE MOUNTAIN **SUMMIT** SOUTH VIEWPOINT
BEER	DIFFICULTY
NORTH SOUND GOOSETOWN BROWN	HIKING
MAP	DURATION OF THE HIKE
MOUNT VERNON PARKS FOUNDATION WWW.LITTLEMOUNTAINPARK.ORG	(LOOP) **1-2 HOURS** **4 MILES** (6.4KM)
PASS NEEDED	ELEVATION GAIN
NONE	610 FEET (186M)

BROWN ALE

ALCOHOL 7% CONTENT

MAHOGANY BROWN

ROASTY, NUTTY

DRY COCOA, SMOKY, CARAMEL

BITTERNESS

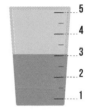

— 5
— 4
— 3
— 2
— 1

SWEETNESS

— 5
— 4
— 3
— 2
— 1

DESCRIPTION OF THE ROUTE

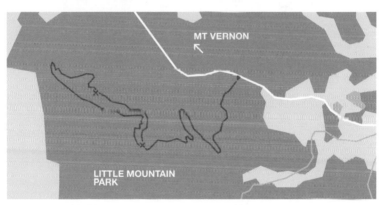

MT VERNON

LITTLE MOUNTAIN PARK

Aptly named Little Mountain tops out at 934 feet (284 meters) above sea level. This giant green hill — surrounded by 522 acres of forested park land — is located just a few miles outside Mount Vernon's downtown core, yet feels much farther from the city. A paved road leads to the sub-1,000 foot summit, where Skagit Valley views await from mountaintop overlooks. And while driving to the top can be pleasant, it is far more rewarding to hike. Especially if you're hitting the brewery afterwards.

Little Mountain Park's trail network has grown considerably in recent years. Since 2009, the Mount Vernon Trail Builders have logged over 12,000 volunteer hours here, building shared-use trails for hikers, runners, and mountain bikers. This is the place to go if you're looking to discover new trails in Mount Vernon.

For a fun "lollipop" loop, park at the east trailhead. Begin along the easy-going Nature Trail before meeting the Cairn Trail, where the elevation gain begins. Take a left on the La-Z-Boy Trail, which was named after a recliner found nearby — see if you can find it! Climb a set of switchbacks before meeting the road and restrooms. Continue up to a large bend in the road with parking and a "To Trails" sign.

Head up the shared Bonnie and Clyde Trail, yielding to any bikers you may encounter. This trail begins with a moderate climb before mellowing out and reaching west around the mountainside. Along the way you'll encounter an abandoned car — surely inspiration for this trail's name. Reach a junction at approximately 2.1 miles (3.3 kilometers). To the left, Sidewinder switchbacks gently up the mountain, with wide berms for downhill mountain biking. Head right for the short, steep, hiker-only Ginny's Trail. Take a short detour at the top of Ginny's Trail (go left) to check out the North Viewpoint, where you can see Mount Baker on a clear day. Then walk up the road a short distance to reach the south summit overlook.

From the top of Little Mountain, gaze over fertile fields and the Skagit River towards Fidalgo and Whidbey Islands. When you're ready to complete this loop, head southeast from the lookout towards two looming communication towers. Follow the signed Ridge Trail down, approximately half a mile, to the road junction before returning to your car. Watch your step! This trail is steep and can be quite slippery after a good northwest rain.

This is just one suggestion for hiking at Little Mountain Park; there are many ways to reach the top. The park contains at least two dozen short, interconnected trails, so download a map from Mount Vernon Parks Foundation and chart your own course.

TURN BY TURN DIRECTIONS

1. Leave the east parking lot along the Nature Trail.
2. At 0.2 miles (0.3 km), turn right onto the Cairn Trail.
3. At 0.7 miles (1.1 km), turn left onto the La-Z-Boy Trail.
4. At 1 mile (1.6 km), stay right on the La-Z-Boy Trail until you reach the road.
5. At 1.1 miles (1.7 km), reach the road. Continue up the road (left).
6. At 1.2 miles (1.9 km), continue onto the signed Bonnie and Clyde trail.
7. Follow Bonnie and Clyde to Ginnie's Trail at 2.1 miles (3.3 km), then turn right.
8. At 2.2 miles (3.2 km), turn left on the North Viewpoint Trail.
9. Reach the North Viewpoint at 2.3 miles (3.7 km).
10. Follow the North Viewpoint Trail around to the road.
11. At 2.4 miles (3.8 km), reach the South Viewpoint.
12. Head south towards the communication towers for the signed Ridge Trail.
13. Follow the Ridge Trail, staying right at all junctions.
14. At 2.9 miles (4.6 km), reach the road junction and return the way you came.

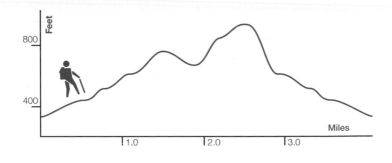

TRAILHEAD DRIVING DIRECTIONS

From I-5 take Exit 225. Head east on Anderson Road for 1 mile (1.6 kilometers), then turn right onto E. Blackburn Road. Continue 0.3 miles (0.5 kilometers) and stay right for Little Mountain Road. After 0.9 miles (1.4 kilometers) on Little Mountain Road, turn into the east trailhead parking area on the right.

NORTH SOUND BREWING

Whether you're coming in for a gameday growler fill or a post-Tulip Festival pint, North Sound Brewing is a favorite craft brewery for the Skagit Valley. With 14 beers on tap, there's something for every craft beer fan. The brewery also features a rotating cask ale inspired by the owner's travels in the UK and Ireland. North Sound isn't afraid to mix things up either — ask your beertender for a mixed-beer!

TRAIL CONTACT INFORMATION
City of Mount Vernon
910 Cleveland Ave.
Mount Vernon, WA 98273
+1 360 336-6215
www.mountvernonwa.gov

RESTAURANT
District Brewing
520 Main St.
Mount Vernon, WA 98273
+1 360 873-6714
www.districtbrewco.com
Pizza, wings, salad, and beer in Mount Vernon's historic Lyric Theater building.

BREWERY
North Sound Brewing
17406 State Route 536
Mount Vernon, WA 98273
+1 360-982-2057
www.northsoundbrewing.com
Bring in food from a nearby restaurant to pair with North Sound's unfiltered brews.

TOURIST ATTRACTIONS INFO
Mount Vernon Chamber of Commerce
301 West Kincaid St.
Mount Vernon, WA 98273
+1 360 428-8547
www.mountvernonchamber.com/visitors

Calm Water Massage
312 Pine St.
Mount Vernon, WA 98273
+1 360-873-8643
www.calmwatermassage.com
Relax after your hike with a therapeutic massage.

MANASTASH RIDGE

FOLLOW THE UNRELENTING WESTBERG TRAIL UP MANASTASH RIDGE
TO A MEMORIAL SITE WITH OPEN VIEWS OVERLOOKING
THE KITTITAS VALLEY TO THE STUART RANGE.

WA
STATE OF WASHINGTON

STARTING POINT	DESTINATION
WESTBERG TRAIL	**MANASTASH RIDGE**

BEER	DIFFICULTY
IRON HORSE IRISH DEATH	**HIKING**

MAP	DURATION OF THE HIKE
WA DNR - YAKIMA	**2-3 HOURS 4 MILES** (6.4KM)

PASS NEEDED	ELEVATION GAIN
NONE	**1,700 FEET** (518M)

DARK STRONG ALE

BLACK

CARAMEL, TOFFEE

CHOCOLATE, BROWN SUGAR, TOASTED MALT

BITTERNESS   SWEETNESS

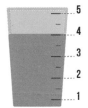

5
4
3
2
1

5
4
3
2
1

DESCRIPTION OF THE ROUTE

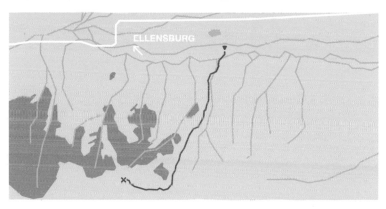

ELLENSBURG

Running approximately 50 miles (80 kilometers) east-west through Central Washington, Manastash Ridge forms the southern boundary of the Kittitas Valley. A handful of hiking trails and jeep roads climb the ridge at various points. Two highways traverse it, running north-south between Ellensburg and Yakima. For those unfamiliar with the area, it can be difficult to find the best hiking route. So we asked a ranger. The verdict? Manastash Ridge's Westberg Trail is the local hiking hotspot.

A single glance at any topo map will tell you everything you need to know about the hike up Manastash Ridge. The way is simply up, across dozens of contour lines, from 1,900 feet (579 meters) above sea level to over 3,500 feet (914 meters). There are no switchbacks. This may change over time, as erosion and runoff ruts have become so bad that the Washington departments of Natural Resources and Fish and Wildlife are considering improvements. For now, the trail retains its steep pitch, 20-foot wide sections, and unmarked route. Be sure to bring a map!

Westberg Trail begins along an old jeep road, separated from private land by wooden fences. Deer can sometimes be seen grazing in this area. Cross over an irrigation canal spanned by twin timbers to reach the trailhead. From here the trail takes off uphill, gently at first but gaining steam all the while. The first junction is at 0.3 miles (0.5 kilometers) — continue straight for the top of the ridge.

As you climb, the distant sounds of off-road vehicles and the pop of hunting rifles may be detected. This land is multi-use, meaning you'll find everyone from off-roaders and mountain bikers to hunters out here. Respect the land and other users by staying on the trail, and wear bright colors if hiking during hunting season (fall). Also watch for rattlesnakes — they are notorious here, especially during the heat of summer.

Because of summer snakes, heat, and lack of a water source, it's best to hike this trail fall-spring. There is no tree cover; the trail is entirely exposed to the elements. Rainy-day runoff has created large ruts in the trail, which users often go around — inadvertently widening the trail in places. With all these warnings and potential issues, it may seem that hiking Manastash Ridge is simply not worth the trouble. But it absolutely is.

Views from the ridge improve every step of the way. Spring and early summer wildflowers keep the trail colorful, while wildlife keeps you on your toes. If not deer and snakes, you're very likely to see a few birds — especially red-tailed hawks. Sagebrush abounds. Hiking through this desert landscape is a markedly different experience from trekking west of the Cascades. As an added bonus, it's often sunny in Ellensburg when it's raining in Seattle.

Atop the ridge, you'll find some uncommon summit sights. First, an ammo can with a notebook inside. This unofficial trail register has reportedly been here for years, since long before the geocaching craze. Sign your name and see what others have written. Beyond, a solitary stake rises from a rock pile in memory of this trail's namesake, Ray Westberg. A well-known wrestling coach in Ellensburg, Ray passed away in 1997 and is memorialized here. Smaller monuments dot the mountainside. All together they look across the valley, at wind turbines spinning beneath snow-capped mountains — a place of peaceful rest for all.

TURN BY TURN DIRECTIONS

1. From the signed Ridge Trail parking area, walk to the end of Cove Road.
2. Begin your hike at the road-end gate.
3. At 0.1 miles (0.16 km), cross over the irrigation ditch and continue straight up the trail.
4. At 0.3 miles (0.5 km), continue straight at the junction.
5. At 1 mile (1.6 km), reach the 1-mile marker post.
6. At 1.5 miles (2.4 km), continue straight at a second junction.
7. At 2 miles (3.2 km), reach the top of the ridge and memorial site.
8. Return the way you came.

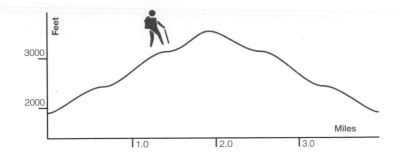

TRAILHEAD DRIVING DIRECTIONS

Take I-90 Exit 101 near Thorp Fruit & Antique Mall. After exiting, turn right and continue along Thorp Highway to Cove Road. Turn right, and follow Cove Road to its road-end parking area, signed "Ridge Trail" on the right-hand side.

IRON HORSE BREWERY

Perhaps the only thing Iron Horse Brewing in Ellensburg takes seriously is making beer. From its wild website to signs around the brewery reading "Your BFF", the brewery has a tongue-in-cheek approach to marketing — but it's all business when it comes to brewing. As it's one of the largest producers of beer in Washington State, you can ask almost any Washingtonian beer drinker and they'll tell you exactly what the brewery's famed Irish Death tastes like. The downtown pub closed in 2020, but the brewery is on track to open a tasting room in the downstairs of its production facility in 2022.

TRAIL CONTACT INFORMATION
Washington Department of Natural Resources
713 Bowers Rd.
Ellensburg, WA 98926
+1 509-925-8510
www.dnr.wa.gov/recreation

BREWERY/RESTAURANT
Iron Horse Brewery Production Facility
1621 Vantage Hwy.
Ellensburg, WA 98926
+1 509-834-7838
www.ironhorsebrewery.com
Production facility with Taproom
expected to open 2022.

TOURIST ATTRACTIONS INFO
My Ellensburg
609 N Main St.
Ellensburg, WA 98926
+1 509-925-2002
www.myellensburg.com

MAPLE PASS LOOP

SOAK UP SOME OF THE FINEST VIEWS IN THE STATE ON THIS EPIC, 7-MILE CIRCUIT AMONG JAGGED CASCADE PEAKS, LUSCIOUS LAKES, AND — SEASONALLY — GOLDEN LARCHES GALORE.

STARTING POINT

RAINY PASS PICNIC AREA

DESTINATION

MAPLE
PASS

BEER

OLD SCHOOLHOUSE METHOW BLONDE

DIFFICULTY

MOUNTAIN HIKING

MAP

GREEN TRAILS MOUNT LOGAN NO. 49

DURATION OF THE HIKE

(LOOP) 4 HOURS
7.5 MILES (12KM)

PASS NEEDED

NORTHWEST FOREST PASS

ELEVATION GAIN

2,000 FEET (609M)

BLONDE ALE

PALE GOLD

**BISCUIT,
SOFT FLORAL**

**LIGHT MALT,
BREADY, HERBAL
BITTERNESS**

BITTERNESS	SWEETNESS

DESCRIPTION OF THE ROUTE

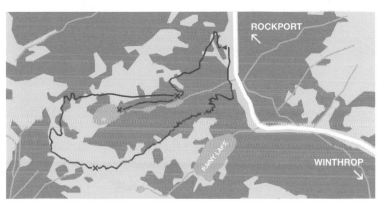

A long-time Washington classic, Maple Pass Loop is simply astonishing. Its long list of pros include diverse scenery — ranging from summer wildflowers to early winter snow — along with old-growth forest and wildlife-spotting, all on a lovely non-repeating loop trail. Not to mention its accessibility — the scenic North Cascades Highway is paved, making for a delightful drive during its open season between May and November. As for cons? We can think of few, besides the fact that Maple Pass is only hikeable July - October most years due to snow. As with most classic hikes, do this one on a weekday to beat the crowds.

From the large Rainy Pass parking area, follow "Lake Trail" signs to the Lake Ann and Maple Pass Loop Trail. At this junction, you can go either way. Hiking the loop counterclockwise is best for a gentler approach, so head right into the second-growth forest. At 1.2 miles (1.9 kilometers), the trail to the left leads half a mile out to Lake Ann, a pretty lake in the cirque beneath Maple Pass. Don't bypass this detour. It's worth the extra mileage to sit by Lake Ann's serene shores, taking a rest while gazing up at the ridgeline you'll ascend to.

Back at the Maple Pass Trail junction, continue upward to Heather Pass. A junction at 3.1 miles (4.9 kilometers) swings off to the northwest — tempting, but save it for another day. Continue straight to reach Maple Pass. The way is steep, with a few switchbacks thrown in for good measure. Watch for pika scurrying among the talus here, especially in the autumn as they frantically prepare their winter dwellings. Atop the ridge, bird's-eye views await in every direction. Peer down upon Lake Ann, marvelling at the progress you've made since sitting near its eastern shores.

Wonder and wander along the ridgeline, contemplating the curiously named peaks surrounding you. Corteo and Frisco. Black and Stiletto. In the distance, Glacier Peak reaches for the southwestern skyline. This massive glaciated vanilla cone is the most isolated of Washington's stratovolcanoes, and potentially the most dangerous. According to the US Geological Survey, the probability of a new eruption in any given year is roughly one in a thousand.

From the nearly 7,000-foot (2,133 meter) high point on Frisco Mountain's shoulder, relax before beginning your descent. Watch for marmots sunning themselves and ptarmigan strutting about. Then switchback down the ridge, keeping an eye out for Rainy Lake off to the right. This final stretch drops about 1,700 feet (518 meters) in 2.8 miles (4.5 kilometers). Once you hit pavement, take a left to complete the loop. The trail to the right reaches Rainy Lake in half a mile, but most hikers are content viewing it from several hundred feet above.

Hike this trail during autumn for vibrant fall colors. The larches in particular are a big draw, turning golden-yellow for a brief period of time during October. Don't forget your camera!

TURN BY TURN DIRECTIONS

1. Walk south from the Rainy Pass parking area a short distance to the signed trailhead.
2. Take the path to the right to hike Maple Pass Loop counter-clockwise.
3. At 1.2 miles (1.9 km) from the trailhead, turn left for Lake Ann.
4. Reach Lake Ann at 1.7 miles (2.7 km), then turn around and retrace your steps to the junction.
5. At 2.2 miles (3.5 km), turn left to continue up to Maple Pass.
6. At 3.1 miles (4.9 km), continue straight at a junction.
7. At 7.2 miles (11.5 km), turn left onto the paved path.
8. At 7.5 miles (12 km), return to the trailhead and retrace your steps to the parking lot.

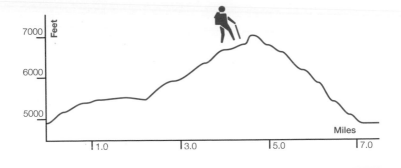

TRAILHEAD DRIVING DIRECTIONS

From I-5 in Burlington, take Highway 20 east for approximately 50 miles (80 kilometers). The signed Rainy Pass trailhead will be on the south (right) side of the road.

OLD SCHOOLHOUSE BREWERY

This is the kind of schoolhouse all of us wish we attended. Old Schoolhouse Brewery slings beers to thirsty patrons inside a historic building that looks straight out of a Western. Located on the banks of a bend in the Chewuch River, the riverside patio is a popular spot to unwind. On weekends, the brewery gets elbow-to-elbow packed, and after one taste of its beer, it's easy to see why. Try anything from the award-winning Brewer's Reserve series.

TRAIL CONTACT INFORMATION
Okanogan-Wenatchee National Forest
Methow Valley Ranger District
24 West Chewuch Rd.
Winthrop, WA 98862
+1 509-996-4003
www.fs.usda.gov

ACCOMMODATIONS
North Cascades Mountain Hostel
209 Castle Ave.
Winthrop, WA 98862
+1 509-699-0568
www.ncascadesmtnhostel.com
Affordable bunk rooms and private cabins in Winthrop with a fun community feel.

BREWERY/RESTAURANT
Old Schoolhouse Brewery
155 Riverside Ave.
Winthrop, WA 98862
+1 509-996-3183
www.oldschoolhousebrewery.com
The pub grub menu features burgers and other eats, each with a recommended beer pairing.

TOURIST ATTRACTIONS INFO
Winthrop Chamber
+1 509-996-2125
www.winthropwashington.com

MARYMERE FALLS
LAKE CRESCENT LOOP

NO VISIT TO OLYMPIC NATIONAL PARK IS COMPLETE WITHOUT A SHORT HIKE OUT TO MARYMERE FALLS, COMBINED WITH A STROLL ALONG THE SHORES OF GLACIALLY-CARVED LAKE CRESCENT.

STARTING POINT	DESTINATION
STORM KING **RANGER** STATION	**MARYMERE** FALLS AND LAKE CRESCENT
BEER	DIFFICULTY
BARHOP CITRA SONIC IPA	**WALKING**
MAP	DURATION OF THE HIKE
LOOK UP WWW.NPS.GOV	(LOOP) **1.5-2 HOURS** **2.7 MILES** (4.3KM)
PASS NEEDED	ELEVATION GAIN
NONE	**500 FEET** (152M)

INDIA PALE ALE

1 QUART (32 FL. OZ.)

PALE AMBER

CITRUS RIND, PINE

ORANGE ZEST, PINE, GRAPEFRUIT PEEL

BITTERNESS   SWEETNESS

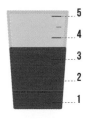 

DESCRIPTION OF THE ROUTE

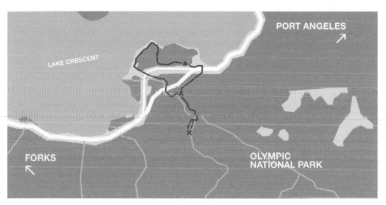

In a massive national park full of trails, waterfalls, mountains, and lakes, how do you choose where to spend your time? Sometimes, it comes down to ease of access. And if you're approaching Olympic National Park from Port Angeles, it doesn't get much easier than this. 20 miles (32 kilometers) west of Port Angeles on the scenic Highway 101, Lake Crescent and Marymere Falls offer an exceptional sampling of the park's diverse offerings.

As is often the case with drive-up destinations, this area gets more than its fair share of crowds — especially during summer. Fortunately, Lake Crescent and Marymere Falls are accessible year-round. We recommend a weekday stroll during fall, winter, or spring for the best waterfall flows, and an opportunity to enjoy this pristine area alone.

Park at the Storm King Ranger Station and follow the paved Marymere Falls Nature Trail east. If it's open, the ranger station is a good first stop to pick up a map and check trail conditions. However, this building is not regularly staffed and is closed most of the year. Mount Storm King looms overhead, offering an alternate hiking destination for those feeling ambitious. Its summit trail gains 1,700 feet (500 meters) in just under 2 miles (3 kilometers) — a short but steep thigh-pumper best saved for a clear, dry day.

Continue past the ranger station, skirting the lakeshore before passing beneath Highway 101 via a pedestrian tunnel. As you stroll through the old-growth forest, see how many trees you can identify. Cedar, hemlock, and maples grace the trail. At 0.5 miles (0.8 kilometers), an enormous boulder marks the Mount Storm King Trail junction. Continue straight here for the falls.

Cross Barnes Creek via the sturdy, rusty-railed bridge, then immediately cross a wooden footbridge over Falls Creek and climb 200 feet (61 meters) to the falls' upper viewpoint. A short loop here allows you to view 90-foot (27 meter) Marymere Falls from its base, and from above. These picturesque falls plunge in a narrow chute before fanning out on the moss-covered rocks below. They are named after the sister (Mary) of homesteader Charles Barnes, whose family first settled the area in the 1890s.

After completing the small loop around the falls, cross back over the bridges and head back to the junction at 1.3 miles (2 kilometers). Turn left here to follow Barnes Creek to Lake Crescent Lodge. For over 100 years, Lake Crescent Lodge has invited explorers to come on in and sit by the fire. Consider staying here if you have time, or grab a bite to eat at the restaurant.

Back on the trail, head north to Barnes Point. This lovely spot offers outstanding panoramic views of Lake Crescent and its surrounding mountains. Directly ahead, stare down Pyramid Peak — a potential hiking destination for another day. Head back along the Moments in Time Trail to complete the loop. Interpretive signs along the way tell the stories of ages and industries past — an inviting glimpse into the storied history of Lake Crescent.

TURN BY TURN DIRECTIONS

1. Head east from the parking lot along the Marymere Falls Nature Trail.
2. At 0.45 miles (0.7 km), reach a junction. Stay left for the falls.
3. At 0.5 miles (0.8 km), meet the Mount Storm King Trail.
   Continue straight for the falls.
4. At 0.7 miles (1.1 km), reach a junction with the Barnes Creek Trail.
   Turn right for the falls.
5. At 0.8 miles (1.2 km), reach the small waterfall loop. Go left to reach the base of the falls, then visit the upper viewing area and return to close the loop.
6. Cross back over the bridges, heading back in the direction you came.
7. At 1.3 miles (2 km), return to the first junction.
   Turn left for Lake Crescent Lodge.
8. At 1.75 miles (2.7 km), cross Lake Crescent Road and continue on the trail.
9. At 1.9 mile (3 km), reach Lake Crescent Lodge.
   Turn right and follow the shore trail north.
10. At 2.1 miles (3.3 km), meet the Moments in Time Trail.
    Stay left to reach Barnes Point.
11. From Barnes Point, continue southeast on the Moments in Time Trail.
12. At 2.3 miles (3.7 km), stay left at the junction.
13. Follow this trail back to the parking lot at 2.7 miles (4.3 km).

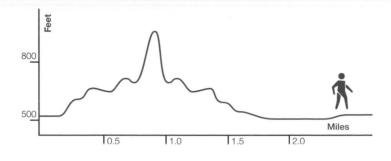

TRAILHEAD DRIVING DIRECTIONS

From Port Angeles, take US 101 west 20 miles (32 kilometers). Turn right for the signed Lake Crescent Lodge and Marymere Falls. Continue a quarter mile (0.4 kilometers), then turn right to reach the parking area near the Storm King Ranger Station.

BARHOP BREWING

Just across the street from the ferry terminal, Barhop Brewing serves up the suds to go with its waterfront views and selection of artisan pizza. This former nanobrewery now brews enough to keep its seafaring patrons satisfied, including international visitors from the Victoria ferry. Old road signs and vintage bar signs decorate the walls, while a rusty bicycle hangs from the ceiling. The Barhop brewery also has a bustling location in Sequim!

TRAIL CONTACT INFORMATION
Olympic National Park Visitor Center
3002 Mount Angeles Rd.
Port Angeles, WA 98362
+1 360-565-3130
www.nps.gov/olym/planyourvisit/
visitorcenters.htm

ACCOMMODATIONS
Red Lion Hotel Port Angeles
221 N Lincoln St.
Port Angeles, WA 98362
+1 360-452-9215
www.redlion.com/port-angeles
Comfy, affordable waterfront hotel just a hop, skip, and a jump from Barhop Brewing.

BREWERY/RESTAURANT
Barhop Brewing
124 W. Railroad Ave.
Port Angeles, WA
+1 360-797-1818
www.barhopbrewing.com

TOURIST ATTRACTIONS INFO
Port Angeles Visitor Center
121 East Railroad Ave.
Port Angeles WA 98362
+1 360-452-2363
www.visitportangeles.com

MOUNT PILCHUCK

HIKE, SCRAMBLE OVER ROCKS, AND CLIMB THE FINAL STEPS TO
MOUNT PILCHUCK'S MILE-HIGH LOOKOUT TOWER FOR UNPARALLELED
PANORAMAS FROM THE CASCADE MOUNTAINS TO PUGET SOUND.

WA
STATE OF WASHINGTON

STARTING POINT	DESTINATION
MOUNT PILCHUCK TRAILHEAD	**MOUNT PILCHUCK**
BEER	DIFFICULTY
SKOOKUM MURDER OF CROWS	**MOUNTAIN** HIKING
MAP	DURATION OF THE HIKE
GREEN TRAILS 109 GRANITE FALLS WA	**3-4 HOURS** **5.2 MILES** (8.3KM)
PASS NEEDED	ELEVATION GAIN
NORTHWEST FOREST PASS	**2,200 FEET** (670M)

OAK AGED STOUT

ALCOHOL 9% CONTENT

 DARK BROWN

 ROASTED, OAK, CHOCOLATE

 CHOCOLATE, DARK FRUIT, WHISKEY

BITTERNESS   **SWEETNESS**

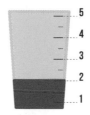 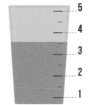

DESCRIPTION OF THE ROUTE

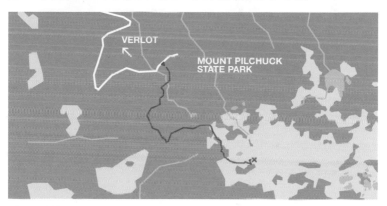

Formerly a ski resort, Mount Pilchuck is now one of the most popular hiking destinations in Washington State. Pilchuck's fame is due to its accessibility — about an hour's drive east of the I-5 corridor — and legendary panoramic views. This classic trail has been featured in guidebooks for decades; hundreds of thousands have reached Pilchuck's summit. Yet despite those crowds, it's worth the trek.

Unfortunately, Pilchuck's ease of access is all too inviting for inexperienced hikers. Many injuries occur here. It's easy enough to twist an ankle on this rocky trail, so watch your footing and take it slow. Route-finding can be tricky in June when the trail is still blanketed in snow. Save this one for July - November for the best (and safest) conditions. The road to Mount Pilchuck closes seasonally in November or December.

The trail begins along a road once used to access Mount Pilchuck Ski Area. Opened in the 1950s, the ski area operated for nearly 30 years before shuttering due to unreliable snow levels and land lease issues.

Today, the US Forest Service and Washington State Parks jointly manage Mount Pilchuck, adding to the oft-confusing predicament of, "Which pass do I need?" Since the parking area and trailhead are within Mount Baker-Snoqualmie National Forest, you'll need a Northwest Forest Pass to park here.

Walk through the National Forest for a quarter mile before entering Mount Pilchuck State Park. The trail gains elevation steadily, wiggling its way south, before turning somewhat abruptly north at a scree slope. At this one-mile point, stay left to continue on the main trail. Continue upwards through forest, heather-decorated talus fields, and ever-improving views towards Mount Pilchuck's restored fire lookout.

These slopes are an ideal habitat for the undeniably adorable American Pika. Listen for the telltale loud "meep!" and keep your eyes peeled for quick movements. About the size of large russet potato, pika are a relative of the rabbit with large, round ears. They spend their days scurrying through the rock fields and collecting vegetation to dry in large "hay piles," which they will eat through the long winter ahead. They are quite possibly the cutest wildlife species in all the Pacific Northwest.

Atop Mount Pilchuck, scramble carefully over boulders and up a short, steep ladder to reach the deck of the lookout. Originally built in 1921, it now houses a mini-museum full of historical photographs and information. Take shelter inside if the weather is unpleasant, or walk around the deck for views in every direction. On overcast days, you may just find yourself above the clouds.

First and foremost, the volcanoes. To the north, distant Mount Baker is visible on clear days. Glacier Peak stands tall to the east, while Mount Rainier looms even larger down south. Because Pilchuck is positioned at the western edge of the Cascade Mountains, it offers views of Puget Sound islands and the Olympic Mountains in addition to these massive Cascade volcanoes.

TURN BY TURN DIRECTIONS

1. Begin along the signed Mount Pilchuck Trail.
2. At 1.0 miles (1.6 km), continue left along the trail.
3. At 2.6 miles (4.1 km), reach the summit lookout.
4. Return the way you came.

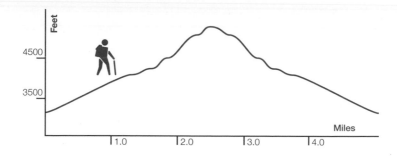

TRAILHEAD DRIVING DIRECTIONS

From Granite Falls, head east for 12 miles (19 kilometers) along Mountain Loop Highway. After crossing a bridge, turn right onto the gravel Forest Road 42. Proceed about 7 miles (11 kilometers) to the road-end trailhead parking area.

SKOOKUM BREWERY

Like many homebrewers, Ron Walcher dreamed of opening his own brewery. He's one of the few who've made it a reality. Starting out as a rustic "brewery in the woods," Skookum Brewery gained a following through word of mouth in the Arlington area. Before long, the brewery had to expand to keep up with demand, and opened its current taproom in 2012. Just like the Chinook name suggests, Skookum's brews are "big, bold, strong."

TRAIL CONTACT INFORMATION
Mount Baker-Snoqualmie National Forest
Verlot Public Service Center
33515 Mtn. Loop Hwy.
Granite Falls, WA 98252
+1 360-691-7791
www.fs.usda.gov

ACCOMMODATIONS
Quality Inn Arlington
5200 172nd St. NE
Arlington, WA 98223
+1 360-403-7222
www.choicehotels.com
Affordable rooms located one mile
from Skookum Brewery.

BREWERY/RESTAURANT
Skookum Brewery
17925 59th Ave. NE
Arlington, WA 98223
+1 360-403-7094
www.skookumbrewery.com
Rotating food trucks available on-site.

TOURIST ATTRACTIONS INFO
Snohomish County Tourism
East Visitor Information Center
1301 First St.
Snohomish, WA 98290
+1 360-862-9609
www.snohomish.org

PINNACLE PEAK LOOKOUT

TAKE A SHORT, STEEP TREK TO A FORMER FIRE LOOKOUT SITE WHERE A NEWLY-CONSTRUCTED REPLICA NOW STANDS.

STARTING POINT

CAL MAGNUSSON TRAIL

DESTINATION

PINNACLE PEAK LOOKOUT

BEER

COLE STREET CASCADIAN RYE

DIFFICULTY

HIKING

DURATION OF THE HIKE

1-2 HOURS
2.4 MILES (3.9KM)

MAP

PINNACLE PEAK TRAIL MAP
WWW.KINGCOUNTY.GOV

PASS NEEDED

NONE

ELEVATION GAIN

1,000 FEET (305M)

ALCOHOL 7.7% CONTENT

CASCADIAN DARK ALE

  BLACK

CHAR, SPICE, PINE

 RESIN, ROAST, RYE SPICE

BITTERNESS   **SWEETNESS**

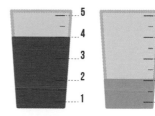

5	5
4	4
3	3
2	2
1	1

DESCRIPTION OF THE ROUTE

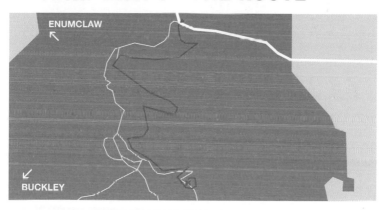

ENUMCLAW

BUCKLEY

One mile south of Enumclaw, an 1,800-foot (549 meter) volcanic cone rises from the White River valley. Known by many names, this geological knob is protected by 375-acre (151 hectare) Pinnacle Peak Park — a place of historical interest and natural beauty just outside the city.

Locals named the knob "Mount Pete" after an early 1900s Enumclaw settler. Over the years, "Pete" became "Peak", and locals still refer to the place as Mount Peak. Around 1929, a 30-foot (9 meter) fire lookout tower was constructed near the top of the mountain, officially called Pinnacle Peak Lookout. Various lookout towers were located atop Pinnacle Peak in the following years, including an Aircraft Warning Station during World War II. In 1966, the Pinnacle Peak Lookout was decommissioned and removed from the site — ending 37 years of fire detection.

Pinnacle Peak remained lookout-free for over 50 years. Popular hiking trails led to the top, but there wasn't much to see at the former lookout site besides old concrete footings and overgrown views. Then, in 2016, a local volunteer group was formed with the goal of rebuilding a lookout atop Pinnacle Peak. The Mt. Peak Historical Fire Lookout Association raised funds through government grants and private donations, partnering with King County Parks to construct a replica of Pinnacle Peak's 1966 lookout tower.

Completed in 2021, the new Pinnacle Peak Lookout brings back a historic landmark — and improved views — to the top of Pinnacle Peak. Various trails lead to the top. Perhaps the most popular is the Cal Magnusson Trail, named after a local mountaineer. This steep little trail climbs 1,000 feet (305 meters) in just over a mile to the top of Pinnacle Peak.

From the trailhead, begin your steady ascent through the ancient forest. Big cedar and Douglas fir trees line the trail, along with maidenhair and sword fern. Watch your footing, especially on the way down, as there are lots of roots and rocks to navigate. The trail can also be extremely slippery when wet! Trekking poles are helpful for the descent.

After turning left onto an old road at 0.9 miles, the trail opens up considerably. Continue climbing past walls of columnar basalt. Formed by the rapid cooling of lava, these honeycomb-shaped rocks are fairly common in the volcanic Cascades.

You'll be at the base of the tower in no time. Climb another 25 feet (7.5 meters) up to the viewing platform, where nice views of the valley and Cascade foothills await. Mount Rainier might even make an appearance — though we can neither confirm nor deny its visibility from the lookout. We visited during a foggy February day when the lookout was completely socked in. Trip reporters say that the best view of Rainier is from a side trail southeast of the lookout.

For an alternate route, the south trailhead is located at SE Mud Mountain Road and SE 481 Street. A parking lot built here in 2017 offers restrooms and can accommodate additional vehicles. Hiking from the southern trailhead makes for a longer, gentler approach to Pinnacle Peak.

TURN BY TURN DIRECTIONS

1. Take the Cal Magnusson Trail from the signed trailhead.
2. At 0.9 miles (1.4 km), turn left onto the wide trail.
3. At 1.1 miles (1.8 km), reach the base of the lookout and ascend the tower. Return the way you came.

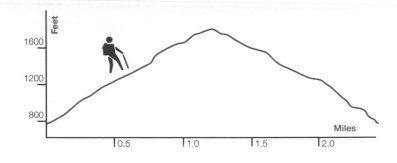

TRAILHEAD DRIVING DIRECTIONS

From Highway 167 in Puyallup, take Highway 410 east for 14.8 miles (23.8 kilometers) towards Enumclaw. Turn right onto SE 456th St/Warner Avenue and continue for 1.2 miles (1.9 kilometers). Then turn right onto 276th Avenue SE and continue 0.9 miles (1.4 kilometers) to the trailhead at the corner of 276th Avenue SE and SE 472nd Street. Limited shoulder parking is available.

COLE STREET BREWERY

Less than a 10-minute drive from Pinnacle Peak Lookout trailhead, Cole Street Brewery is an ideal stop for a post-hike beer. Enumclaw's first craft brewery, Cole Street offers a space for locals and visitors to relax and enjoy a beer in a charming downtown location. In the summer, the brewery's production facility opens an outdoor patio space with unobstructed views of Mt. Rainier. With events like comedy nights, cribbage tournaments, and weekly trivia, Cole Street is a hub for Enumclaw activity.

TRAIL CONTACT INFORMATION
King County Parks
+1 206-477-4527
parksinfo@kingcounty.gov
www.kingcounty.gov/services/parks-recreation/parks.aspx

BREWERY
Cole Street Brewery
1627 Cole St
Enumclaw, WA 98022
+1 253-951-6656
www.colestreetbrew.com

RESTAURANT
The Historic Mint Restaurant & Alehouse
1608 Cole St.
Enumclaw, WA 98022
+1 360-284-2517
www.thehistoricmint.com
Originally established in 1906 and reopened in 2013, The Mint offers a full menu of sandwiches, burgers, American entrees, and 28 beers on tap. Family-friendly and located just steps from Cole Street Brewery.

TOURIST ATTRACTIONS INFO
Enumclaw Area Chamber of Commerce
1421 Cole St.
Enumclaw, WA 98022
+1 360-825-7666
www.visitenumclaw.com

POINT DEFIANCE SPINE TRAIL

EXPLORE THE HEART OF TACOMA'S POINT DEFIANCE PARK TO DISCOVER OLD-GROWTH FOREST, WILDLIFE, AND VIEWS OUT TO THE WATERS OF THE TACOMA NARROWS.

STARTING POINT	DESTINATION
RHODODENDRON GARDEN PARKING FOR THE SPINE TRAIL	**GIG HARBOR VIEWPOINT**

BEER	DIFFICULTY
E9 TACOMA BREW	**WALKING**

MAP	DURATION OF THE HIKE
LOOK UP WWW.METROPARKSTACOMA.ORG	**1-2 HOURS 2.6 MILES** (4.2KM)

PASS NEEDED	ELEVATION GAIN
NONE	**MINIMAL**

KÖLSCH

PALE GOLD

CRACKER,
DRIED FLOWERS

CRACKED MALT,
CRACKER, HERBAL

BITTERNESS	SWEETNESS

DESCRIPTION OF THE ROUTE

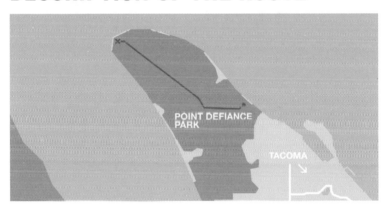

Point Defiance Park might be an urban green-space, but its 760 acres are home to a number of animals and crisscrossed by miles of hiking trails. "Tacoma's Great Pride," as it was dubbed in an 1892 newspaper headline, Point Defiance Park contains multiple attractions outside of hiking. Perhaps most recognized is Point Defiance Zoo and Aquarium, but the grounds also contain several gardens and a promenade along the beach.

The 1.3 mile (2 kilometer) long Spine Trail cuts a straight path through the middle of the park, exploring its deep wooded core. A wide gravel-surfaced trail, the Spine trail is rolling, with only two sections of significant changes in grade. With old growth conifers and abundant moss, the trail offers hikers plenty of green year-round.

Start from the parking for the Rhododendron Gardens along Five Mile Road. The Spine Trail begins here, marked on all trail signs as a light blue circle. The first 200 feet (60 meters) of trail run through the eastern edge of the Rhododendron Gardens. These gardens have 198 cultivated varieties of Washington's state flower, grown in a wild setting. During the spring and summer when the garden is in bloom, it's worth taking a stroll through.

The trail frequently crosses two additional main trails in the area, the Outside Loop and the Inside Loop. Each intersection is well signed, but the Spine Trail's straight bisection of the park makes it easy enough without signage — when in doubt, simply continue straight. After rain, watch out for standing water on the trail, or muddy sections that may occur. Despite this occasional issue, the trail is well maintained.

The residents of the Point Defiance Zoo aren't the only animals in the park, and on quiet days you might encounter one of the many wild creatures that seek a home in this wooded oasis. Elusive and shy red foxes have been spotted in the park, but you're much more likely to come across a mule deer grazing on the side of the path. For unfortunate reasons, you're almost guaranteed to see one or more raccoons (we spotted ten during a single visit). Despite the number of signs warning against feeding wildlife, raccoons in the area have become accustomed to human handouts. Though they may look friendly, please remember that these are wild animals and can become aggressive if they feel threatened.

At 1.3 miles (2 kilometers), you'll reach the Gig Harbor Viewpoint. Though partially obstructed by a fence that guards against the dangerous drop of steep 200-foot (60 meter) sea cliffs, the houses of Gig Harbor are visible, and you might see bald eagles soaring above the waves, or catch sight of a whale out in the channel. Refill your water bottle at the picnic structure, and head back the way you came.

Once you return to your vehicle, an optional side trip to Owen Beach is an easy add-on. Continue on Five Mile Road, turning right at the Y for Owen Beach parking lot. From here, you can explore the shores of the beach, scramble over driftwood, and watch the ferries as they navigate the Narrows.

TURN BY TURN DIRECTIONS

1. About 200 feet (60 m) from the parking lot, continue straight at an intersection with the Outside Loop Trail.
2. At 0.1 miles (0.16 km), continue straight at an intersection with the Inner Loop Trail.
3. At 0.2 miles (0.3 km), continue straight at an intersection.
4. At 0.3 miles (0.5 km), continue straight at an intersection.
5. At just over 0.3 miles (0.5 km), cross Five Mile Road to continue straight.
6. At 0.5 miles (0.8 km), cross Five Mile Road to continue straight.
7. At 0.6 miles (0.9 km), continue straight at an intersection with the Outside Loop Trail.
8. At just over 0.6 miles (0.9 km), continue straight at an intersection with an unnamed trail.
9. At 0.8 miles (1.2 km), continue straight as the trail crosses the Inside Loop Trail.
10. At just over 0.8 miles (1.2 km), continue straight at an intersection.
11. At 1.1 miles (1.7 km), continue straight as the trail crosses the Inside Loop Trail.
12. Arrive at the Gig Harbor Viewpoint at 1.3 miles (2 km).
13. Return the way you came.

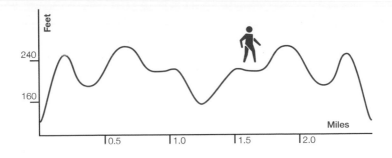

TRAILHEAD DRIVING DIRECTIONS

On I-5 South, take Exit 132 (Highway 16 West). Exit at 6th Avenue (Exit 3) and turn left. Take the next right onto Pearl Street. Follow Pearl Street into Point Defiance Park.

E9 BREWING CO.

Tacoma's first craft brewery, E9 started in 1995 as a humble brewery attached to neighborhood tavern Engine House 9. Located in a restored firehouse, it is still a great option for a family-friendly dining experience. Under current ownership since 2011, the brewery has diversified with a highly-respected barrel program featuring sours and farmhouse ales. Craft beer lovers should visit the production facility in Tacoma's Brewery District to experience E9 Pizza and Beer Works. Visiting both locations showcases the history and current innovations of this long-loved brand.

TRAIL CONTACT INFORMATION
Metro Parks Tacoma
4702 S 19th St.
Tacoma, WA 98405
+1 253-305-1000
www.metroparkstacoma.org/
point-defiance-park

RESTAURANT
E9 Firehouse and Gastropub
611 N Pine St.
Tacoma WA, 98406
+1 253 272 3435
www.ehouse9.com
Family-friendly restaurant in a historic firehouse. The original brewery location since 1995.

TOURIST ATTRACTIONS INFO
Travel Tacoma
1516 Commerce St
Tacoma, WA 98402
+1 253-284-3254
www.traveltacoma.com

BREWERY
E9 Brewing Co.
2506 Fawcett Ave.
Tacoma, WA 98402
+1 253 383 7707
www.e9brewingco.com
Production facility and taproom serving delicious pizza and craft beers, located in Tacoma's Brewery District. Ages 21+ only.

ACCOMMODATIONS
Hotel Murano
1320 Broadway
Tacoma, WA 98402
253-238-8000
www.hotelmuranotacoma.com
Modern glass-art-inspired hotel conveniently located downtown near several breweries.

RAILROAD GRADE

THIS STEADY GRADE ALONG THE EDGE OF A GLACIAL MORAINE LEADS TO THE TERMINUS OF EASTON GLACIER, WHERE IT BECOMES A STEEP CLIMBER'S ROUTE FOR SUMMITING 10,781-FOOT MOUNT BAKER.

STARTING POINT	DESTINATION
PARK BUTTE TRAILHEAD	**RAILROAD GRADE**
BEER	DIFFICULTY
BIRDSVIEW 7BBL IPA	**MOUNTAIN** HIKING 
MAP	DURATION OF THE HIKE
GREEN TRAILS 45 HAMILTON	**4 HOURS 7 MILES** (11.2KM)
PASS NEEDED	ELEVATION GAIN
NORTHWEST FOREST PASS	**2,000 FEET** (609M)

ALCOHOL 7% CONTENT

INDIA PALE ALE

UNFILTERED AMBER

CITRUS, GRASSY, PINE

BISCUITY, PINE, ORANGE

BIRDSVIEW
Brewing Company

BITTERNESS	SWEETNESS
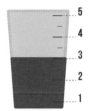	

DESCRIPTION OF THE ROUTE

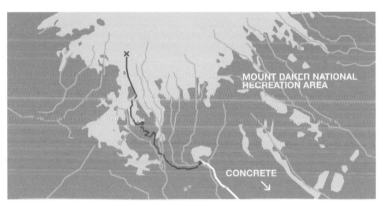

MOUNT BAKER NATIONAL RECREATION AREA

CONCRETE

You'll find few trails more memorable than Railroad Grade on Mount Baker's southside. One of just a few Mount Baker summit routes, Railroad Grade approaches Easton Glacier by way of an exposed, rocky path between alpine meadows and a cavernous creekbed, with mountain views all around.

First, a word of warning. Those with a significant fear of heights may be better off spending their day at the brewery, or hiking nearby trails like the Park Butte and the Scott Paul Trails. Railroad Grade is potentially dangerous, and all hikers should proceed with caution. That said, it's worth the effort.

Begin along the well-maintained Park Butte Trail, strolling past picnic tables and crossing a permanent bridge over Sulphur Creek into colorful Schreibers Meadow. Lined with heather and wildflowers in early summer, the trail becomes a boardwalk here before returning to dirt. This first mile is easy and passes in and out of forest, offering occasional glimpses of Mount Baker, whose indigenous name is Koma Kulshan: the "Great White Watcher." Cross the seasonal bridge over glacier-fed Rocky Creek, or carefully ford if the bridge is absent.

After approximately 2 miles (3.2 kilometers), the forest opens up to yet another wildflower-strewn meadow, Morovitz. At 2.4 miles (3.8 kilometers), reach the Park Butte/Railroad Grade junction. Turn right and head up the stone steps. You'll pass some backcountry campsites along the way and a signed "trail to water," which leads to a reflective tarn. At approximately 3 miles (4.8 kilometers), reach Railroad Grade.

Named for its steady ascent toward Easton Glacier, Railroad Grade has as much in common with train tracks as Mount Baker does with breadmaking. Don't waste your time searching for railroad spikes here. Instead, peer over the precipitous edge at Rocky Creek below, then begin the steady climb toward Easton Glacier.

Depending on snow levels, you may be able to hike half a mile or more up the grade. Visit during late summer and early fall for the best trail conditions. At 3.5 miles (5.6 kilometers), High Camp is a good place to turn around. The trail deteriorates from here, becoming a steep climber's path.

Back at the Park Butte/Railroad Grade junction, consider the trek up to Park Butte Lookout. It's another 1.3 miles (2 kilometers) from here with significant elevation gain, so you should only proceed if you have the time and energy to do so. But what a reward. This historic 1930s fire lookout stands at 5,450 feet (1,161 meters) with classic views over the Nooksack Valley, the Mount Baker Wilderness, and of course Koma Kulshan itself.

TURN BY TURN DIRECTIONS

1. Leave the parking area on the signed Park Butte Trail.
2. At 1.8 miles (2.8 km), turn left at the Scott Paul Trail junction.
3. At 2.4 miles (3.8 km), turn right to ascend the stone steps.
4. At 3 miles (4.8 km), reach Railroad Grade.
   Proceed with caution towards Mount Baker.
5. At 3.5 miles (5.6 km), reach High Camp.
   Turn around here and return the way you came.

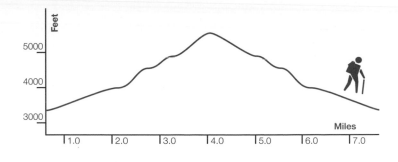

TRAILHEAD DRIVING DIRECTIONS

From Burlington (Exit 230 on I-5), head east on the North Cascades Highway (SR-20) for 23 miles (37 kilometers). After Milepost 82, turn left onto Baker Lake Road. Continue 12.3 miles (19 kilometers) to FR 12. Turn left on FR 12, continuing 3.7 miles (5.9 kilometers) to FR 13. Turn right on FR 13 and proceed 5.3 miles (8 kilometers) to the trailhead parking area.

BIRDSVIEW BREWING

Located on North Cascades Highway near the bottom of Baker Lake Road, Birdsview Brewing is a most welcome and convenient post-hike stop. The family-owned, octagon-shaped brewery offers small batch brews and pub food, with mountain views to boot. Outside, Birdsview's beer garden is a pastoral place to relax on sunny days. Get the sample tray to try a little bit of everything.

TRAIL CONTACT INFORMATION
Mt. Baker Ranger District Office
810 State Route 20
Sedro-Woolley, WA 98284
+1 360-856-5700
www.fs.usda.gov

ACCOMMODATIONS
Rasar State Park
38730 Cape Horn Rd.
Concrete, WA 98237
+1 360-826-3942
www.parks.state.wa.us/571/rasar
Located behind Birdsview Brewing on the Skagit River, this scenic park offers a variety of campsites and cabins for overnight stays.

BREWERY/RESTAURANT
Birdsview Brewing
38302 State Route 20
Concrete, WA 98237
+1 360-826-3406
www.birdsviewbrewingcompany.com
Menu offers burgers, sandwiches, salads, and more.

TOURIST ATTRACTIONS INFO
North Cascades Park and
Forest Information Center
810 State Route 20
Sedro-Woolley, WA 98284
+1 360-854-7200
www.nps.gov
This station is operated jointly with the Mt. Baker Ranger District Office (see trail contact information) and North Cascades Institute.

ROCK TRAIL

DESCEND A SERIES OF STAIRS ALONG SANDSTONE CLIFFS
AND AROUND MOSS-COVERED BOULDERS BEFORE TAKING A BREATHER
AT A LOST LAKE OVERLOOK.

STARTING POINT	DESTINATION
CYRUS GATES OVERLOOK (ROCK TRAIL TRAILHEAD)	**LOST LAKE**
BEER	DIFFICULTY
KULSHAN RUSSIAN IMPERIAL STOUT	**HIKING**
MAP	DURATION OF THE HIKE
CHUCKANUT MOUNTAIN RECREATION MAP	**2-3 HOURS 4 MILES** (6.4KM)
PASS NEEDED	ELEVATION GAIN
DISCOVER PASS	**700 FEET** (213M)

ALCOHOL CONTENT 9%

RUSSIAN IMPERIAL STOUT

MIDNIGHT BLACK

SMOKE, COFFEE

ROAST, CHOCOLATE, DARK FRUIT

BITTERNESS	SWEETNESS

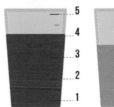

DESCRIPTION OF THE ROUTE

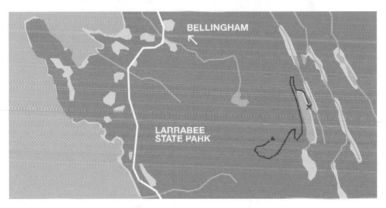

A playground for the budding geologist in all of us, Larrabee State Park's Rock Trail gets up close to the sandstone cliffs that make up the Chuckanut range. Add in a series of staircases to descend several hundred feet and you might find yourself huffing and puffing on the way back up. At the bottom, meet up with the South Lost Lake connector and take a short forest stroll to the shores of long and narrow Lost Lake. A jewel of the Chuckanut Mountains, Rock Trail is the ideal year-round hike.

Begin at the Cyrus Gates Overlook, where you can organize your daypack and stretch while gazing out at a view of the San Juan Islands. An interpretive sign at the viewpoint will help you identify the islands out in Chuckanut Bay below. The trail begins at the south end of the parking lot, heading immediately under tree cover. In 0.1 miles (0.16 kilometers), come to the beginning of the Rock Trail.

The majority of this trail's 100 or so stairs happen within the first stretch, aiding in the steep loss of elevation — and eventual gain on the way back up! When you reach the bottom of the stairs, you'll see where the trail gets its name: sandstone cliffs rise above, pocked with cubbyholes and delicate maidenhair ferns clinging to the surface.

The trail rolls and switchbacks, skirting and passing between formidable mossy erratics left behind by glacial flow. At 0.8 miles (1.2 kilometers), you'll find one boulder complete with a cave — if you packed a flashlight, explore inside for a bit of spelunking. After three more staircases and switchbacks each, the trail will level out until at 1.2 miles (1.9 kilometers) it converges on the South Lost Lake Trail. Turn left and head to the north end of Lost Lake.

The trail passes through marshy bits, skunk cabbage growing on either side. To the left of the trail, you'll come across a massive root system from a downed tree that lost its purchase in the soft, wet earth near the lake. Once you reach the shore, head uphill on a rooty foot trail surrounded by salal bushes. At the top of the hill, you'll find the perfect lunch spot — a bald rock shelf overlooking the dark green waters of Lost Lake. Stop for lunch or a snack before returning the way you came.

Retracing your path, what was an easy downhill hike turns into a bit of a work-out. Take your time and allow water breaks when needed between staircases. But each stair that helps hikers explore this unique corner of the Chuckanuts is thanks to one of the hundreds of volunteers who logged more than 2,000 hours to build this trail. Cheers to that!

TURN BY TURN DIRECTIONS

1. Head south on the Connector Trail at the end of Cyrus Gates Overlook parking lot.
2. At 0.15 miles (241 m), come to the Rock Trail trailhead and continue straight.
3. At 1.2 miles (1.9 km), the Rock Trail meets up with the South Lost Lake Trail; turn left.
4. At 1.6 miles (2.5 km), turn right to continue on East Lost Lake Trail.
5. At 1.9 miles (3 km), turn left uphill on the footpath.
6. At 2.0 miles (3.2 km), arrive at Lost Lake viewpoint.
7. Return on the same route to Cyrus Gates Overlook parking lot.

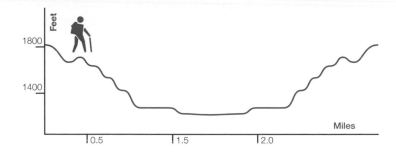

TRAILHEAD DRIVING DIRECTIONS

From Chuckanut Drive (SR-11) turn onto HiLine Road; a sign indicates Cleator Road. At the end of the paved road section, continue onto the gravel Cleator Road. Follow Cleator Road for 3.5 miles (5.6 kilometers) to the parking lot at Cyrus Gates Overlook.

KULSHAN FLAGSHIP & K2

Founded in 2012, Kulshan is one of Whatcom County's fastest growing breweries. This award-winning brewery opened a second location in 2015, "K2," equipped with a 30-barrel brewhouse to meet demands for its brews. Its continued popularity led to the opening of Trackside, a seasonal beer garden in Bellingham's evolving downtown waterfront. Committed to sustainability with a staff full of outdoor enthusiasts, Kulshan takes its name from the indigenous name for nearby Mount Du
Dukei. Kulshan's taphouses host live music and feature a rotating caravan of local food trucks.

TRAIL CONTACT INFORMATION
Larrabee State Park
245 Chuckanut Dr.
Bellingham, WA 98229
+1 360-676-2093
www.parks.state.wa.us/536/Larrabee

ACCOMMODATIONS
Fairhaven Village Inn
1200 10th St.
Bellingham, WA 98225
+1 877-733-1100
www.fairhavenvillageinn.com
Charming historic hotel with water views.

BREWERY/RESTAURANT
Kulshan Flagship
2238 James St
Bellingham, WA 98225
+1 360-389-5348

"K2"
1538 Kentucky Street
Bellingham, WA 98229
www.kulshanbrewery.com

TOURIST ATTRACTIONS INFO
Bellingham Whatcom County Tourism
904 Potter St
Bellingham, WA 98225
+1 800-487-2032
www.bellingham.org

SAINT EDWARD
STATE PARK LOOP

EXPLORE THE HISTORIC FORMER GROUNDS OF A CATHOLIC SEMINARY,
WITH A HIKE DOWN TO THE SHORE OF LAKE WASHINGTON.

STARTING POINT	DESTINATION
SAINT EDWARD MAIN PARKING LOT	**LAKE** WASHINGTON
BEER	DIFFICULTY
CAIRN SEAPLANE IPA	**WALKING**
MAP	DURATION OF THE HIKE
SAINT EDWARD STATE PARK	(LOOP) **1 HOUR** **2 MILES** (3.2KM)
PASS NEEDED	ELEVATION GAIN
DISCOVER PASS	**358 FEET** (109M)

INDIA PALE ALE

 CLEAN DEEP GOLD

 MALT, GRAPEFRUIT

PINE, CITRUS, MANGO

BITTERNESS   **SWEETNESS**

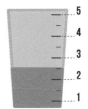

DESCRIPTION OF THE ROUTE

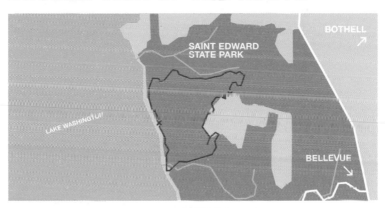

Once the hallowed grounds of a Catholic seminary, Saint Edward State Park is 316 acres of forested hillside and undeveloped lakeshore, crisscrossed by hiking trails. The regal brick seminary building still stands at the heart of the park as a backdrop for family picnics, leisurely walks, and the occasional cricket match.

Completed in 1930 as the final major project of Bishop O'Dea of the Seattle Catholic Archdiocese, Saint Edward Seminary was created as a boys' school and an institution to train Catholic priests. The school closed in 1976, and the land was formally dedicated as a state park in 1978. In 2021, after years of restoration, the Seminary building reopened as the Lodge at St. Edward State Park.

From the main parking lot, make your way around the seminary building to find a paved walkway. Across the lawn from the paved roundabout, you'll find the Perimeter Trail. A dirt path open to hikers and bikers alike, the Perimeter Trail circumnavigates the Great Lawn — a large grassy field created by seminary students. Head south on the trail to meet up with the Grotto Trail. Like the Great Lawn, many of the park's trails were constructed by seminarians.

At 0.2 miles (0.3 kilometers), you'll come to the Grotto that gives this part of trail system its name. Take the steps down to check it out. A stone alcove built by seminarians, the Grotto is set back into the hillside, shaded by trees and ferns. This quiet garden once offered a place for prayer and meditation, and now is a picturesque highlight. Back on the Perimeter Trail, you'll come to the trailhead for the Grotto Trail at 0.3 miles (0.5 kilometers).

The steepest trail in Saint Edward, The Grotto Trail is also one of the most beautiful. Narrow and rocky, the dirt trail follows the edge of a lush gully. Bigleaf maples shade the trail, the filtered sunlight taking on a green hue. Licorice ferns grow from the mossy trunks of trees, and sword ferns sprawl across the forest floor.

At 0.6 miles (0.9 kilometers), the Grotto Trail veers to the right and turns into the Beach Trail. The Beach Trail traverses the park's 3,000 feet (914 meters) of beach along Lake Washington. The water is shallow enough for wading, or find a sunny spot to watch the boating traffic on the lake. This area is popular with families, so you shouldn't expect silence beside the lake. Back on the trail, you'll wander through cottonwood trees and blackberry bushes until you reach the North Trail at 1.1 miles (1.7 kilometers).

Also quite steep, the North Trail climbs up the far side of the park's boundary. Watch for nettles along the trail, and keep climbing until you reach the upper parking lot at 1.7 miles (2.7 kilometers). Cross the parking lot and meet back up with the Perimeter Trail as it bisects the Native Plant Garden in the middle of the parking lot. Stay on the Perimeter Trail to close the loop at 2.0 miles (3.2 kilometers) and complete your hike.

TURN BY TURN DIRECTIONS

1. From the main parking lot, head around the side of the seminary building, across the Great Lawn from the roundabout.
2. Start on the Perimeter Trail at its intersection with the Seminary Trail. Head south.
3. At 0.3 miles (0.5 km), turn right onto the Grotto Trail at the trailhead.
4. At 0.6 miles (0.9 km), turn right onto the Beach Trail.
5. At 1.1 miles (1.7 km), turn right onto the North Trail.
6. At 1.7 miles (2.7 km), continue straight through the upper parking lot to the Perimeter Trail.
7. At 2.0 miles (3.2 km), close the loop and head back to the main parking lot.

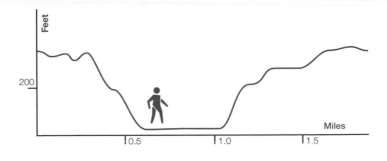

TRAILHEAD DRIVING DIRECTIONS

From Bothell Highway (522) turn South onto 68th Avenue. 68th Avenue will turn into Juanita Drive. Turn right onto NE 145th Street at the entrance to St. Edward State Park. Keep right to stay on 145th. Continue straight to the main parking lot by the swimming pool.

CAIRN BREWING

Located on the northern shore of Lake Washington, Cairn Brewing is the only true production brewery in Kenmore. Since May 2016, Cairn has served the Northshore neighborhood with a wide selection of beer styles and a focus on community. The large (dog-friendly!) open taproom blends into the brewing space, and pints are served directly from brite tanks. Have a seat at one of the large picnic tables, or find a sunny spot in the beer garden and enjoy one of their 18 rotating beers on tap. Cairn is also the only brewery where one of the authors of this guide might pour you a pint!

TRAIL CONTACT INFORMATION
Saint Edward State Park
14445 Juanita Dr. N.E.
Kenmore, WA 98028
+1 425-823-2992
www.parks.state.wa.us/577/saint-edward

RESTAURANT
HodgePodge Cafe
6016 Bothell Way NE Ste. J
Kenmore, WA 98028
+1 425-949-8802
www.thehodgepodgecate.com
Comfort food that can be ordered in at
Cairn Brewery!

TOURIST ATTRACTIONS INFO
Explore Bothell
18415 101st Ave. NE
Bothell, WA 98011
+1 425-486-3256
www.explorebothell.com

BREWERY
Cairn Brewing
7204 NE 175th St. Bldg. A
Kenmore, WA 98028
+1 425 949 5295
www.cairnbrewing.com

ACCOMMODATIONS
McMenamins Anderson School Hotel
18607 Bothell Way NE
Bothell, WA 98011
+1 425-368-5661
www.mcmenamins.com/andersonschool

SKYLINE LOOP

AMONG THE MOST ICONIC AND TRODDEN TRAILS IN WASHINGTON, THE SKYLINE TRAIL AT MOUNT RAINIER NATIONAL PARK SHOWCASES WILDFLOWERS, WATERFALLS, GLACIERS, AND PANORAMIC MOUNTAIN VIEWS GALORE.

STARTING POINT	DESTINATION
HENRY M. JACKSON VISITOR CENTER	**PANORAMA POINT AND UPPER SKYLINE TRAIL**
BEER	DIFFICULTY
PACKWOOD BREWING **TREE LINE**	**HIKING**
MAP	DURATION OF THE HIKE
GREEN TRAILS PARADISE NO. 270S, MOUNT RAINIER NATIONAL PARK: LOOK UP WWW.NPS.GOV	(LOOP) **3-5 HOURS** **5.5 MILES** (8.8KM)
PASS NEEDED	ELEVATION GAIN
NATIONAL PARKS PASS	**1,700 FEET** (518M)

INDIA PALE ALE

GOLDEN ORANGE

LEMON ZEST,
TROPICAL FRUIT

PINEY, GRAPEFRUIT
RIND, MANGO

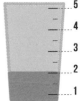

BITTERNESS	SWEETNESS
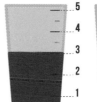	

DESCRIPTION OF THE ROUTE

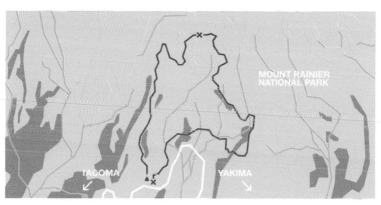

Summer hiking at Paradise is an unforgettable experience, and Skyline Trail is the cream of the crop. This near-perfect non-repeating loop offers almost everything a hiker could ask for. Massive mountain views? Wildlife scurrying about? Glaciers? Wildflowers too numerous to name? All present and accounted for. But Paradise is no secret, and Skyline Trail can be overrun with summer crowds. Go early or visit on a weekday if possible. Summer weekends are a circus.

Grab a trail map from the Jackson Visitor Center before heading out. The network of trails at Paradise can be confusing, and you don't want to end up Paradise Lost! Climb the stone steps north towards Mount Rainier. If the mountain is out, you'll know it: Rainier towers 9,000 feet (2,741 meters) overhead. Washington's tallest peak, Mount Rainier tops out at 14,410 feet (4,392 meters). On a clear day, it will knock your hiking socks off from the parking lot.

Follow the Skyline Trail signs to make your way around the loop.

Hiking in either direction is pleasant; we suggest going clockwise for big views from the get-go. Climb steeply to start, watching for wildflowers along the way. Mid-July through early August is usually the best time for wildflower-spotting at Paradise, with hundreds of varieties to identify. Rainier's subalpine meadows are home to snow-white Avalanche Lily, yellow Mountain Monkeyflower, purple Cascade Aster, and Pink Mountain Heather — to name just a few.

After a mile (1.6 kilometers) of steady climbing, reach the Glacier Vista junction. This is a popular photo-op spot, and a worthy detour from the main trail. Glacier Vista's 6,300-foot (1.6 meter) overlook is the closest you'll get to the Nisqually Glacier on this trail. Of Rainier's 27 major glaciers, Nisqually is the easiest to access — and therefore the most visited. Waterfalls stream from neighboring Wilson Glacier. If you're not yet convinced that this is Paradise, continue climbing.

In another half mile (0.8 kilometers), the trail mellows out for a quarter mile (0,4 kilometers) before reaching Panorama Point. If ever there was an aptly-named overlook, this is it. Facing south, Panorama Point stands at nearly 7,000 feet (2,133 meters) with expansive mountain views. The "Chain of Volcanoes" visible from here on a clear day includes Mount Adams, Mount Hood, and Mount St. Helens. In the foreground, the Tatoosh Range and Paradise Valley are laid out before you.

From Panorama Point, take the Upper Skyline Trail to reach 7,000 feet (2,137 meters). This detour off the main route avoids a potentially dangerous snowfield crossing. Descend from this high point to loop back through more meadows, streams, and waterfalls to the Paradise parking lot. Along the way, you may encounter Rainier's fearless population of hoary marmots running amok in the meadows or basking in
the sun on a high rock. Listen for their tell-tale whistle as you walk.

On the way back, two short waterfall detours are absolutely worth your time. The first is Sluiskin Falls at 3.7 miles (5.9 kilometers), just beyond the Stevens Van Trump Historic Monument. This 155-foot falls is arguably the most spectacular at Paradise. Further along, Myrtle Falls is accessed by a short, steep spur right around the 5-mile (8 kilometer) mark. Hike down for an iconic Rainier shot: the mountain above and falls below, a picture-perfect snapshot of Paradise.

TURN BY TURN DIRECTIONS

1. Begin by heading north from Jackson Visitor Center on the Skyline Trail.
2. At 0.1 miles (0.16 km), reach a 4-way junction. Continue north on the Skyline Trail.
3. Immediately come to a second junction with the Alta Vista Trail.
   Continue straight on the Skyline Trail.
4. At 0.6 miles (0.9 km), meet the Alta Vista Trail again.
   Continue straight on the Skyline Trail.
5. At 0.9 miles (1.4 km), come to another junction and stay straight on the Skyline Trail.
6. At 1 mile (1.6 km), meet the Glacier Vista Trail. Continue straight on the Skyline Trail.
7. At 1.5 miles (2.4 km), come to a junction and continue straight on the Skyline Trail.
8. At 1.8 miles (2.8 km), reach Panorama Point. Head north, and left at
   the junction for the Upper Skyline Trail.
9. At 2 miles (3.2 km), reach a 4-way junction. Turn right for the Upper Skyline Trail.
10. At 2.5 miles (4 km), continue straight at a junction.
11. At 3 miles (4.8 km), continue straight on the Skyline Trail.
12. At 3.65 miles (5.8 km), continue straight on the Skyline Trail.
13. At 4.1 miles (6.5 km), continue straight on the Skyline Trail.
14. At 4.4 miles (7 km), continue straight on the Skyline Trail.
15. At 5 miles (8 km), continue straight on the Skyline Trail.
16. At 5.2 miles (8.3 km), continue straight on the Skyline Trail and follow
    it back to Jackson Visitor Center.

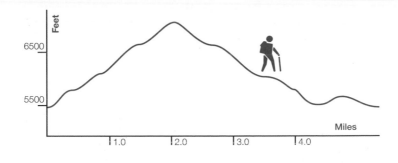

TRAILHEAD DRIVING DIRECTIONS

From Tacoma, drive east on SR 512 to SR 7. Head south on SR 7 to SR 706 in Elbe. Then go east on SR 706 through Ashford to the Nisqually Entrance of Mount Rainier National Park. Follow the signs to Paradise, where several large parking lots are available.

PACKWOOD BREWING CO.

Housed in a renovated 1930s-era general store, Packwood Brewing Company is now a brewpub offering hikers and skiers a place to warm up (or cool down) with a pint. The rustic lodge feel echos the "parkitecture" theme of nearby Mt. Rainier haunts such as Longmire and Paradise, and it comes as no surprise that Mount Rainier is visible from the beer garden. Packwood Brewing also hosts live music frequently and serves up tasty pub fare alongside six year-round brews and rotating seasonals. If it's in season, check out the Mountain Goat Coffee Porter — brewed in collaboration with a local Packwood Roastery.

TRAIL CONTACT INFORMATION
Mount Rainier National Park
55210 238th Ave. East
Ashford, WA 98304
+1 360-569-2211
www.nps.gov/mora

TOURIST ATTRACTIONS INFO
Henry M Jackson Memorial
Visitor Center at Paradise
+1 360-569-2211
www.nps.gov/mora/
planyourvisit/paradise.html

BREWERY
Packwood Brewing Co.
12298 US 12,
Packwood, WA 98361
+1 360-496-0845
www.packwoodbrewingco.com/home
The closest brewpub to Paradise!

ACCOMMODATIONS
National Park Inn at Longmire
47009 Paradise Rd. E
Ashford, WA 98304
+1 360-569-2275
www.mtrainierguestservices.com/
accommodations/national-park-inn
Cozy, rustic rooms in the Longmire
Historic District at Mount Rainier
National Park.

SNOQUALMIE FALLS TRAIL

TAKE A SHORT HIKE DOWN TO THE LOWER OBSERVATION DECK TO WITNESS THE EPIC SIGHT OF WASHINGTON'S ICONIC SNOQUALMIE FALLS.

STARTING POINT

SNOQUALMIE FALLS UPPER OBSERVATION DECK

DESTINATION

SNOQUALMIE FALLS LOWER OBSERVATION DECK

BEER

SNOQUALMIE
STEAM TRAIN PORTER

DIFFICULTY

WALKING

MAP

GREEN TRAILS MAP 205S RATTLESNAKE MOUNTAIN

DURATION OF THE HIKE

LESS THAN AN HOUR
1.4 MILES (2.2KM)

PASS NEEDED

FREE PARKING IN UPPER LOT (LOCATED ACROSS SKY BRIDGE). $7 PARKING IN MAIN LOT.

ELEVATION GAIN

250 FEET (76M)

PORTER

ALCOHOL CONTENT 5%

 BLACK

 ESPRESSO, COCOA POWDER, BAKER'S CHOCOLATE

ROASTED, CHAR, CHOCOLATE

STEAM TRAIN PORTER

SNOQUALMIE FALLS BREWING

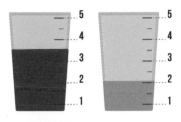

BITTERNESS	SWEETNESS
5 4 3 2 1	5 4 3 2 1

DESCRIPTION OF THE ROUTE

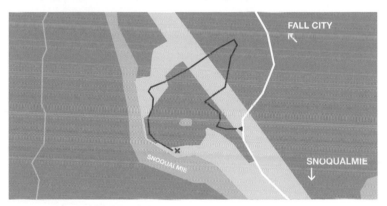

FALL CITY

SNOQUALMIE

SNOQUALMIE

Snoqualmie Falls is a thunderous site that brings in an annual count of over 1.5 million visitors. A curtain waterfall that plummets 200 foot (81 meters) from an abrupt cliff, Snoqualmie Falls is not only awe-inspiring — it helps to power many homes and businesses in the Puget Sound area. Don't just settle for the observation deck views of this beauty. Instead, hike down the short, moderately steep path to the lower observation deck to get a closer look.

Due to its massive size, the flow at the falls varies seasonally depending on the swell of the Snoqualmie River. In the summer the flow is low, yet still powerful enough to send mist up into the faces of excited visitors. In fall and early spring, the flow is high, sometimes creating enough spray to obscure the bottom half of the falls in an impenetrable mist. The Snoqualmie People who first inhabited this region believed that these mists carried prayers up to the Great Creator and viewed the falls as a sacred place.

From the upper parking lot, follow the signs towards the observation deck just a few yards past the gift shop. On weekends this area can be crowded, so a weekday visit is recommended. From the upper deck, gaze across the expanse to the nearly eye-level falls, with the historic Salish Lodge perched on the cliff's edge. Head back towards the gift shop, but turn left at the junction just before you reach it. This is the start of the Snoqualmie Falls trail, an easy interpretive trail with signs discussing native plants in the area, as well as detailing the history of the hydroelectric power plant.

Bigleaf maples and Douglas fir tower above the trail, while salal bushes and thimbleberry make up the understory. The path is wide, short, and well maintained, but surprisingly steep! The way down is easy enough, but you might huff and puff on the way back to the parking lot. When you get to the bottom, you'll come across Plant 2, built in 1910. It is not open to the public, but informational signs describe how the rushing of Snoqualmie Falls powers the massive turbines, producing renewable energy. At the base of the falls, entrenched 250 feet (76 meters) below the surface, is Plant 1, the world's first underground power plant.

Follow the trail as it turns to the left. Here, you'll walk along an enclosed boardwalk above the rushing waters of the Snoqualmie River. The flow of the river changes quickly, so this boardwalk was constructed to offer a lower viewing platform, while staying clear of the unpredictable and dangerous waters. At the end of the boardwalk, you'll be treated to a head-on view of Snoqualmie Falls' majesty. The roar, the mist, and the force of cascading waters is phenomenal.

Return using the same route back to the upper parking lot. The best way to avoid the crowds? Park at the lot near the lower observation deck and hike up to the upper platform, checking out the lower deck on the way back to your car.

TURN BY TURN DIRECTIONS

1. From the parking lot, walk up the stairs past the gift shop to the upper observation deck 0.1 miles (0.16 km) away.
2. Walk back towards the gift shop; turn left at the junction.
3. At 0.5 miles (0.8 km), turn left at the junction, turning left again at the next junction to head past Plant 2 towards the boardwalk.
4. Reach the lower observation deck at 0.7 miles (1.1 km).
5. Continue back the same way to the parking lot above.

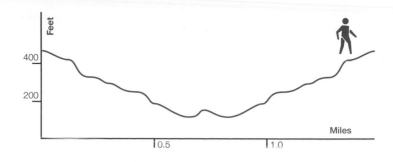

TRAILHEAD DRIVING DIRECTIONS

From Seattle, head east on I-90 to Exit 22 for Preston. Cross over the freeway and turn right onto SE Highpoint Way/Preston Fall City Road. Continue 1.5 miles (2.4 kilometers), coming to a traffic circle after crossing the Snoqualmie River. Turn right at the circle onto SR-202 East, continuing 4.0 miles (6.4 kilometers) until you reach the main parking area ($7 fee) on the right side of the road. For free parking, park across the street and walk across the sky bridge.

SNOQUALMIE FALLS BREWING

Snoqualmie Brewery is part of the foundation of Washington's current craft brewing scene — it opened its doors in 1997 just as microbreweries were taking a downturn. Now with craft beer once again thriving, the brewery's Wildcat IPA is seen as a catalyst for the current hop-forward NW IPA style. The cozy taproom, buzzing with the chatter of both locals and post-Falls tourists alike, is the best place to experience this time-honored Washington craft brewery.

TRAIL CONTACT INFORMATION
Puget Sound Energy
SE 69th Pl.
Snoqualmie, WA 98065
+1 425-831-4445
www.pse.com/inyourcommunity/
toursandrecreation/pages/snoqualmie-
tours.aspx

ACCOMMODATIONS
Salish Lodge
6501 Railroad Ave.
Snoqualmie, WA 98065
+1 425-888-2556
www.salishlodge.com
Perched over the Falls, this Lodge is a historic and beloved Seattle getaway.

BREWERY/RESTAURANT
Snoqualmie Brewery and Taproom
8032 Falls Ave. SE
Snoqualmie, WA 98065
+1 425-831-2357
www.fallsbrew.com
A Washington Craft Beer institution since 1997, with hearty pub grub.

TOURIST ATTRACTIONS INFO
Snoqualmie Valley
Chamber of Commerce
38767 SE River St.
Snoqualmie, WA 98065
+1 425-888-6362
www.snovalley.org

SUGARLOAF AND MOUNT ERIE

EARN ISLAND, SEA, AND LAKE VIEWS FROM SUGARLOAF AND
MOUNT ERIE, TWIN SUMMITS RISING OVER 1,000 FEET ABOVE SEA LEVEL
ON FIDALGO ISLAND.

STARTING POINT	DESTINATION
SUGARLOAF PARKING AREA	**MOUNT ERIE**

BEER	DIFFICULTY
ANACORTES IPA	**HIKING**

MAP	DURATION OF THE HIKE
ANACORTES COMMUNITY FOREST LANDS	**3 HOURS** **5 MILES** (8KM)

PASS NEEDED	ELEVATION GAIN
NONE	**1,200 FEET** (365M)

INDIA PALE ALE

 HAZY ORANGE

 GRAPEFRUIT, GRASS, PINE

MALT, CITRUS PEEL, PINE

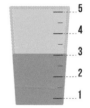

BITTERNESS   SWEETNESS

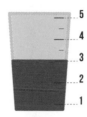

5
4
3
2
1

5
4
3
2
1

DESCRIPTION OF THE ROUTE

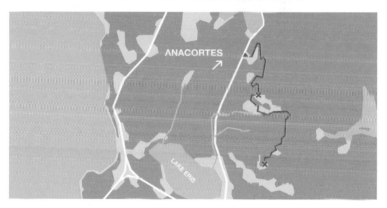

ANACORTES

LAKE ERIE

Sure, you can drive to the summit of Mount Erie. The road is steep and winding — a delightful drive if you're not in the mood for a workout. But hiking to the top is half the fun. Navigating this extensive network of trails, you gain two summits in just 5 miles (8 kilometers), roaming up and down through the Anacortes Community Forest Lands (ACFL) with map in hand. From each summit, expansive island and bay views await. As an added bonus, these low-elevation peaks are generally accessible year round.

Begin along the trail to Sugarloaf, gaining over 600 feet (182 meters) in the first mile. It starts out gently — a peaceful tree-covered stroll — before suddenly ramping up the elevation. Sugarloaf's summit can be reached in half an hour, but your heart will surely be a-pumping. An opening in the trees at 0.8 miles (1.3 kilometers) provides some welcome R&R, along with the first island views over Burrows Bay. Catch your breath before tackling the final quarter mile to the top. Panoramas from the south-facing summit overlook include Kiket Island to the east and antennae-topped Mount Erie straight ahead. Lake Erie, Burrows Bay, and sea as far as the eye can see are laid out to the west. Once you've had your fill, it's time to tackle that pesky view-blocking mountain to the south. One glance across will tell you everything you need to know about Mount Erie: the only way up is to go back down. Retrace your steps to the gated junction you walked through on the way up. Head left on trail #215. You can also go right here for trail #226 — both trails eventually lead to Mount Erie. We highly recommend printing or purchasing an ACFL map for hiking in this area. Without one, the numbered trails can become quite confusing!

Lose a few hundred feet hiking down Sugarloaf before gaining them back — and then some. Mount Erie is higher than Sugarloaf, with even more expansive views over the land and sea. At the top, you'll reach the road-end parking lot. Cross the road and walk toward the antennae, where a short trail leads to the big payout. How many islands, lakes, and bays can you spot? A love-lock decorated sign announces their names: Kiket, Skagit, Goat, and Hope Islands between Similk and Skagit Bays. Lakes Campbell, Pass, and Erie. Peer over Deception Pass — its iconic bridge hidden from here — to Whidbey Island Naval Air Station.

Take your time exploring the viewpoint at the other end of the parking lot and then head back down the way you came. It's possible to avoid climbing back up Sugarloaf by looping back around its east side. This is where your ACFL map will come in handy — choose your own route back to the parking lot, or even add on a detour to nearby Whistle Lake.

 # TURN BY TURN DIRECTIONS

1. Head east from the parking area on the signed trail #215.
2. At 0.2 miles (0.3 km), stay right at the junction.
3. At 0.5 miles (0.8 km), go right at the junction to stay on trail #215.
4. Continue straight on trail #215 to a wooden gate at approximately 1 mile (1.6 km).
5. Head through the gate onto trail #238 to a wide-open viewpoint at 1.1 miles (1.7 km).
6. Head back to the gate junction and turn left onto trail #215. Head south.
7. At 1.5 miles (2.4 km), reach Mt. Erie Road. Turn left and walk 0.1 mile (0.16 km) up the road.
8. At 1.6 miles (2.5 km), turn left onto trail #26.
9. At 1.8 miles (2.8 km), turn right onto trail #216. Follow it to the parking area at 2.6 miles (4.1 km).
10. Explore the two viewpoints, then return on trail #216 the way you came.

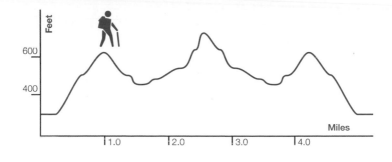

TRAILHEAD DRIVING DIRECTIONS

Take I-5 Exit 230 for Highway 20 and head west for 10 miles (16 kilometers); then turn left to stay on Highway 20. Turn right onto Campbell Lake Road; then turn right onto Heart Lake Road near Mount Erie Grocery. Less than a mile from the grocery store, turn right into the gravel parking lot at Ray Auld Drive.

ROCKFISH GRILL & ANACORTES BREWERY

Anacortes is "The Gateway to the San Juan Islands"; you can sip on a craft beer from Anacortes Brewery while you wait for the ferry to arrive. Established in 1994, it is the tenth oldest continuously operating brewery in Washington state. They not only brew beer and cook a mean pizza at the Rockfish Grill — the pub also hosts live music. With a great happy hour to boot, Anacortes Brewing is an ideal spot for your post-hike pint.

TRAIL CONTACT INFORMATION
Anacortes Parks & Recreation Department
904 6th St.
Anacortes, WA 98221
+1 360-293-1918
www.cityofanacortes.org

ACCOMMODATIONS
Majestic Inn & Spa
419 Commercial Ave.
Anacortes, WA 98221
+1 360-299-1400
www.majesticinnandspa.com
Upscale hotel one block from Anacortes Brewery with a seasonal rooftop lounge.

BREWERY/RESTAURANT
Rockfish Grill & Anacortes Brewery
320 Commercial Ave.
Anacortes, WA 98221
+1 360-588-1720
www.anacortesrockfish.com
Brews, woodfired pizza, live music, and more in Old Town Anacortes.

TOURIST ATTRACTIONS INFO
Anacortes Visitor Information Center
819 Commercial Ave. A
Anacortes, WA 98221
+1 360-293-3832
www.anacortes.org

WINCHESTER MOUNTAIN AND TWIN LAKES

A SHORT, BUT MODERATELY STEEP CLIMB TO A FORMER FIRE LOOKOUT WITH COMMANDING VIEWS OF MOUNTS BAKER AND SHUKSAN, THE BORDER PEAKS, AND SAPPHIRE-BLUE TWIN LAKES BELOW.

STARTING POINT	DESTINATION
TWIN LAKES	**WINCHESTER LOOKOUT**

BEER	DIFFICULTY
NORTH FORK ESB ON NITRO	**HIKING**

MAP	DURATION OF THE HIKE
GREEN TRAILS #14 MOUNT SHUKSAN	**2 HOURS** **3.4 MILES** (5.4KM)

PASS NEEDED	ELEVATION GAIN
NORTHWEST FOREST PASS	**1,300 FEET** (396M)

EXTRA SPECIAL BITTER

ALCOHOL CONTENT 5.3%

AMBER

ROAST, HONEY

CREAMY, TOASTED MALT

BITTERNESS	SWEETNESS
5	5
4	4
3	3
2	2
1	1

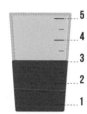
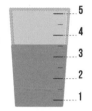

DESCRIPTION OF THE ROUTE

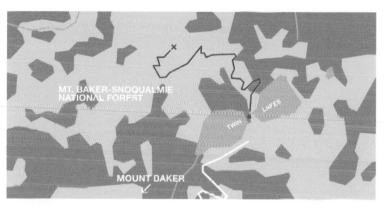

MT. BAKER-SNOQUALMIE NATIONAL FOREST

TWIN LAKES

MOUNT BAKER

Starting between the blue-green shores of twin alpine lakes, climbing up slopes overrun by mountain blueberries, you'll find a view dominated by mountain peaks — a considerable reward for less than two miles of hiking. If you can make it up the road first.

The Winchester Mountain Trail begins at the top of Twin Lakes Road: a primitive forest road with a final two miles that could easily be confused for an off-roading route. With a high clearance vehicle (four-wheel drive doesn't hurt!) you can carefully make your way up to the trailhead. Calm lakes greet you at the top of the road.

The trail begins with a bit of incline for the first 0.3 miles (0.5 kilometers). In late summer and early fall, the mountainside is a patchwork of green and red as the blueberry bushes turn crimson. Pluck a few on your way up the trail until you reach the junction with the High Pass trail; then veer to the left and the trail begins to switchback through more berry bushes.

At nearly a mile (1.6 kilometers) you'll come to the only challenging part of the trail, where it crosses a narrow rocky slope. Make the traverse and watch your footing, then come to the crest of the slope. At the top, you'll find a spectacular view of the surrounding mountains and a historic fire lookout.

With its four sturdy sides and wooden shutters, the Winchester Lookout is always fun to explore. Built in 1935 as a fire lookout for the Forest Service, it fell into disrepair after it was decommissioned. But in 1982, it was restored by the Mount Baker Club and is now open to the public for overnight stays. Equipped with cots, a stove, and bare cooking essentials, all you need to pack-in are sleeping bags, food, and water — and hope you're lucky enough to claim it for the evening!

From inside or outside the lookout, the views are incredible. To the north, you'll see Mount Larrabee, with the American and Canadian Border Peaks just behind. To the south, double-peaked Goat Mountain rises just beyond the Twin Lakes, and in the distance snow-covered Mounts Shuksan and Baker appear. Take in your fill of the view and return back down the way you came.

It never hurts to have camping supplies in the car when heading out to Winchester — there are several primitive sites along the lake, each with tent pad and picnic table. Bring your own water as there isn't any available at the trailhead, and all trash needs to be packed out. On clear nights, the Milky Way is brilliantly visible from both the lookout and the lakes — just another feature of this trail.

TURN BY TURN DIRECTIONS

1. Begin at the Winchester Mountain trailhead between Twin Lakes.
2. At 0.2 miles (0.3 km), meet up with the High Pass Junction; continue left towards Winchester Lookout.
3. At 0.9 miles (1.4 km), continue straight at the unmarked junction.
4. At 1.7 miles (2.7 km), arrive at the Winchester Lookout.
5. Return on the same route.

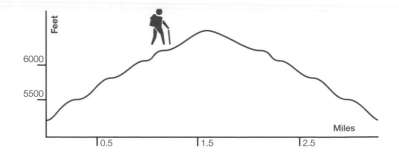

TRAILHEAD DRIVING DIRECTIONS

On Mount Baker Highway (SR 542), drive 12.5 miles (19 kilometers) past the Glacier Public Service Center to Twin Lakes Road. Turn left onto the gravel forest road and drive 7 miles (11 kilometers) to its end at Twin Lakes. After passing the Yellow Aster Butte trailhead at 4.5 miles (7.2 kilometers) the road is very rough — high clearance vehicles are mandatory and four-wheel drive advised.

NORTH FORK BREWERY

The North Fork Brewery is many things — a pizzeria, a beer shrine, and a favorite post-hike choice on the Mount Baker Highway. A Whatcom County institution since 1997, the brewery offers hearty grub, warm atmosphere, and tasty brews that have become just another part of the adventure for many. Because North Fork's pizza, beer, and quirky, laid-back atmosphere are so renowned, it's common to see a line out the door on summer weekends. Admire the extensive craft beer memorabilia while you relax and drink some delicious brews.

TRAIL CONTACT INFORMATION
US Forest Service
Glacier Public Service Center
10091 Mt. Baker Hwy.
Glacier, WA 98244
+1 360-599- 2714

ACCOMMODATIONS
Blue T Lodge
10459 Mt Baker Hwy.
Glacier, WA 98244
+1 360-599-9944
www.bluetlodge.com
Small six-room inn, pet friendly,
with free wi-fi.

BREWERY/RESTAURANT
North Fork Brewery
6186 Mt. Baker Hwy.
Deming, WA 98244
+1 360-599-2337
www.northforkbrewery.com

TOURIST ATTRACTIONS INFO
Bellingham Whatcom County Tourism
904 Potter St.
Bellingham, WA 98225
+1 800-487-2032
www.bellingham.org

5

BRITISH COLUMBIA

ABBY GRIND

EXPERIENCE A FAVORITE BC OUTDOOR ACTIVITY (GRINDING!)
AS YOU MAKE YOUR WAY UP THE STEEP SWITCHBACKS OF ABBY GRIND TO A
VIEWPOINT TAKING IN THE FRASER VALLEY AND SURROUNDING PEAKS.

STARTING POINT	DESTINATION
ABBY GRIND PARKING LOT	**ABBY GRIND LOOKOUT**

BEER	DIFFICULTY
OLD ABBEY SCOTTISH MONK	**HIKING**

MAP	DURATION OF THE HIKE
NONE AVAILABLE	**1-2 HOURS 2.4 MILES** (3.8KM)

PASS NEEDED	ELEVATION GAIN
NONE	**1,420 FEET** (433M)

BELGIAN-STYLE SCOTCH ALE

ALCOHOL 6.5% CONTENT

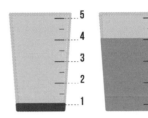

RUBY-BROWN

BISCUIT, TOASTED GRAIN

CARAMEL, DARK FRUIT, HINT OF PEAT

BITTERNESS   SWEETNESS

5
4
3
2
1

5
4
3
2
1

DESCRIPTION OF THE ROUTE

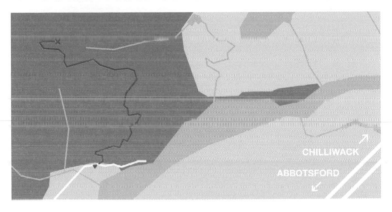

CHILLIWACK

ABBOTSFORD

Vancouver's Grouse Grind is one of the most iconic trails in British Columbia. It is often called "Nature's stairmaster." Hikers, trail runners and fitness buffs put themselves to the test on this gruelling climb up Grouse Mountain. With its popularity, other "Grinds" have popped up, offering alternatives for those intimidated by Grouse, and less demanding terrain to train on.

Abby Grind offers a great training course for those in the Fraser Valley. Located just outside of Abbotsford, this Grind gains just over 1,400 feet (430 meters) of elevation in 1.2 miles (1.9 kilometers). For trail runners, it's just long enough to get the heart pounding, and short enough for an after-work run.

While Abby Grind may be a thigh-pumping, huff and puff-inducing scramble, you shouldn't be surprised to see the same focused runner speed by again as they climb the trail 2-3 times in a single session. This is a prime example of "hike your own hike." Always take Abby Grind at your own pace. As you begin from the parking lot, you might be startled at first by gunshots nearby. Don't worry — these are only from the nearby shooting range you drove past on your way to the trailhead. These shots do, however, disturb the peaceful forest setting for some. As you wind your way up the trail, the noise will diminish, only to be replaced by a brisk wind on the eastern slope of the hillside. Also noticeable is the smell of manure, which you may find yourself mucking through to the trailhead. Welcome to the valley!

In the first section of the trail, you quickly get a feel for what the Abby Grind is: a hard packed single-track dirt trail, zigzagging sharply between trees. Along the way, there are progress signs posted on trees along the trail at ¼, ½, and ¾ marks. You'll either praise or curse these signs, as you calculate just how much further it is to the top. Though the trail is densely forested, there are a few viewpoints ideal for a breather along the trail. You'll reach the first at 0.6 miles (1.0 kilometer), signed as the KM Mountain View. From here, you'll be able to see Mount Cheam, Lady Peak, Mount Archibald, and Knight Peak.

After this welcome break, you'll quickly arrive at the halfway point at 0.7 miles (1.1 kilometers). This section is the steepest part of the trail — wide and outfitted with a length of assist ropes. Once you reach the end of this straight stretch, the trail returns to its somewhat moderate grade.

At 0.9 miles (1.4 kilometers), you'll reach the three-quarters mark. From here the trail levels out as you continue towards the overlook. At 1.1 miles (1.8 kilometers), you'll come to a junction where you should keep straight for the Lookout. Abby Grind terminates at 1.2 miles (1.9 kilometers) at the bald rock face of the Lookout. From here, you'll have views down the Fraser Valley, and a partial view of Mount Baker in Washington State. The view is slightly obscured by three massive Douglas Firs that act like natural frames for different sections of the landscape. Rest up from your grind before heading back to the parking lot via the same path. In steep sections, try serpentining down the path in order to avoid slipping or tripping.

TURN BY TURN DIRECTIONS

1. From the parking area, head to the unmarked trailhead at the base of the hill.
2. At 0.6 miles (1.0 km), come to the KM Mountain View point.
3. At 0.7 miles (1.1 km), come to the Halfway Point.
4. At 0.9 miles (1.4 km), come to the Three-Quarters Point.
5. At 1.1 miles (1.8 km), come to the junction with Taggart Peak trail; continue straight to the Lookout.
6. Reach the Lookout at 1.2 miles (1.9 km). Return the way you came.

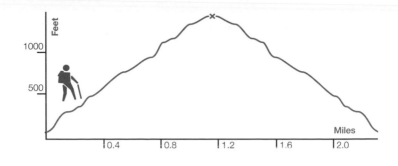

TRAILHEAD DRIVING DIRECTIONS

From Abbotsford, head east on Trans-Canada Highway (BC-1) east. Take Exit 95 for Whatcom Road; turn left onto Whatcom Road. Turn right onto N Parallel Rd, and continue onto Eldridge Rd. Turn right onto Atkinson Road and continue onto N Parallel Road. Turn left onto McDermott Road, and continue onto Lakemount Road. Abby Grind Parking is on the left just past the Abbotsford Fish and Game Club.

OLD ABBEY ALES

Inspired by the name of the town it calls home, Old Abbey Ales brewed its first batch of beer in its Abbotsford facility in 2015. With a rotating selection of 15 beers, Old Abbey Ales offers everything from a Raspberry Sour to a Belgian-twist on the Scotch Ale. Sourcing hops from nearby Chilliwack, B.C.-grown malts, and using locally grown fruits, Old Abbey Ales makes beers that are a product of local ingredients. A friendly staff, high ceilings, and a fireplace lounge will invite you to pull up a bar stool, sip on a brew, and stay awhile.

TRAIL CONTACT INFORMATION
Fraser Valley Regional District
45950 Cheam Ave.
Chilliwack, BC V2P 1N6
+1 604-702-5000
www.fvrd.ca

BREWERY
Old Abbey Ales
30321 Fraser Hwy. #1A
Abbotsford, BC V4X 1T3
+1 604-607-5104
www.oldabbeyales.com

TOURIST ATTRACTIONS INFO
Tourism Abbotsford
34561 Delair Rd.
Abbotsford, BC
+1 604-859-1721
www.tourismabbotsford.ca

ACCOMMODATIONS
Clarion Hotel & Conference Centre
36035 North Parallel Rd.
Abbotsford, BC V3G 2C6
+1 604 870 1050
clarionabbotsford.com

EAGLE BLUFFS

BIRD'S-EYE VANCOUVER VISTAS AWAIT AT THE END
OF THIS QUINTESSENTIALLY NORTHWEST TREK UP STEEP SLOPES
AND PAST SUBALPINE LAKES IN CYPRESS PROVINCIAL PARK.

STARTING POINT	DESTINATION
CYPRESS CREEK DAY LODGE	**EAGLE BLUFFS**
BEER	DIFFICULTY
GREEN LEAF WEIZENHOWER WHEAT	**HIKING**
MAP	DURATION OF THE HIKE
NATIONAL TOPOGRAPHIC SYSTEM 92G6	**3-4 HOURS 5.6 MILES** (9KM)
PASS NEEDED	ELEVATION GAIN
NONE	**1,000 FEET** (305M)

WITBIER

CLOUDY GOLDEN

PEAR,
CITRUS ZEST

ORANGE, LIGHT
CORIANDER SPICE,
SELTZER DRY

BITTERNESS	SWEETNESS
5 4 3 2 1	5 4 3 2 1

DESCRIPTION OF THE ROUTE

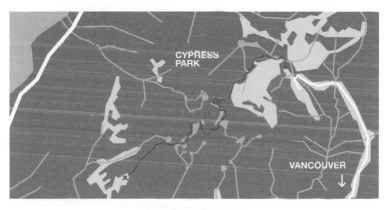

Ski resorts offer some of the most accessible summer hikes in British Columbia. Wide, paved access roads lead to high mountain lodges, where trails take you even higher. Eagle Bluffs is a fine example. Just 17.4 miles (28 kilometers) from downtown Vancouver, the trailhead can be reached in 30 minutes on a good traffic day. The easy access combined with the promise of outdoor adventure make for a popular hiking destination, especially during summer weekends.

The trail takes off from Cypress Creek Day Lodge. Notice the Olympic rings and inukshuk here — relics from Vancouver's 2010 Winter Olympics. Follow the Baden Powell trail as it runs roughly parallel to several Black Mountain ski runs, all accessed by the Eagle Express chairlift. You may wish you were riding the Eagle Express as you gain over 800 feet (244 meters) in the first mile, climbing steep switchbacks over loose, rocky terrain on the wide path. Unfortunately, the chairlift takes summers off. But your destination is more than worth the effort.

After climbing the initial set of switchbacks, you'll come to a wide gravel area at around 0.8 miles (1.3 kilometers). The ski run to your left is known as "Maëlle Rickers, Gold" during snowier months, after Canadian snowboarder Maëlle Ricker. In 2010, Maëlle became the first Canadian woman to win a gold medal on home soil at the Olympics.

Listen closely, and you may hear the call of pika in this rocky area.

After 1.1 miles (1.8 kilometers), the trail reaches a high point of 3,900 feet (1,189 meters). Here, you are presented with a choice. The trail splits, forming a loop right in the middle of your hike. Head left towards Theagill and Sam Lakes. From here on out, the trail becomes a rollercoaster with some flat areas, short uphill climbs, and rocky downhill drops. Boardwalks keep your feet dry between lakes as you walk through the mountain hemlock forest. Beyond the lakes, scramble down a final steep section, using your hands to grab nearby trees for balance. Once you clear this final obstacle, Eagle Bluffs is just a few minutes down the trail.

Suddenly, a vast scene emerges. Awed by the swift transition from dense tree cover to full exposure, first-timers reach for their cameras and sunglasses without fail. Standing upon the bluffs feels transcendent. Look down upon the city of Vancouver, capped by Stanley Park and connected to the North Shore by Lions Gate Bridge. A variety of vessels hang out in Burrard Inlet, whose waters meet Howe Sound at Lighthouse Park directly below. Bowen Island drifts offshore to the east, across from Horseshoe Bay. The entire landscape is a painting of modern civilization, set against the backdrop of swirling waters, emerald islands, and majestic mountains as far as the eye can see.

Watch for wildlife from the rocks. Enormous ravens and tiny chipmunks frequent Eagle Bluffs, each fearlessly seeking some trail mix. Don't indulge them. If these animals become dependent on humans for food, how will they survive the harsh, snowy winters?

Back on the trail, you'll reach the loop junction at 3.7 miles (6 kilometers). Go left to check out Cabin Lake — the most picturesque of them all. Then head up to the Yew Lake Lookout for a final view down into Howe Sound — and across to the Lions — before returning to the trailhead.

TURN BY TURN DIRECTIONS

1. From Cypress Creek Day Lodge, follow the signed Baden Powell Trail west.
2. At 0.1 miles (0.1 km), turn left at the first two junctions.
3. At 0.15 miles (0.2 km), turn right onto the Baden Powell trail.
4. At 0.2 miles (0.3 km), turn left and begin climbing.
5. At 1.1 miles (1.8 km), turn left on the Baden Powell trail.
6. At 1.3 miles (2.1 km), stay right on the Baden Powell trail.
7. At 1.8 miles (2.9 km), stay left on the Baden Powell trail.
8. At 2.8 miles (4.5 km), reach Eagle Bluffs.
9. Return via the same trail for a 5.6-mile (9 km) roundtrip hike.
10. **Optional:** At 3.7 miles (6 km), turn left onto the Cabin Lake Trail to return via the lollipop loop.
11. At 4 miles (6.5 km), reach Cabin Lake. Turn around here.
12. At 4.1 miles (6.6 km), turn left to reach the Yew Lake viewpoint, then turn around.
13. At 4.3 miles (6.9 km), turn left on the Cabin Lake trail.
14. Take a second left onto the Baden Powell trail.
15. Follow the Baden Powell trail back to the trailhead at 5.6 miles (9 km).

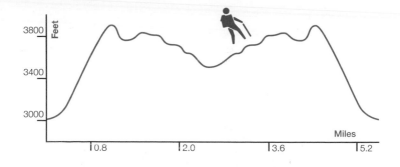

TRAILHEAD DRIVING DIRECTIONS

Take British Columbia Highway 1 BC 1 to Exit 8 for Cypress Provincial Park. Merge right onto Cypress Bowl Road and continue for 9.3 miles (15 kilometers) to the parking lot beneath Cypress Creek Day Lodge.

GREEN LEAF BREWING

Located in North Vancouver's Lonsdale Quay Market, Green Leaf Brewing Co. has focused on sustainability and creating innovative beer from local ingredients since it opened its doors in 2013. Green Leaf has a well-rounded taplist with everything from IPAs to sours. Rustically chic, the brewery also serves house-made Kombucha and ginger beer.

TRAIL CONTACT INFORMATION
Cypress Provincial Park
+1 604-926-5612
*www.env.gov.bc.ca/bcparks/explore/
parkpgs/cypress*

RESTAURANT/HOTEL
Lonsdale Quay Market
123 Carrie Oates Ct.
North Vancouver, BC V7M 3K7
www.lonsdalequay.com
Choose from a variety of food vendors on the North Vancouver waterfront. Lodging available upstairs at the Lonsdale Quay Hotel.

BREWERY
Green Leaf Brewing
Lonsdale Quay Market North Vancouver BC V7M 3K7
+1 604-984-8409
www.greenleafbrew.com
Located conveniently inside the Lonsdale Quay Market.

TOURIST ATTRACTIONS INFO
North Vancouver Visitor Centre
Lonsdale Quay Market
+1 604-656-6491
www.vancouversnorthshore.com
Located inside the Lonsdale Quay Market (ground floor, north end).

GOLD CREEK FALLS

HIKE PAST THE ICONIC GOLDEN EARS AS YOU FOLLOW GOLD CREEK ON AN EASY FORESTED WALK TO THE RUSHING WATERS OF GOLD CREEK FALLS.

STARTING POINT	DESTINATION
LOWER FALLS TRAILHEAD	**GOLD CREEK FALLS**

BEER	DIFFICULTY
MISSION SPRINGS BLUE COLLAR PALE ALE	**WALKING**

MAP	DURATION OF THE HIKE
LOOK UP WWW.ENV.GOV.BC.CA	**2 HOURS** **3.4 MILES** (5.5KM)

PASS NEEDED	ELEVATION GAIN
NONE	**200 FEET** (61M)

ENGLISH
PALE ALE

 PALE GOLD

CARAMEL,
GRASS, SPICE

BREADY, MALTY,
FLORAL HOP

BITTERNESS

5
4
3
2
1

SWEETNESS

5
4
3
2
1

DESCRIPTION OF THE ROUTE

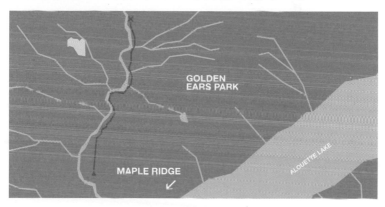

Just an hour and a half outside of Vancouver, Golden Ears Provincial Park is teeming with fun-seekers on summer weekends. Coming out in force, packing beach blankets and coolers, these Vancouverites head to North Beach on Alouette Lake to escape the city. Many extend the fun by setting up camp at one of the three campgrounds in the park.

But if you venture beyond the shores of Alouette, you'll find trails that explore around the Golden Ears mountain group. The park is named for Golden Ears — a twin summit massif that reaches 5,630 feet (1,716 meters). There is a trail to the top, but it's long and difficult — many hikers backpack it, setting up camp at Panorama Ridge. For those looking to see the beauty of this park on a leisurely hike, there couldn't be a better option than Gold Creek Falls.

A parking lot for the Lower Falls Trail is located at the end of Golden Ears Parkway — the lot fills up quickly on summer weekends, so either arrive early or plan to park across the bridge, along the side of Golden Ears Parkway.

Following Gold Creek as it winds through Alouette Valley, you'll walk the Lower Falls Trail out to the rushing cascades of Lower Gold Creek Falls. The trail is gentle and almost entirely flat as it makes its way through the coastal western hemlock forest. It's also wide and well maintained, which makes it popular with families — don't be surprised if you find yourself passing a stroller on the way.

Along the trail, remnants of the area's logging past take the form of large red cedar stumps, weathered but still there some 90 years later.
In the summer, this shady forest helps beat the heat, but in the spring and late fall the trail can get very muddy.

At 0.8 miles (1.3 kilometers), you'll come to one of the most iconic viewpoints in the park. Turn left off of the main trail to the viewpoint trail. Above a bend in Gold Creek, look to the west to see the Golden Ears mountain group. The twin peaks of Golden Ears are to the north, the blunt Edge Peak nearest, and the Blanshard Needle to the south.
The sandy shores along this part of the creek are a favorite picnic spot; you might spy children splashing in the shallows.

At 1.7 miles (2.7 kilometers), you'll arrive at the viewing platform for Gold Creek Falls. They rush strongly even in the summer, so you'll be able to feel the spray on your face as you take in the falls. Thrill seekers will scale the rocky edge of the falls up to the pool just above — but as tempting as the swimming hole is, keep in mind the reports of people getting caught in the rush and going over the falls. Instead, wander a bit back down the trail to one of a few side trails that lead to large boulders, perfect for dipping in toes and sunning on the rocks. Return the way you came.

TURN BY TURN DIRECTIONS

1. From the parking lot, head to the Lower Falls Trail at the northwest corner of the lot.
2. At 0.8 miles (1.3 km), turn left onto the viewpoint side trail. Return to the main trail.
3. At 1.7 miles (2.7 km), arrive at Gold Creek Falls.
4. Return the way you came.

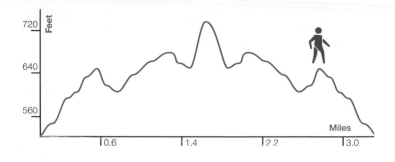

TRAILHEAD DRIVING DIRECTIONS

From the Vancouver area on Highway 1, take Exit 57 for 192 Street N. Turn left onto 192nd, then right onto Golden Ears Way. Continue on this road to the park entrance, and then continue on Golden Ears Parkway to the parking lot at the end of the road.

MISSION SPRINGS BREWING COMPANY

When you walk into Mission Springs Brewing Company, you might wonder for a moment if you've accidentally wandered into an old junk store — a pickup hangs from the ceiling and hubcaps and tools line the walls. The brewpub has been brewing its line-up of award-winning beers since 1996. One of B.C.'s oldest breweries, Mission Springs is not only a popular watering hole, but a favorite restaurant for the lower mainland. With crisp, easy-drinking takes on classic styles, its beers are great for kicking back and relaxing.

TRAIL CONTACT INFORMATION
British Columbia Ministry of Environment
B.C. Parks
+1 604-466-8325
www.env.gov.bc.ca/bcparks/explore/
parkpgs/golden_ears

BREWERY/RESTAURANT
Mission Springs Brewing Company
7160 Oliver St.
Mission, BC V2V 6K5
+1 604 820-1009
www.missionsprings.ca

ACCOMMODATIONS
Gold Creek Campground
24480 Fern Crescent
Maple Ridge, BC V4R 2S1
+1 800-689-9025
www.discovercamping.ca
Open year-round with full service sites
within Golden Ears Provincial Park.

TOURIST ATTRACTIONS INFO
Maple Ridge Visitor Center
190 - 22470 Dewdney Trunk Rd.
Maple Ridge, BC V2W 2E2
+1 604-467-7320
www.mapleridge.ca/330/tourism

INLAND LAKE LOOP TRAIL

DAY HIKE AN EASY AND ACCESSIBLE SECTION OF THE SUNSHINE COAST TRAIL — CANADA'S LONGEST HUT-TO-HUT HIKE.

STARTING POINT	DESTINATION
INLAND LAKE BOAT LAUNCH	**INLAND LAKE**
BEER	**DIFFICULTY**
TOWNSITE SUNCOAST PALE ALE	**WALKING**
	DURATION OF THE HIKE
MAP	**3 HOURS 8.4 MILES** (13,5KM)
INLAND LAKE PROVINCIAL PARK MAP WWW.BCPARKS.CA	
PASS NEEDED	**ELEVATION GAIN**
NONE	**MINIMAL**

ENGLISH PALE ALE

 AMBER BROWN

 FLORAL, HERBAL

 BISCUIT, HERBAL BITTERNESS, SMOOTH

BITTERNESS **SWEETNESS**

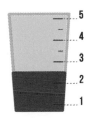 

DESCRIPTION OF THE ROUTE

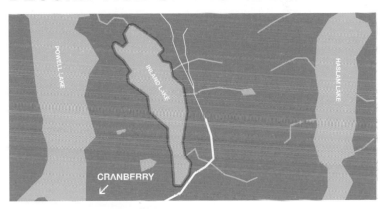

Sepurated from Vancouver, BC by the Salish Sea, the Sunshine Coast is a world away from the bustle of the big city. Quaint coastal communities connected by scenic highways and ferries make their home here. The island-like coast is only accessible by boat or plane and offers prime year-round hiking opportunities. Ferry across to Powell River from Vancouver Island, or take two ferries from West Vancouver to get there. Once across the waters, the town of Powell River welcomes you with all 112 miles (180 kilometers) of the Sunshine Coast Trail (SCT).

Canada's longest hut-to-hut hike, the SCT runs from Desolation Sound all the way to Saltery Bay. This rollercoaster trail rambles from sea level to an elevation of 4,265 feet (1,300 meters) with countless climbs and descents along the way. An increasingly popular thru-hike, the SCT treats backpackers to over a dozen shared-use huts — ranging from open-sided shelters to fully enclosed cabins. Built and maintained by a supportive community, the SCT is a source of inspiration for locals and visitors alike.

Set out on the Inland Lake Loop from Inland Lake Provincial Park for an easy introduction to the SCT. This level 8.4-mile (13.5 kilometer) loop is great for bikers as well as hikers, with bridges, boardwalks, and two accessible huts along the peaceful lakeshore. The crushed gravel path is wheelchair-accessible.

Beginning from the boat launch, walk north through a picnic area where restrooms and additional parking are available. The forested trail follows Inland Lake north to a totem pole at 1.8 miles (2.9 kilometers) — carved by Tla'amin First Nation artist Jackie Muksamma Timothy. Shortly after the carving, you'll meet the trail to Confederation Lake — a steep climb through old-growth forest. Skip it and continue along the lakeshore, watching and listening for bald eagles overhead.

Next you'll reach Anthony Island — worth a short side trip across the bridge. Check out the Anthony Island SCT hut here, which gives priority to users with mobility issues. Back on the main trail, pass benches, a picnic shelter, and a canoe portage as you round the loop. Part of the Powell Forest Canoe Route, Inland Lake is one of eight lakes connected by portages on the Sunshine Coast. Paddlers can spend five days or more camping and canoeing the 35-mile (56 kilometer) route.

You'll encounter a second accessible hut, Inland Lake West, at 6.5 miles (10.4 kilometers). Look across the lake from here for views of Mount Mahony and Loon Bluffs. Then continue around the lake back to the trailhead. After completing the loop, it's a 20-minute drive back to Powell River for SCT-inspired Townsite brews.

TURN BY TURN DIRECTIONS

1. Beginning from the boat launch parking area, walk north on the Inland Lake Trail.
2. At 2 miles (3.2 km), reach the Confederation Lake junction. Stay left for Inland Lake.
3. At 2.3 miles (3.0 km), turn left to visit Anthony Island. Then continue north on the Inland Lake Trail.
4. At 5.1 miles (8.2 km), reach the canoe portage junction. Stay left on the Inland Lake Trail.
5. At 7.8 miles (12.5 km), reach a junction with the Lost Lake Trail and stay left for Inland Lake.
6. At 8.4 miles (13.5 km), return to the trailhead.

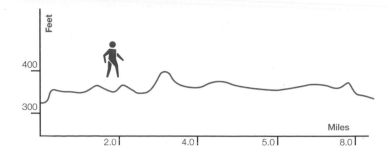

TRAILHEAD DRIVING DIRECTIONS

From Powell River, take Manson Avenue north to Cassiar Street. Turn right, then turn left onto Yukon Avenue. Continue for 0.6 miles (1 kilometer); then turn right onto Haslam Street. Drive 1.4 miles (2.2 kilometers) and then take a slight left, following signs for Inland Lake Provincial Park. Continue 2.2 miles (3.5 kilometers) and then turn right at the Haywire Bay/Inland Lake intersection. After 1.2 miles (1.9 kilometers), turn left at the next fork and descend to the boat launch parking area.

TOWNSITE BREWING

Townsite Brewing is housed in an art deco brick building constructed in 1939. Inside, Belgian brewmaster Cédric Dauchot has been crafting saisons, sours, and Belgian brews for the local Powell River community since 2012. With an expanded outdoor beer garden and a warm, rustic tasting room, the brewery is a haven for this remote community— and for the beer lovers who seek out its award-winning tap list. Try the Sunshine Coast-inspired Suncoast Pale Ale or Tin Hat IPA — both sure to satisfy thirsty hikers after a day on the trail.

TRAIL CONTACT INFORMATION
Inland Lake Provincial Park
Operated by Wilderness Recreation
Services Ltd.
www.bcparks.ca

RESTAURANT
Shingle Mill Pub & Bistro
6233 Powell Pl.
Powell River, BC V8A 4S6
+1 604-483-3545
www.shinglemill.ca
Waterfront dining on the shores of Powell Lake,
with an excellent selection of local beers.

TOURIST ATTRACTIONS INFO
Powell River Visitor Center
4760 Joyce Ave.
Powell River, BC V8A 3B6
+1 604-485-4701
www.tourism-powellriver.ca/visit

BREWERY
Townsite Brewing
824 Ash Ave.
Powell River, BC V8A 4R4
+1 604-483-2111
www.townsitebrewing.com

ACCOMMODATIONS
The Old Courthouse Inn
6243 Walnut St.
Powell River, BC V8A 4K4
+1 604-483-4000
www.oldcourthouseinn.ca
Eight-room B&B in a restored 1939
Tudor-style building. Located across the
street from Townsite Brewing.

IONA JETTY

AN AVIATION LOVER'S DREAM: HIKE ALONG IONA JETTY TO WATCH THE WAVES AND SHOREBIRDS AND GET A JOLT FROM THE ROAR OF PLANES LANDING AND TAKING OFF AT NEARBY VANCOUVER INTERNATIONAL AIRPORT.

STARTING POINT	DESTINATION
PARKING LOT BY SOUTH POND	**IONA JETTY**
BEER	DIFFICULTY
FUGGLES AND WARLOCK THE LAST STRAWBERRY	**WALKING**
MAP	DURATION OF THE HIKE
LOOK UP WWW.METROVANCOUVER.ORG	**2 HOURS 5 MILES** (8KM)
PASS NEEDED	ELEVATION GAIN
NONE	**MINIMAL**

ALCOHOL 4.9% CONTENT

STRAWBERRY WIT

 ROSE GOLD HAZE

 STRAWBERRY, LEMONADE, WHEAT

 STRAWBERRY, SELTZER, WHEAT

BITTERNESS	SWEETNESS
5	5
4	4
3	3
2	2
1	1

DESCRIPTION OF THE ROUTE

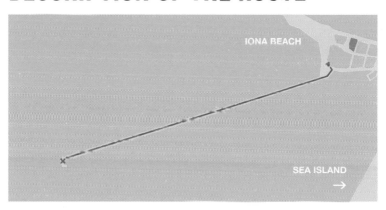

IONA BEACH

SEA ISLAND
→

Herons wade through the shallows on long legs, and waterfowl dive below the surface of the icy waters of the Strait of Georgia. Seals bob offshore. None of them seem to be disturbed by the jet coming in for a landing overhead. Iona Jetty reaches 2.5 miles (4.0 kilometers) straight through this landscape on a windswept trail.

Iona Beach makes up the west side of Iona Island and is home to a diverse ecology of wildlife including marshlands, intertidal zones, and sand dunes. It's not truly an island anymore, since a land bridge was created to connect it as a peninsula to Sea Island, where Vancouver International Airport is located. This close proximity to the airport actually adds to the "scenery" along the trail. Many come out to the area to plane-spot, logging the different types of aircraft that land at or take off from the airport.

From the parking lot near the South Pond, you can't miss the jetty — it shoots out from the beach in a straight line, along a raised gravel paved trail. The jetty is actually formed by a pipeline coming from the nearby water-treatment plant (the locals have plenty of alternate names for Iona Jetty because of this). However, between Iona and the industrial North Jetty, the fertile Iona Beach area is now home to over 300 species of birds that come to the beach to seek shelter and food. If you like, take the time to explore along the beach as well, but please be mindful of the animals that make the beach their home.

The trail itself is incredibly straightforward, following the jetty to its end and back. Take in views of the North Shore Mountains and Vancouver Island along the way. The trail is completely exposed — which is both a positive aspect and a drawback. Wide open skies above allow for expansive views of migrating birds in the Pacific Flyway, sharing airspace with all the jets overhead. But the trail can also experience strong winds, even on calmer weather days. Bundle up!

There are several wind shelters along the trail that allow for a short reprieve from blustery conditions. Near the end of the trail at 2.4 miles (3.9 kilometers) there's a restroom. The wind shelters also make for a good early turn around point if the brewery beckons before you reach the end.

TURN BY TURN DIRECTIONS

1. From the parking lot, turn towards the water and find the Iona Jetty Trailhead. Continue onto the Jetty.
2. At 0.8 miles (1.3 km), reach the first wind shelter.
3. At 1.6 miles (2.5 km), reach the second wind shelter.
4. At 2.4 miles (3.9 km), come to the restroom.
5. At 2.5 miles (4.0 km), reach the end of the Jetty.
6. Return the way you came.

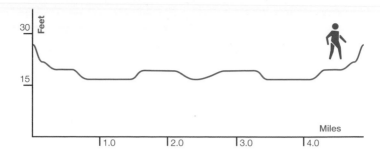

TRAILHEAD DRIVING DIRECTIONS

On BC-99 North from Richmond, take Exit 39 for Bridgeport Road, and turn left onto Bridgeport Road. Then use the right two lanes to take the exit for the Main Terminal. Then turn right onto Grant McConachie Way East. Turn right onto Templeton Street. Templeton Street will turn into Ferguson Road. Iona Beach Park is located at the end of Ferguson Road.

FUGGLES & WARLOCK

Fuggles & Warlock Craftworks wants the geek in each of us to pull up a stool, enjoy a pint pulled by lightsaber tap, and face-off in an old school video game battle. It's all about "Keeping Beer Weird." Here you'll find a line-up of brews that are just a little off-center for their style — in a good way. Combining names like "The Last Strawberry" and "Beam Me Up" with label designs inspired by anime and videogames, Fuggles and Warlock appeals to beer nerds and good old fashioned nerds alike. And a taste of the beer alone is a treasure well worth the journey.

TRAIL CONTACT INFORMATION
Metro Vancouver Parks
4330 Kingsway
Burnaby, BC V5H 4G8
+1 604-432-6200
www.metrovancouver.org

RESTAURANT
Kirin Seafood Restaurant
7900 Westminster Hwy., 2nd Fl
Richmond, BC V6X 1A5
+1 604-303-8833
www.kirinrestaurant.com
Every Richmond visit should include dim sum, and Kirin is one of the best.

TOURIST ATTRACTIONS INFO
Visit Richmond Visitor Centre
3811 Moncton St.
Richmond BC V7E 3A7
+1 604-271-8280
www.visitrichmondbc.com

BREWERY
Fuggles & Warlock
103-11220 Horseshoe Way
Richmond, B.C. V7A 4V5
+1 604-285-7745
www.fuggleswarlock.com
Anime- and videogame-inspired brewery that brews award-winning and novel beers.

ACCOMMODATIONS
La Quinta Inn Vancouver Airport
8640 Alexandra Rd.
Richmond, BC Y6X1C4
+1 604-276-2711
www.laquintarichmondvancouverairport.com
Clean, comfortable and affordable, close to the trail.

JOCELYN HILL

HUSTLE UP HOLMES PEAK AND JOCELYN HILL FOR EVER-EXPANDING VIEWS OVER THE FINLAYSON ARM FJORD.

STARTING POINT	DESTINATION
CALEB PIKE TRAILHEAD	**JOCELYN HILL**

BEER	DIFFICULTY
CATEGORY 12 GOLDEN RATIO	**HIKING**

MAP	DURATION OF THE HIKE
GOWLLAND TOD PROVINCIAL PARK MAP WWW.BCPARKS.CA	**3 HOURS 5.5 MILES** (8.8KM)

PASS NEEDED	ELEVATION GAIN
NONE	**970 FEET** (296M)

BELGIAN TRIPEL

GOLDEN

PEAR, BUBBLEGUM

BANANA,
SPUN SUGAR,
CANDIED PEAR

BITTERNESS   SWEETNESS

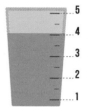

DESCRIPTION OF THE ROUTE

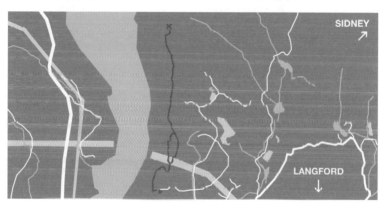

Accessible within 30 minutes drive of downtown Victoria, Gowlland Tod Provincial Park protects 3,163 acres (1,280 hectares) of seashore and uplands on Vancouver Island. Hike to the heart of this cherished green space with a trek to Jocelyn Hill.

From the Caleb Pike Trailhead in Gowlland Tod Provincial Park, follow signs (and orange trail markers) toward Jocelyn Hill. The hike begins beneath tree cover, losing a bit of elevation before picking up the pace. You'll gain over 300 feet (91 meters) climbing to Holmes Peak for nice first views of the Finlayson Arm (and some freeway noise from across the waters). Enjoy a water and snack break — this is just the warmup.

You might notice trees with reddish, flaking bark along this trail. Known as madronas in the United States, they are called arbutus (or sometimes manzanita) here in British Columbia. Whatever you call these unique trees, they are native to the western coastal areas of North America, found from British Columbia to California. Feel how smooth they are beneath the bark.

Descend Holmes Peak by continuing north along the ridge. At 1.4 miles (2.2 kilometers) the grade steepens again — now you'll begin climbing up Jocelyn Hill. Listen for ravens in the trees and enjoy partial water views along the way. Soon you'll be high enough to see the Olympic Mountains across the Salish Sea in Washington.

There's no clear end to the trail — it continues north and makes various loops — so we called it a day at the open overlook at 2.75 miles (4.4 kilometers). After a steep and rocky final push, find a spot to sit and survey the fjord. This is Finlayson Arm, part of the greater Saanich Inlet, which cuts through Vancouver Island to form the Saanich Peninsula. The fjord replenishes its marine waters once a year, creating a unique environment for marine wildlife. Watch for whales!

Take it easy on the descent. This trail can be slippery in places, especially when it's wet. You can mix up your return route by taking the Lower Jocelyn Loop and Holmes Peak Bypass trails. Holmes Peak may be worth bypassing if you don't feel like hiking up and over it again. Or simply return the way you came — the views are best along the ridge.

TURN BY TURN DIRECTIONS

1. Beginning from the Caleb Pike Trailhead, follow signs west, then north (turn right) for Jocelyn Hill.
2. At 0.7 miles (1.1 km), turn left and follow the Ridge Trail to Holmes Peak.
3. At 1.2 miles (1.9 km), turn left to continue on the Ridge Trail to Jocelyn Hill.
4. At 2.75 miles (4.4 km), reach the summit of Jocelyn Hill. Retrace your steps to the previous junction.

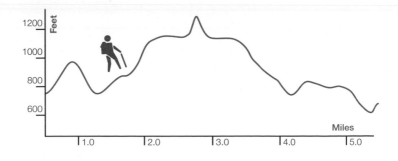

TRAILHEAD DRIVING DIRECTIONS

From Victoria, take Trans-Canada Highway/BC-1 North. Take Exit 14 toward Langford/Highlands. Merge onto Millstream Road and continue north for 4.1 miles (6.6 kilometers). Turn left onto Caleb Pike Road, continue for 0.4 miles (0.6 kilometers), and park in the Provincial Park parking lot on the right.

CATEGORY 12 BREWING

A step into this bright and cheery taproom is a step into a literal beer laboratory. With a Ph.D. in microbiology and biochemistry, Category 12's head brewer and founder Michael Kuzyk is constantly optimizing and obsessing over brewing better beer — from unfiltered big Belgian brews to hoppy Northwest ales. As Michael's wife and co-owner Karen puts it, "Life's too short to drink beer you don't like." We wholeheartedly agree.

TRAIL CONTACT INFORMATION
Gowlland Tod Provincial Park
Operated by R.L.C. Enterprize Ltd.
+1 250-474-1336
office@rlcparks.ca
www.rlcparks.ca

BREWERY/RESTAURANT
Category 12 Brewing
2200 Keating Cross Rd. C
Saanichton, BC V8M 2A6
+1 250-652-9668
www.category12beer.com
Enjoy inventive flatbreads, sandwiches, and other indulgences from the Category 12 Bistro.

ACCOMMODATIONS
Hotel Rialto
653 Pandora Ave.
Victoria, BC V8W 1N8
+1 800-332-9981
www.hotelrialto.ca
Elegant rooms (and free breakfast) in the heart of downtown Victoria, within walking distance of several pubs.

TOURIST ATTRACTIONS INFO
Tourism Victoria Visitor Center
812 Wharf St.
Victoria, B.C. V8W 1T3
+1 800-663-3883
www.tourismvictoria.com

LYNN CANYON

CAPILANO ISN'T THE ONLY SUSPENSION BRIDGE IN BC — TAKE A SWINGING WALK ACROSS LYNN CREEK CANYON AND VISIT THE DEEP BLUE 30 FOOT POOL.

STARTING POINT

PARKING LOT IN FRONT OF THE ECOLOGY CENTER

DESTINATION

TWIN FALLS LOOP TRAIL

BEER

BRIDGE BREWING ALL OUT STOUT

DIFFICULTY

WALKING

DURATION OF THE HIKE

(LOOP) **1 HOUR**
1.5 MILES (2.4KM)

MAP

LOOK UP
WWW.LYNNCANYONECOLOGYCENTRE.CA

PASS NEEDED

NONE

ELEVATION GAIN

300 FEET (91M)

STOUT

 DARK BROWN

 TOASTED GRAIN,
BROWN BREAD,
CACAO NIBS

 DARK CHOCOLATE,
CHAR, COFFEE

BITTERNESS   SWEETNESS

DESCRIPTION OF THE ROUTE

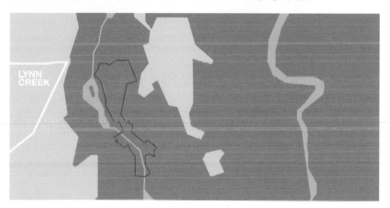

LYNN CREEK

Capilano Suspension Bridge is one of Vancouver's Landmarks, thrilling guests as they dangle high above the canyon below. But even during a downpour, the bridge is packed with tourists, and you might find yourself in yet another line-up instead of taking in the scenery. Which is why Lynn Canyon Park and Suspension Bridge might be one of the most valuable gems in the Vancouver area.

Located east of Capilano in North Vancouver, the park is a popular forest getaway. Its several hiking trails, including a section of the famed Baden Powell Trail, crisscross both sides of the canyon, mostly under dense tree cover. The park's scenery and ruggedly green landscapes have even appeared in a variety of TV shows and movies.

From the main parking lot, follow the road northeast to reach the suspension bridge. You'll pass by the park's cafe where they serve drinks and food seasonally. Almost immediately, you'll be able to spot the bridge. For those afraid of heights, crossing the bridge might involve seeking out some inner courage. The narrow bridge sways and jostles to the delight of thrill seekers, but its sturdy construction and net sides will reassure even the most trepidatious. And the walk is breathtaking: to the right, a waterfall cascades down the canyon wall, and to the left the rushing waters of Lynn Creek descend from a deep pool through a series of rapids. If you dare to linger, the view at midspan is the best.

Once across the bridge, at just under 0.1 miles (0.1 kilometers), the trail forks. Head to the left and walk along the dirt trail towards the 30 Foot Pool. At 0.3 miles (0.5 kilometers), you'll come to a clearing in the trees on the shore of the creek. Ahead, you'll find the deep blue waters of the 30 Foot Pool. The area is an incredibly popular swimming hole in the summer months. But posted next to the pool is a sobering statistic of the injuries and deaths of those who have cliff-jumped here and in other parts of the park. Take a short dip, dip your toes, or just take in the sight from the rocks along the shore — but above all stay safe.

Next is the most difficult part of the trail. A series of staircases leads back up to the top of the canyon. Catch your breath when needed, reaching the end of the stairs at 0.6 miles (1.0 kilometer). Here, turn right and continue back down the creek. When you reach the junction with the trail towards the suspension bridge at 0.9 miles (1.4 kilometers), continue straight to make a loop to view Twin Falls. Here, the trail continues on a boardwalk through the trees, steadily climbing downhill on another set of stairs. At 1.3 miles (2.0 kilometers), you'll come to the Twin Falls and a bridge that crosses right over the top of them. Head down off to the left of the trail for the best views of the falls, then cross the bridge and turn right on the Centennial Trail to arrive back at the parking lot in 1.5 miles (2.4 kilometers).

If you'd like to learn more about the flora and fauna of the area or pick up a paper map for yourself, head into the Park's Ecology Center. The center has a variety of hands-on activities and detailed info on the many animals that live in the area.

TURN BY TURN DIRECTIONS

1. From the parking lot, head to the right toward the suspension bridge.
2. At just under 0.1 miles (0.16 km), turn left.
3. Come to the 30 Foot Pool at 0.3 miles (0.5 km). Continue up the stairs.
4. At 0.6 miles (1.0 km), turn right after the stairs.
5. At 0.7 miles (1.1 km), continue straight at the trail junction.
6. At 0.9 miles (1.4 km), continue straight on the Baden Powell Trail.
7. At 1.3 miles (2.0 km), turn right to cross the Twin Falls Bridge; then turn right onto the Centennial Trail.
8. Arrive back at the parking lot in 1.5 miles (2.4 km) to close the loop.

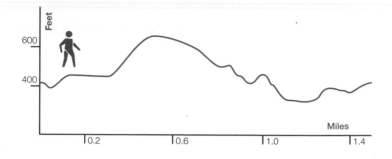

TRAILHEAD DRIVING DIRECTIONS

Take Trans-Canada Highway BC 1 until you reach Exit 19. Follow Lynn Valley NE East past the Mountain Highway intersection, and then continue to Lynn Valley Road. Watch for the Lynn Canyon Ecology Centre sign on the right hand side of the road. Turn right onto Peters Road, and you will find the main entrance at the end of the road.

BRIDGE BREWING COMPANY

Named after the formidable Iron Workers Bridge, Bridge Brewing Company is located nearby in North Vancouver. It was the city's first nanobrewery, but is now cranking out beers in kegs and bottles alike. The taproom is a mixture of warm wood and steel, giving everything a very industrial feel: it's a cozy place to drink a pint. Try the sample tray to experience the brewery's take on both hoppy pale ales and dark beers.

TRAIL CONTACT INFORMATION
District of North Vancouver
Recreation and Leisure
355 West Queens Rd.
North Vancouver, BC V7N 4N5
+1 604-990-2311
www.dnv.org/recreation-and-leisure

TOURIST ATTRACTIONS INFO
North Vancouver Visitor Centre
Lonsdale Quay Market
604-656-6491
www.vancouversnorthshore.com

Lynn Canyon Ecology Centre
3663 Park Rd.
North Vancouver, BC V7J 3G3
+1 604-990-3755
www.lynncanyonecologycentre.ca

BREWERY
Bridge Brewing Company
1448 Charlotte Road
North Vancouver, BC, V7J 1H2
+1 604-770-2739
www.bridgebrewing.com
Vancouver's first nanobrewery, now a highly producing microbrewery and taproom.

RESTAURANT
Tommy's Cafe
1308 Ross Rd.
Vancouver, BC V7J 1V2
+1 604-988-0174,
www.tommycaters.com
Great for breakfast and lunch.

ACCOMMODATIONS
Holiday Inn and Suites North Vancouver
700 Old Lillooet Rd.
North Vancouver, BC V7J 2H5
+1 877-859-5095
www.hinorthvancouver.com
Comfortable lodging close to both Lynn Canyon and Bridge Brewing Company.

SEA TO SUMMIT ASCENT TRAIL

SCRAMBLE UP THIS CHALLENGING TRAIL TO THE SUMMIT LODGE
— NEARLY 3,000 FEET ABOVE HOWE SOUND — AND RIDE BACK DOWN IN
AN ENCLOSED GONDOLA TO SAMPLE BC BREWS IN NEARBY SQUAMISH.

STARTING POINT	DESTINATION
SEA TO SUMMIT TRAILHEAD	**SUMMIT LODGE**
BEER	**DIFFICULTY**
HOWE SOUND RAIL ALE	**MOUNTAIN** HIKING 
MAP	**DURATION OF THE HIKE**
PAPER MAPS AVAILABLE AT SEA TO SKY GONDOLA SEATOSKYGONDOLA.COM	**3-5 HOURS 4.6 MILES** (7.4KM)
PASS NEEDED	**ELEVATION GAIN**
NONE	**3,012 FEET** (980M)

NUT BROWN

BROWN

CARAMEL,
DRIED FRUIT

MALTY, NUTTY,
SMOOTH

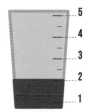

BITTERNESS

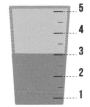

SWEETNESS

DESCRIPTION OF THE ROUTE

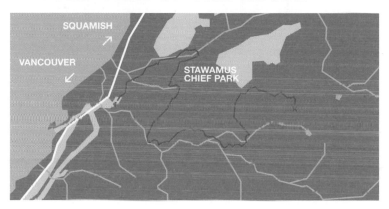

Sea to Summit Ascent. It's a sexy trail name, no doubt — alliterative and alluring, the stuff of daydreams. But this trail is no fantasy. Those who set out on the Sea to Summit Ascent will climb from 115 feet (35 meters) above sea level to 2,900 feet (884 meters) above sea level in 4.6 miles (7.4 kilometers) one-way. Perhaps somewhat underrated in terms of difficulty, the Sea to Summit Trail gains 3,000 feet over terrain so steep that fixed ropes and chains are in place to assist you.

Yet the payoff is oh-so worth it. Trailside waterfalls gush with snowmelt, and views of Howe Sound improve with every mile. Gondolas pass quietly overhead — a reminder that your hike is only one-way. Fortunately, most of the route is under tree cover, so you are sheltered from the elements. Summit Lodge awaits at the top, with plenty of attractions to keep you busy all day.

Park at Darrell Bay for free long-term parking. Alternatively, you can park in the Sea to Sky Gondola lot for 3 hours of free parking — but you'll want more than 3 hours for this hike. From the Darrell Bay parking area, cross the street into Shannon Falls Provincial Park. Take a gander at BC's third-tallest waterfall before following the signed Connector Trail towards Sea to Summit.

Once on the Sea to Summit Ascent, you'll climb steep staircases, cross bridges, and scramble over rocks, enjoying a mix of flat and downhill sections to balance things out along the way. This is one trail where the estimated 3-5 hours hiking time is no exaggeration. Take your time, and remember that it's smooth sailing once you reach the top.

Your destination, Summit Lodge, sits on a ridge northwest of Mount Habrich. Most visitors make their first stop at the viewing deck for sweeping vistas of Howe Sound, the Coast Mountains, and the emerald forests below. Next to the viewing deck, the 100-meter-long Sky Pilot Suspension Bridge is considered a "must-do" for all visitors due to its unique photo opportunities and easy access.

If you have any energy left, several easy walking trails are worth exploring. The Spirit Trail takes off from the Sky Pilot Suspension Bridge, offering interpretive information along the way. Learn about the Squamish First Nation's history and culture on this short, 0.3-mile (400 meters) long loop. For a longer walk, try the 1-mile (1.6 kilometer) Panorama Trail loop. Allow an hour to explore this trail's various viewpoints, including the Chief Overlook Platform. True to its name, this deck offers unparalleled views of Squamish's granite monolith, the Stawamus Chief.

When you've finished exploring, grab a beer and a bite to eat at Summit Lodge. Or simply ride the gondola down for your next adventure at Howe Sound Brewery. Either way, you'll need to purchase a download pass for the gondola. Hiking back down the Sea to Summit Ascent is not recommended.

TURN BY TURN DIRECTIONS

1. From Darrell Bay, cross the street into Shannon Falls Provincial Park.
2. After viewing the falls, begin your hike by heading north on the signed Connector Trail.
3. At 0.5 miles (0.8 km), cross the Oleson Creek Bridge; stay right at a junction.
4. At 1 mile (1.6 km), stay right at the junction.
5. At 3.0 miles (4.8 km), turn left at the wide trail to head uphill.
6. At 3.2 miles (5.1 km), turn left at the junction.
7. Reach Summit Lodge at 4.6 miles (7.4 km).

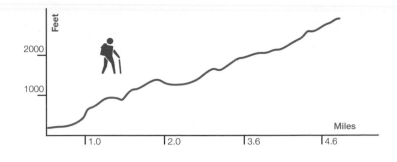

TRAILHEAD DRIVING DIRECTIONS

From Vancouver, head northwest on BC-99 to Trans-Canada Highway/
BC-1 W/BC-99. Merge onto the highway to continue west, then north for
approximately 31 miles (50 kilometers). Turn left into the Darrell Bay
parking area, directly across from the entrance to Shannon Falls.

HOWE SOUND BREWERY AND INN

Located in Squamish, BC, with views of the Stawamus Chief, Howe
Sound Brewing was designed in partnership with John Mitchell, the
"grandfather of micro-brewing in Canada." Over 20 years later, the
brewery continues to diversify its line-up of award-winning Northwest
ales. Howe Sound Brewery is also home to the Howe Sound Inn — letting
craft beer fans have a pint before heading upstairs to a room with a view
of majestic Howe Sound.

TRAIL CONTACT INFORMATION
Sea to Sky Gondola
36800 Hwy. 99
Squamish, BC V0N 3G0
+1 604-892-2551
www.seatoskygondola.com

TOURIST ATTRACTIONS INFO
Squamish Adventure Centre
38551 Loggers Lane
Squamish, BC, V8B 0H2
+1 604-815-4994
www.exploresquamish.com

**BREWERY/RESTAURANT/
ACCOMMODATIONS**
Howe Sound Brewery and Inn
37801 Cleveland Ave.
Squamish, BC V8B 0A7
+1 604-892-2603
www.howesound.com
Howe Sound does it all. Dine in their large,
rustic-feel restaurant and stay upstairs in a
room with a view of the Stawamus Chief.

SENDERO DIEZ VISTAS

A CHALLENGING RIDGE CLIMB BETWEEN BUNTZEN LAKE AND THE INDIAN ARM SALTWATER FJORD TO SOME OF THE FINEST VISTAS IN THE VANCOUVER AREA.

STARTING POINT	DESTINATION
BUNTZEN LAKE PARKING LOT	**DIEZ VISTAS**

BEER	DIFFICULTY
YELLOW DOG CHASE MY TAIL PALE ALE	**MOUNTAIN** HIKING 

MAP	DURATION OF THE HIKE
LOOK UP WWW.BCHYDRO.COM	**3-4 HOURS 5 MILES** (8KM)

PASS NEEDED	ELEVATION GAIN
NONE	**1,900 FEET** (579M)

PALE ALE

GOLDEN

PINE, GRAPEFRUIT

ORANGE ZEST,
GREEN MANGO

BITTERNESS   SWEETNESS

DESCRIPTION OF THE ROUTE

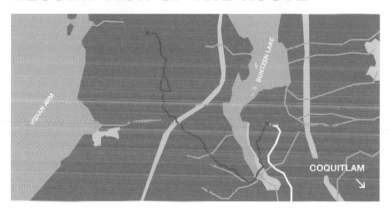

Sendero Diez Vistas, Spanish for "Ten Views Trail," is a classic Vancouver hike. Beginning at Buntzen Lake's shore, the trail charges up Buntzen Ridge through mossy forests to views aplenty before circling back along the lake in an 8.3 mile (13.3 kilometer) loop. Below, we describe an abbreviated 5 mile (8 kilometer) hike to the best viewpoints along the Sendero.

Begin your hike by following the flat, easy Buntzen Lake Trail south for half a mile to the floating bridge. This bridge rises and falls with the lake's fluctuating water levels throughout the year. Once across the bridge, get ready to climb. The Diez Vistas trail takes off from here, gaining 1,400 feet (427 meters) in 1.4 miles (2.3 kilometers). This is a technical trail — a carpet of roots and rocks draped over steep slopes. At times it becomes a full-on scramble, so be ready to use all fours!

The route is mostly straightforward, but some areas can be a bit confusing. When in doubt, look for orange trail markers tacked to the trees. Small orange squares line the trail, making it difficult to stay lost for long.

After climbing steadily through the forest, the trail passes through a clearing beneath power lines. Continue on up to a series of switchbacks and the steepest part of the trail. Here you'll find fixed ropes in place to assist your climb, and to keep you from falling down a significant drop on one side.

After navigating the ropes, you'll come to a junction. Head left to reach a somewhat obscured view — a taste of what's to come. From here you can look down on Belcarra Peninsula and Jug Island. Next up is the Cima Amanecer viewpoint, followed by — in our opinion — the best vista on the Sendero. From this wide, unobscured vantage point you can look across the Indian Arm at Deep Cove. Vancouver and Burnaby with their high-rise buildings look like tiny toy towns in the distance.

This is a great lunch spot, and the best place to turn around if you're not up for the entire loop. At the time of research, the East Buntzen Lake Trail was closed, so we opted to call it quits here. There's no shame in doing so. You've already hiked the toughest section of the Sendero, and hiking out-and-back allows for additional views over Buntzen Lake. While you won't see the full ten vistas, many are overgrown from here on out.

After passing Cima Amanecer on your way back, head left at the junction. The trail drops rather steeply to Punta Del Este, a nice viewpoint over Buntzen Lake. Deer frolic in the forest here, coming out before sunset for their evening meal. Check out Punta Aprecio for limited views south to Burnaby Mountain before rejoining the main trail. Return the way you came.

TURN BY TURN DIRECTIONS

1   From the parking area, head south on the Buntzen Lake Trail.
2   Continue straight at all junctions.
3   At 0.5 miles (0.8 km), cross the floating bridge.
4   After crossing the bridge, walk aross the road and continue straight on the Diez Vistas Trail.
5   At 0.75 miles (1.2 km), continue straight on the Diez Vistas Trail.
6   At 1.5 miles (2.4 km), continue straight beneath the power lines.
7   At 1.9 miles (3.1 km), go left at the junction.
8   At 2.1 miles (3.4 km), go left at the junction.
9   At 2.5 miles (4 km), reach the best vista. Turn around here.
10   At 2.9 miles (4.7 km), go left at the junction.
11   At 3.1 miles (5 km), go left at the junction.
12   Return the way you came.

TRAIL CONTACT INFORMATION
BC Hydro
333 Dunsmuir St.
Vancouver, BC, V6B 5R3
+1 800-224-9376
www.bchydro.com/recreation

ACCOMMODATIONS
The Simon Hotel at Simon Fraser University
8888 University Dr.
Burnaby, BC V5A 1S6
+1 778-782-4503
www.sfu.ca/stayhere/accommodations/hotel/overview.html
Comfy, no-frills accommodations on the top floor of the highest building in the Vancouver area.

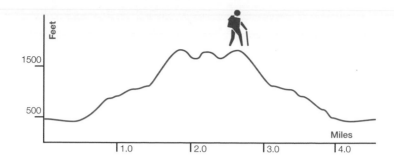

TRAILHEAD DRIVING DIRECTIONS

From Port Moody, take BC-7A east. Turn north onto Ioco Road. At the second major intersection on Ioco, bear left to stay on Ioco. Follow Ioco Road until you come to a stop sign at 1st Avenue. Turn right onto 1st Avenue and then bear right immediately at the fork for Sunnyside Road. Follow Sunnyside Road up the hill to its end. Turn left into the parking area, and park in the southwest corner of the large parking lot.

YELLOW DOG BREWERY

A giant golden lab greets you as you enter Yellow Dog Brewing Co.'s taproom — or at least a large photograph of one does. Part of Port Moody's Murray Street Brewery Row, Yellow Dog was actually the first brewery to open in the area in 2014. Now joined by a handful of other breweries mere steps away, Yellow Dog still maintains its alpha status with a line-up of hop-forward ales. For dog and beer lovers alike, this family-owned brewery is a Port Moody must!

TOURIST ATTRACTIONS INFO
Tri Cities Chamber of Commerce
1209 Pinetree Way
Coquitlam, BC, V3B 7Y3
+1 604-464-2716
www.tricitieschamber.com

Burnaby Mountain Park
800 Burnaby Mountain Pkwy.
Burnaby, BC V5A 1G9
+1 604-294-7450
www.burnaby.ca/things-to-do/
explore-outdoors/parks/burnaby-
mountain-conservation-area.html
Worth a side trip for excellent Vancouver
metro views and a visit to the Kamui
Mintara "Playground of the Gods."

BREWERY
Yellow Dog Brewery
2817 Murray St. #1
Port Moody, BC, V3H 1X3
+1 604-492-0191
www.yellowdogbeer.com
Dog-themed brewery in Port Moody's
Brewery Row.

RESTAURANT
Pajo's Restaurant
2800 Murray St.
Port Moody, BC, V3H 1X3
+1 604-469-2289
www.pajos.com/locations/pajos-at-
rocky-point-park-port-moody
Classic Canadian fish and chips,
located across the street from
the brewery in Rocky Point Park.

STANLEY PARK

TAKE IN THE SIGHTS OF ONE OF THE WORLD'S MOST FAMOUS PARKS
AND WALK ALONG STANLEY PARK'S ICONIC SEAWALL FOR VIEWS
OF ENGLISH BAY AND SECOND-GROWTH FORESTS.

STARTING POINT	DESTINATION
SECOND BEACH PARKING AREA	**STANLEY PARK SEAWALL LOOP**
BEER	DIFFICULTY
STEAMWORKS FLAGSHIP IPA	**WALKING**
MAP	DURATION OF THE HIKE
LOOK UP WWW.VANCOUVER.CA	(LOOP) **3 HOURS** **6.1 MILES** (9.8KM)
PASS NEEDED	ELEVATION GAIN
PAY PARKING LOTS IN THE PARK	**260 FEET** (79M)

INDIA PALE ALE

 CLOUDY GOLD

 ORANGES, RESIN, LEMON

JUICY, MANGO, GRAPEFRUIT

BITTERNESS   **SWEETNESS**

DESCRIPTION OF THE ROUTE

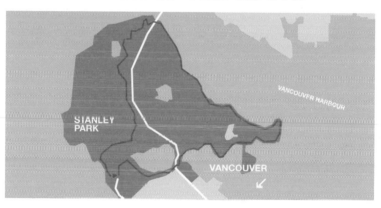

Vancouver's first park, Stanley Park is an emerald-green jewel for the city. A combination of urbanization and second-growth forests, the park is surrounded on three sides by the waters of Vancouver Harbor and English Bay. Stanley Park opened officially in 1888 and was dedicated to Lord Stanley — Canada's Governor General at the time, and donor of the Stanley Cup hockey championship trophy. Today, the park is home to play structures and the Vancouver Aquarium, and is a favorite place for the citizens of Vancouver to get out of the house even on the rainiest of days.

With enough trails to satisfy avid walkers for a week straight, it's a daunting task to pick a route. This is one of our favorites, combining many of the park's iconic landmarks along the famed Seawall, a breathtaking viewpoint, and a forest stroll.

Starting from the parking lot at the Second Beach Picnic area, cross Stanley Park Drive and take the path along the north edge of the pitch and putt field. At 0.2 miles (0.3 kilometers), turn right and continue up the path towards Lost Lagoon. On this stretch of trail, the contrast of the park's natural beauty with the high-rises of downtown is stark. Continue past the placid waters of Lost Lagoon, use the pedestrian underpass, and meet up with the Seawall at 0.8 miles (1.3 kilometers). From here, head left and start on one of Vancouver's most popular walking paths. While on the Seawall, make sure to stay on the designated walking side — the flat pathway is a favorite of rollerbladers and bicyclists (bicycles can be rented in-park if you're looking for a change of pace!).

The south end of the Seawall offers views of Coal Habour — Canada Place in the distance plus the prestigious Vancouver Rowing Club and Royal Vancouver Yacht Club just offshore. At 1.7 miles (2.7 kilometers), the entrance to Deadman's Island appears, gated. The island has historically been used as a burial ground (thus its name), first by the Coast Salish and later by early settlers in the area. The island is now restricted, but still a fascinating site. Another interesting landmark, at 2.0 miles (3.2 kilometers), is the 9 O'Clock Gun, a cannon that goes off every evening at 9pm.

At 2.3 miles (3.7 kilometers) you'll come to one of the quintessential landmarks along the Seawall: the red and white striped Brockton Point Lighthouse. From here, the views of the Burrard Inlet and North Coast Mountains take over. This stretch of the Seawall is one of the most travelled and has appeared in various movies and television shows. It's also at this point that another Vancouver landmark comes into view: the Lionsgate Bridge. As you approach the bridge, you'll leave the Seawall and take a left at 3.7 miles (6.0 kilometers) onto the Avison Trail to the Prospect Point trail. At 3.8 miles (6.1 kilometers), continue straight at the junction. From here, the trail to Prospect Point climbs sharply up the hillside, underneath the Lionsgate Bridge towards the viewpoint. At 4.2 miles (6.8 kilometers), that steep climb will be worth it as you come to the viewpoint.

The breathtaking view from Prospect Point is astounding. The mouth of Burrard Inlet shimmers as you look west towards Lighthouse Park in West Vancouver. The North Coast Mountains rise like a wall in front of you, with both Cypress and Grouse Mountain ahead. Count container ships coming into the harbor, marvel at the impressive Lionsgate Suspension Bridge, and then head into the heart of the park. Cross Stanley Park Drive and take the Prospect Point Trail through the park's most forested expanses. At 4.7 miles (7.6 kilometers) you'll continue straight onto the Bridle Path Trail, which will explore the forest as it works its way back towards Second Beach. At 5.9 miles (9.5 kilometers), the trail meets up with the Seawall once again. Enjoy the calm waters of English Bay as you round Second Beach back to the parking lot at the picnic area, completing the loop at 6.1 miles (9.8 kilometers).

TURN BY TURN DIRECTIONS

1. From the Second Beach picnic area, cross Stanley Park Drive to the trail near the golf course.
2. At 0.2 miles (0.3 km), turn right.
3. At 0.7 miles (1.1 km), use the pedestrian underpass.
4. At 0.8 miles (1.3 km), turn right onto the Seawall.
5. At 3.7 miles (6.0 km), turn left onto the Avison Trail.
6. At 3.8 miles (6.1 km), continue straight onto the Prospect Point Trail.
7. At 4.2 miles (6.8 km), cross Stanley Park Drive to stay on the Prospect Point Trail.
8. At 4.7 miles (7.6 km), continue straight onto the Bridle Path Trail.
9. At 5.9 miles (9.5 km), turn left onto the Seawall.
10. At 6.1 miles (9.8 km), arrive at the parking lot to close the loop.

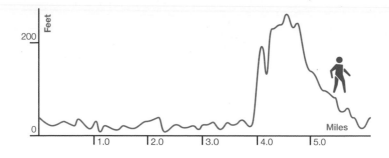

TRAILHEAD DRIVING DIRECTIONS

From downtown Vancouver, take W Georgia/BC-99N. Turn left onto Denman Street, then right onto Beach Avenue. Continue on Beach Avenue until you come to the Second Beach Picnic Area on Stanley Park Drive.

STEAMWORKS BREWING CO.

Steamworks Brewing Co. is a downtown Vancouver "Establishment." Steps away from Gastown and conveniently situated on the Waterfront, Steamworks has an enviable location and a history that is impossible to ignore. The brewpub is a favorite for tourists and locals alike, who fill the restaurant's multiple spacious seating areas every night of the week. Steamworks has recently taken on a "Steampunk-lite" branding, with a nod to the steam pipes that not only run Gastown's iconic steam clock but heat the brew kettles as well.

TRAIL CONTACT INFORMATION
Vancouver Board of Parks and Recreation
2099 Beach Ave.
Vancouver, BC V6G 1Z4
+1 604-873-7000
www.vancouver.ca

ACCOMMODATIONS
Rosellen Suites At Stanley Park
2030 Barclay St.
Vancouver, BC V6G 1L5
+1 604-689-4807
www.rosellensuites.com
Walking distance to Stanley Park.

RESTAURANT
Steamworks Brewing Co.
375 Water St.
Vancouver, BC V6B 5C6
+1 604-689-2739
www.steamworks.com
Convenient location on the Waterfront, with a historic building and great menu.

TOURIST ATTRACTIONS INFO
Tourism Vancouver Visitor Centre
200 Burrard Street Plaza Level
Vancouver, BC V6C 3L6
+1 604-682-2222
www.tourismvancouver.com

TEAPOT HILL

COUNT THE TRAILSIDE TEAPOTS AS YOU MAKE YOUR WAY THROUGH
THIS ENCHANTING FOREST TO A HIGH POINT
OVERLOOKING CULTUS LAKE AND THE COLUMBIA VALLEY.

STARTING POINT	DESTINATION
TEAPOT HILL PARKING AREA	**TEAPOT HILL**
BEER	DIFFICULTY
FARMHOUSE BLACKBERRY PEACH COBBLER	**HIKING**
MAP	DURATION OF THE HIKE
LOOK UP WWW.ENV.GOV.BC.CA	**2 HOURS 3.4 MILES** (5.5KM)
PASS NEEDED	ELEVATION GAIN
NONE	**820 FEET** (250M)

SOUR ALE

 BRIGHT RUBY RED

 BLACKBERRY, SPICE, LEMON ZEST

TART, PASTRY CRUST, BLACKBERRY

BITTERNESS

5
4
3
2
1

SWEETNESS

5
4
3
2
1

DESCRIPTION OF THE ROUTE

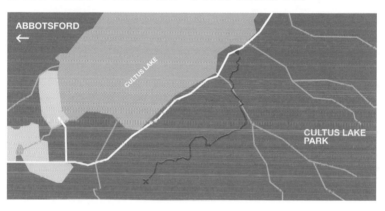

Located south of Chilliwack, BC, near the US-Canada border, Cultus Lake is a buzzing family-fun destination during the summer. Escape the busy campgrounds with a quiet walk in the woods at Teapot Hill. While the trail can certainly be busy on summer weekends, a weekday or off-season hike here is quite charming — as much an exercise for the imagination as it is for the body.

The story goes that in the 1940s, a logger discovered a teapot on this 1,181-foot (360-meter) hill. The name stuck, and in recent years someone (or something?) has taken the liberty of decorating the trail with a variety of ceramic teapots. It's a curious phenomenon, seen as harmless fun by some and a bit of a nuisance by others. While many enjoy counting the pots, occasional shattered vessels are a reminder that not everyone finds them so endearing.

From the parking area, a wide gravel road-turned-trail takes off gradually uphill. You'll pass an outhouse and trail map on the left while walking alongside a trickling stream. Mossy cedar trees line the trail. Watch for colorful mushrooms in autumn, tiger lilies in spring. Trillium, western columbine, and stinging nettle can be found here seasonally as well. At 1 mile (1.6 kilometers), a signed intersection guides you uphill to the right. Here, the hike truly begins.

If you haven't spotted any teapots yet, keep an eye out here. They could be anywhere — hanging from tree branches, sitting upon stumps, resting against tree trunks — or they could be nowhere at all. Perhaps they only show themselves to those who believe? Let your imagination wander. Could they have been placed by furry forest friends, anxiously awaiting your arrival for a tea party in the woods? Why do some people count 50, while others claim to see not a single teapot?

In reality, the teapots really do exist. We counted 27 in November 2016 — three years after Cultus Lake Provincial Park cleaned up the area due to litter concerns. It's a complicated and controversial issue. Should the park allow this whimsical tradition, or ban it in favor of Leave No Trace ethics? For now, it seems a compromise has been reached: teapots line the trail once again. Please respect the natural environment by staying on-trail to view them, and resist any temptation to smash these fragile vessels. If you find a smashed teapot, be a good steward and pack the pieces out to help keep this trail wild.

At the top of Teapot Hill, two viewpoints reward your efforts. Immediately across the lake, Vedder Mountain dominates much of the skyline. Enjoy partially tree-obstructed views north over Cultus Lake and the Fraser Valley towards distant snow-capped Canadian peaks. Peer southwest across the Columbia Valley and beyond to the USA. When you've had your fill of the views, head on back to Chilliwack. While there may not be any trailside tea to quench your thirst here, there's plenty of beer to go around in town.

TURN BY TURN DIRECTIONS

1. The trail begins at the east end of the parking area. Follow it uphill to begin.
2. At 0.7 miles (1.1 km), continue straight at the junction.
3. At 1 mile (1.6 km), turn right at the signed junction.
4. At 1.5 miles (2.4 km), reach the first viewpoint.
5. At 1.7 miles (2.7 km), reach the final viewpoint.
6. Return the way you came.

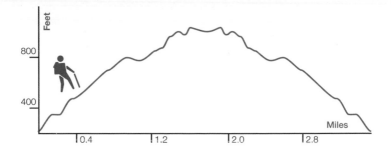

TRAILHEAD DRIVING DIRECTIONS

From Chilliwack, take Vedder Road south. After crossing the Chilliwack River, turn left onto Columbia Valley Highway. Follow this road 5.1 miles (8.3 kilometers) to the parking lot on the left.

FARMHOUSE BREWING CO.

Opened in October 2020, Farmhouse Brewing Co. is a cozy space to enjoy a pint paired with wood-fired pizza. One of the few true farmhouse breweries in British Columbia, Farmhouse Brewing is located on an 11.5-acre farm in rural Chilliwack. Utilizing their own barley, the brewer's create a wide variety of beer styles with a unique emphasis on fruited sours. The heated patio, rustic tasting room, and open lawn greenspace are family-friendly and provide plenty of room to spread out and relax.

TRAIL CONTACT INFORMATION
BC Parks
(Operated by Sea to Sky Park Services Ltd)
+1 604 086 0371
www.env.gov.bc.ca/bcparks/explore/
parkpgs/cultus_lk

TOURIST ATTRACTIONS INFO
Tourism Chilliwack Visitor Centre
44150 Luckakuck Way
Chilliwack, BC, V2R 4A7
www.tourismchilliwack.com

BREWERY/RESTAURANT
Farmhouse Brewing Co.
6385 Lickman Rd.
Chilliwack, BC V2R 4A9
www.farmhousebrewing.co
Farm brewery located nine miles from the Teapot Hill trailhead.

ACCOMMODATIONS
The Royal Hotel
45886 Wellington Ave
Chilliwack, BC V2P 2C7
+1 604-792-1210
www.royalhotelchilliwack.com
Charming downtown Chilliwack hotel established in 1908.

WHISTLER TRAIN WRECK

TAKE A BREAK FROM THE SLOPES TO EXPLORE WHISTLER'S ICONIC TRAIN WRECK SITE — ONE OF THE FEW YEAR-ROUND ACCESSIBLE TRAILS NEAR THE WORLD CLASS WHISTLER BLACKCOMB SKI RESORT.

STARTING POINT	DESTINATION
TRAIN WRECK PARKING AREA	**WHISTLER TRAIN WRECK**

BEER	DIFFICULTY
COAST MOUNTAIN SUNBREAK SAISON	**WALKING**

MAP	DURATION OF THE HIKE
RESORT MUNICIPALITY OF WHISTLER LOOK UP ON WWW.WHISTLER.CA	**1 HOUR 1.3 MILES** (2KM)

PASS NEEDED	ELEVATION GAIN
NONE	**98 FEET** (30M)

ALCOHOL
6.5%
CONTENT

SAISON

 LIGHT YELLOW

LEMON, SWEET HAY, CLOVER

CRACKED PEPPER, LEMON ZEST, CLOVE

BITTERNESS **SWEETNESS**

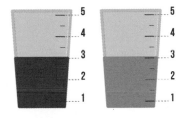

DESCRIPTION OF THE ROUTE

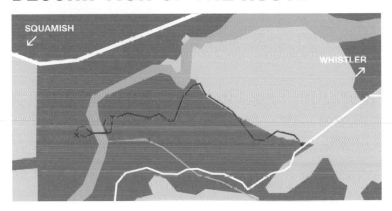

SQUAMISH

WHISTLER

In 1956, a speeding train derailed just south of Whistler, BC. Details of the wreck are murky, but members of a local logging family, Rick and Howard Valleau, have shed light on the event in an interview with Whistler Museum. According to Rick and Howard, a train going 20 mph (32 km/h) over the speed limit crashed and blocked the railway line. The Valleau family was called on to move the cars with logging equipment. They brought in Cats to haul the boxcars off the line, and deposited them in the forest where they rest today.

For many years, a potentially dangerous trail led from Function Junction out to the Train Wreck site. Because it crossed the railroad tracks illegally, CN Rail police issued tickets to trespassing hikers in an attempt to discourage unsafe access. But hikers (and bikers) would go anyway. After seeing unbelievable photos of the tagged-up twisted metal on social media, many were willing to take the risk.

To address these safety concerns and legal issues, the Resort Municipality of Whistler funded a $176,000 suspension bridge project in 2016. This beautiful new bridge connects the Train Wreck to the well-maintained Sea to Sky Trail, opening access to all. There's never been a better time to visit the Train Wreck.

Begin along the wide, gravel Sea to Sky Trail. The trail itself is picture-perfect: beautifully manicured, rolling gently through the woods. It's easy enough to walk with a cup of Tim Horton's in hand, and many visitors do just that. Take a right at the first junction you come to, signed for "Train Wreck Site and Suspension Bridge." This will put you on the Trash Trail, a more primitive dirt path with roots and some mud during rainier months.

At a second junction, go either way to reach the suspension bridge. The trail to the left is quite steep, so it may be easier to head right here. Marvel at the bridge before crossing the raging Cheakamus River. On the other side, you'll arrive at the legendary Train Wreck.

Behold the wreckage: several train cars strewn about the forest, each one covered in graffiti art. Local bikers have turned the area into an impromptu mountain bike park with ramps leading up, over, and down many of the cars. Once you've had your fill, return the way you came.

The Train Wreck Trail is generally hikeable year-round, but may require snowshoes during the winter. Check with the land manager for current conditions.

TURN BY TURN DIRECTIONS

1. From the parking area, head west across the road to the Sea to Sky Trail.
2. At 0.4 miles (0.6 km), turn right at a signed junction.
3. At 0.6 miles (0.9 km), turn right at the junction.
4. Cross the suspension bridge and explore the train wreck site;
    then return the way you came.

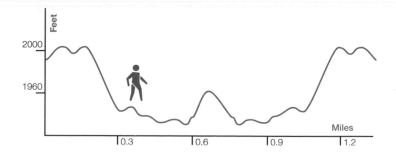

TRAILHEAD DRIVING DIRECTIONS

From Whistler Village, head south on BC-99 and turn left on Cheakamus Lake Road (at Function Junction). After crossing a bridge, turn right onto Jane Lakes Road and follow it 0.3 miles (0.5 kilometers) to the signed "Train Wreck Parking" area on the left.

COAST MOUNTAIN BREWING

Since opening its doors in summer 2016, Coast Mountain has captured the hearts (and taste buds) of beer drinkers living in and visiting the mountain resort town of Whistler. Located just a five-minute drive from the Train Wreck trailhead in Function Junction, Coast Mountain brews hop-forward and sessionable beers perfect for relaxing après-ski or after a summer hike. During your visit, make sure to try one of the small batch sours from their oak barrel program. With cans-to-go, Coast Mountain beers can even join you on your next adventure.

TRAIL CONTACT INFORMATION
Resort Municipality of Whistler
4325 Blackcomb Way
Whistler, B.C. V0N 1B4
+1 604-932-5535
www.whistler.ca/culture-recreation/
parks-trails/train-wreck-bridge

RESTAURANT
Beacon Pub and Eatery
4154 Village Stroll #7
Whistler, BC V0N 1B4
+1 604-962-9333
www.beaconwhistler.com
Gastro-pub menu and 12 craft beers on tap.

TOURIST ATTRACTIONS INFO
Tourism Whistler Visitor Centre
4230 Gateway Dr.
Whistler, BC V0N 1B4
+1 800-944-7853
www.whistler.com

BREWERY
Coast Mountain Brewing
1212 Alpha Lake Rd. #2
Whistler, BC V0N 1B1
+1 604-962-3222
www.coastmountainbeer.ca
Solid brews, friendly staff, and a cozy cabin like taproom in Function Junction.

ACCOMMODATIONS
Crystal Lodge and Suites
4154 Village Green
Whistler, BC V0N 1B4
+1 604-932-2221
www.crystal-lodge.com

SCANDINAVE SPA WHISTLER
8010 Mons Rd.
Whistler, BC V0N 1B8
+1 604-935-2424
www.scandinave.com/en/whistler
Relax post-hike at this expansive outdoor spa.

6

INDEX

BREWERIES

BEERS

7BBL IPA	Birdsview Brewing	156
All Out Stout	Bridge Brewing Co.	210
Anacortes IPA	Rockfish Grill & Anacortes Brewery	176
Blackberry Peach Cobbler	Farmhouse Brewing Co.	226
Blue Collar Pale Ale	Mission Springs Brewing Co.	194
Bracegriddle	The 3 Legged Crane Pub	62
Cascadian Rye	Cole Street Brewery	148
Cetacea	Yachats Brewing	30
Chase My Tail Pale Ale	Yellow Dog Brewery	218
Citra Sonic IPA	Barhop Brewing	140
Dairyland	Haywire Brewing Co.	84
Dark Persuasion	Icicle Brewing Co.	120
Dunkel	Buoy Beer Company	46
E9 Tacoma Brew	E9 Brewing Co.	152
Eliot IPA	Ex Novo Brewing Co.	42
ESB On Nitro	North Fork Brewery	180
Flagship IPA	Steamworks Brewing Co.	222
Golden Ratio	Category 12 Brewing	206
Goosetown Brown	North Sound Brewing	128
Hogsback Oatmeal Stout	Mt. Hood Brewing Co.	78
Homo Erectus IPA	Walking Man Brewing	88
Interurban IPA	Fremont Brewing Co.	100
IPA	pFriem Brewery	54
Irish Death	Iron Horse Brewery	132
Kiwanda Cream Ale	Pelican Pub and Brewery	22
Kriek	De Garde Brewing	26
Life Changer Scottish Ale	River Time Brewing	112
Liquid Vacation	Skyline Brewing	50
Moonlight Ride Blackberry Ale	Rusty Truck Brewing Co.	34
Murder of Crows	Skookum Brewery	144
Methow Blonde	Old Schoolhouse Brewery	136
Nut Crusher Peanut Butter Porter	Wild Ride Brewing	70
Pacemaker Porter	Flyers Restaurant and Brewery	104
Pirate Stout	Santiam Brewing	66
Rail Ale	Howe Sound Brewery and Inn	214
Russian Imperial Stout	Kulshan Flagship & K2	160
Schwarz	Dru Bru	124
Scottish Monk	Old Abbey Ales	186
Seaplane IPA	Cairn Brewing	164
Spruce	Propolis Brewing	108
Standard & Better	Ashtown Brewing Co.	116
Steam Train Porter	Snoqualmie Falls Brewing	172
Sunbreak Saison	Coast Mountain Brewing	230
Suncoast Pale Ale	Townsite Brewing	198
Sweet As Pacific Ale	GoodLife Brewing	58
The Last Strawberry	Fuggles & Warlock	202
The Milkman Knocks Twice	North Jetty Brewing	92
Topcutter IPA	Bale Breaker Brewing Co.	96
Torrential Sour Series	Falling Sky Brew Pub	74
Tree Line	Packwood Brewing Co.	168
Weizenhower Wheat	Green Leaf Brewing	190
Ya Ya Ee IPA	Thunder Island Brewing	38

DIFFICULTY

WALKING	Duration	Loop?	
Barclay Lake	2		84
Beacon Rock	1		88
Cape Disappointment	2		92
Cape Kiwanda	1		22
Cowiche Canyon	2 – 3		96
Discovery Park	2	↺	100
Dry Creek Falls	2		38
Fort Stevens State Park	2 – 3	↺	46
Fort Worden	1 – 2	↺	108
Gold Creek Falls	2		194
Hood River Waterfront	1 – 2		54
Iona Jetty	2		202
Inland Lake Loop Trail	3	↺	198
Lynn Canyon	1	↺	210
Marymere Falls	1 – 2	↺	140
Newberry Caldera	1 – 2	↺	58
North Fork River Walk	2 – 3		62
Point Defiance	1 – 2		152
Stanley Park	3	↺	222
Saint Edward	1	↺	164
Snoqualmie Falls	1		172
Whistler Train Wreck	1		230

HIKING			
Abby Grind	1 – 2		186
Cape Lookout	2 – 3		26
Cape Perpetua	3		30
Cascade Head	2		34
Eagle Bluffs	3 – 4		190
Ebey's Landing	2 – 3	↺	104
Forest Park	2 – 3		42
Garfield Peak	2 – 3		50
Icicle Ridge	2 – 3		120
Jocelyn Hill	3		206
Little Mountain	1 – 2	↺	128
Manastash Ridge	2 – 3		132
Misery Ridge Loop	2 – 3	↺	70
Pinnacle Peak Lookout	1 – 2		148
Rock Trail	2 – 3		160
Spencer Butte	1 – 2		74
Silver Falls	3	↺	66
Sugarloaf-Erie	3		176
Skyline Loop	3	↺	168
Teapot Hill	2		226
Tom Dick and Harry Mountain	3 – 4		78
Winchester Mountain	2		180

MOUNTAIN HIKING			
Green Mountain	6		112
Harry's Ridge	3 – 4		116
Ira Spring Trail	3		124
Maple Pass Loop	4	↺	136
Mount Pilchuck	3 – 4		144
Railroad Grade	4		156
Sea to Summit	3 – 5		214
Sendero Diez Vistas	3 – 4		218

ACKNOWLEDGEMENTS & DEDICATION

Thank you, Monika Saxer, for paving the way and connecting us to Helvetiq. Many thanks to Hadi Barkat, Olivia Chudik, and the entire team at Helvetiq for working with us over the course of many months on this project.

A growing number of fellow writers and editors have inspired and mentored us over the years. We owe much of our professional growth to them.

Eli Boschetto gave us our first feature assignment in *Washington Trails Magazine* a few years ago — a "Boots and Brews" travel piece on our hometown of Bellingham, WA. Thank you, Eli, for offering that early opportunity and for always being just a phone call or email away. Your expertise has been invaluable in our quest. May the force continue to be with you. And to Jessi Loerch — we loved working with you at the *Everett Herald* writing about trails and ales. Now, we have the pleasure of working with you once more at *Washington Trails Magazine.* Thank you for your keen editorial eye and enthusiasm for the stories we want to craft.

We met fellow writers Adam Sawyer and Joe Wiebe on a 2013 Bellingham beer media trip and have looked to them for guidance ever since. Adam, we've loved watching you succeed in seemingly everything you do. Thanks for taking the time to meet with us at every opportunity. From that Portland pizza place to Cape Kiwanda, there's never been a dull moment with the Professional Gentleman of Leisure. Joe, you literally wrote the book on B.C. beer and we set your writing on beer as a benchmark to aspire to. Thanks for always having a moment to send along a brewery recommendation. Your *Craft Beer Revolution* is a constant travel companion on our Canadian travels — ¡Viva la Revolución!

Thank you to the countless destination marketing organizations and lodging partners that assisted us during research. Special thanks to Stephen Hoshaw for going above and beyond each time we've visited Eugene. And of course, we owe a deep gratitude to the 50 breweries in this book. Thanks for making great beer in the Pacific Northwest.

Rachel: I would like to thank my parents for their love and support and for not asking too many questions when I ran off on yet another research trip. I would also like to express my love and thanks to Megan O'Patry, Ed Moore, and Neal Yurick for making me a better beer writer. To Heather Matheson, for being the first person to call me a writer — you showed me how to take an adventure with words. And of course to my co-author and partner: Brandon, your scheming got us here, and our relationship is one of my greatest treasures in life.

Brandon: Thank you, Mom and Dad, for your lifelong love, support, and encouragement. I probably also have you to thank for my hiking passion and good taste in beer. To the rest of my family — Cassi, Ellie, Annaliese, Martin, and Patty — I wrote this book with you in mind. I hope it inspires you to explore and discover in the same ways that you have inspired me. Thanks to my friends for the countless hikes, beers, and laughs we've shared together. And to my partner Rachel for walking this path — and sharing this dream — with me over the years. Here's to many more.

To all those who believed in, encouraged, and supported us along the way: this book is for you.

In addition to all those we thanked in the first edition of this book, we'd like to extend our gratitude to the following friends of Beers at the Bottom:

- Ryan Timm — For believing in *Beer Hiking PNW* and ensuring its space on store shelves.
- Richard Harvell at Bergli Books — Thank you for taking point on this project and assisting us in reviving it.
- Dan Ullom at Brick and Mortar Books — For taking a chance on this title, hosting us in-store, and everything your store provides to the community.
- Bill and Jen Boyd — For your excitement, support, and friendship during this ongoing adventure. And for making beer so good we needed to write about it.
- Tilly — The "purr"-fect office assistant (except for when you're walking across our keeeeeeeeeeeeeeyboards).
- Every patient person who smiled when asked, "Did you know, my daughter wrote a book?"
- Everyone who championed this book by gifting it, attending signing events, writing reviews, chatting with us on podcasts, etc. Interest in the first edition of *Beer Hiking Pacific Northwest* exceeded our expectations as first-time authors. Thank you, fellow beer hikers, for your support. We hope to meet you all at a brewery somewhere, enjoying a post-hike pint. Cheers!

helvetiq.com